The Political Responsibility
of the Critic

JIM MEROD

The Political Responsibility
of the Critic

CORNELL UNIVERSITY PRESS

Ithaca and London

First published 1987 by Cornell University Press.
First published, Cornell Paperbacks, 1989.

International Standard Book Number 0-8014-1976-X (cloth)
International Standard Book Number 0-8014-9555-5 (paper)
Library of Congress Catalog Card Number 86-47977
Printed in the United States of America
*Librarians: Library of Congress cataloging information
appears on the last page of the book.*

*The paper in this book is acid-free and meets the guidelines for
permanence and durability of the Committee on Production Guidelines
for Book Longevity of the Council on Library Resources.*

For
MARTHA,
who taught me to read,
and
VIRGIL,
who taught me patience

Thought is a beacon not a life-raft, and to confuse the functions is tragic. The tragic character of thought—as any perspective will show—is that it takes a rigid mold too soon; chooses destiny like a Calvinist, in infancy, instead of waiting slowly for old age, and hence for the most part works against the world, good sense, and its own object: as anyone may see by taking a perspective of any given idea of democracy, of justice, or the nature of the creative act.

—R. P. Blackmur, "A Critic's Job of Work"

A rational exposition becomes an assertion of authority if no trace remains of the fumbling approaches that made it possible. . . . The political world shuns objective elucidation of its practices as an academic exercise, while the academic world rejects as "political" any testing of its statements against the real.

—Régis Debray, *Critique of Political Reason*

Contents

Preface

We cannot teach the moral sense any more than we can teach abstract thought to a dog. But we can individuate the moral sense by directing it into a specific code or tradition. The socialists today imply this fact when they object to the standard *bourgeois* education, meaning that it channelizes the potentialities of the child into a code which protects the *bourgeois* interests, whereas they would have the same potentialities differently individuated to favor the proletarian revolution.
—Kenneth Burke (1931)

Courage, like wine, bears costly insight. Like Antonio Gramsci, whose radical project accommodates conservative schooling, Kenneth Burke goads reductive materalists no less than textualizing idealists to challenge their own critical evasions. Early in *Criticism and Social Change,* Frank Lentricchia tells the story of Burke's unhappy reception at the first American Writers' Congress, in New York in 1935. The distance between Burke and emerging North American socialist thinking is implicit in his irony above, but the eccentricity of Burke's cultural insurgency left his work, for a half-century, in the twilight of respectful misunderstanding by critics on all sides.

Burke got from Marx and Aristotle a sense of the importance of practical literacy, of critical discourse as equipment for life. To Marx's strategy for adult education he added an Aristotelian emphasis on dramatic ratios and rhetorical dynamics. Burke found in Nietzsche a way to revamp dilapidated concepts: perspectives by incongruity, deliberately deformed or inverted proportions, misaligned arrangements of structure and presentation which breed intellectual and emotional energy. This gambit, which has motivated a century of Western artistic experimentation, has instructed two generations of critics in the United States rarely disturbed by Burke's representational commitment. Burke understood, early in his career, that the use of language is a material event embedded within symbolic and ideological mechanisms. Writing is a political and social act that cannot be detached from the network of practices that motivate it, because reading, itself situated, takes place within cultural directives, subtle and not so subtle assumptions about priority and legitimacy, which repress or censor as well as make possible interpretive activity.

Burke's example as a critic leads us to see that rhetoric does not culminate decisively in the logic and illogic of metaphor. Rhetoric acts on readers and listeners in discernible if sometimes unpredictable ways. Since language used persuasively creates attitudes and positions that have far-reaching consequences, literature, the most complex embodiment of persuasive language, provides access to authoritative strategies of value and policy through which cultures thrive. Complex verbal tactics often culminate as subtle as a snakebite. The power of Burke's example, noted frequently by R. P. Blackmur, nudges critical readers to look at conscious and unconscious claims to authority. Let this book add its whisper to Kenneth Burke's legacy.

In the years since the Indochina wars, the North American critic's authority has been confused by several pressures. One of them is the retrenched but uncertain status of the humanities in the contemporary university and within an increasingly commercialized culture. Another is the troubled state of intellectual exchange in a more and more militarized economy. A third pressure, invented or perfected by critical writers in response to the other two, seems only slightly less intractable: a self-consciously marginal professional identity, authoritative within small intellectual domains that relentlessly subvert traditional authoritative roles. These pressures have not destroyed critical and pedagogical authority, but they have produced among critics a political consciousness that can be thought of as emphatically uncertain. They have led to a self-contesting yet no less codified, professionally enforced "authority of the margin," as John Carlos Rowe has shown. Numerous literary tactics—appeals to honesty, tolerance, self-criticism, indeterminacy, the alien position of creative identity or the exotic solidarity of beleaguered groups (the exiled integrity of nondominant ideas and peoples and cultures)—now seek to salvage an undermined or flatly discredited cultural authority for the working critic.

This assessment recognizes how vulnerable critical strategies are to absorption by the cultural and political energies they oppose. If this text serves any purpose within the simultaneous authorizing and deauthorizing of intellectual resistance to forces that can be named, if not easily thwarted, it may be in the incongruity of its concern to make criticism a pedagogical counterforce dedicated, with the whole of its professional and institutional capacity, to intelligent public discourse. My working assumption is this: Humanist knowledge, critical authority, and radical political ambition will not accomplish significant cultural change solely by self-conscious analytic techniques. They will not alter democratic institutions by intellectual dexterity alone. If criticism in the United States is to de-idealize its aims and habits, if its traditional role as an adjunct to the authority of artistic detachment is to be brought toward an active transformational purpose, professional critics will have to pursue a variety of collective scholarly and pedagogical practices across intellectual fields. To say this is to encourage the best energies on each side of the antagonism that in 1935, at the Writers' Congress in Madison Square Garden, put Burke's call for radical critical intervention *within* bourgeois culture (inside the conflict then spreading among capitalist institutions) at odds with left-wing appeals to solidarity. Collective practices are perpetually subject to critical harassment; and yet scholars and theorists have a social impact, incremental though it is, complexly mediated, which demands the quarrelsome cooperation of minds working across institutional as well as intellectual boundaries.

This book has benefited from comments by some of the best readers any writer could hope to find. I owe heartfelt appreciation to Jonathan Arac, Donald Marshall, and Richard Ohmann. Without their encouraging suspicions, these pages would be poorer. I have been given caring, careful, and forthright attention by Tom Jeffers, Marjorie Roemer, and Richard Onorato. To Gene Goodheart I owe the respect of adversarial differences neither hidden nor exaggerated. My special thanks to Bernhard Kendler, whose editorship brought this book to completion. Anne-Marie Feenberg gave encouragement bolstered by understanding of the traditions and institutional limits under survey. Barbara Salazar lent these pages the clarity of her generous intelligence. My sons, Jim and Matt, have given companionship of a kind that makes a writer's life whole. More than anyone, Maeve Elliott knows the cost of the arguments under way here. Least incongruous of all my debts, a final tribute to students at Brandeis (such as Lisa Shiffman, writing from China, soon at Oxford) who have proved that criticism is "about questioning, the risks of daring to question and the responsibilities of those who question."

JIM MEROD

Rancho La Costa, California

The Political Responsibility
of the Critic

1

On the Road to Work:

Introduction

The reigning perspective in departments of literature throughout the United States continues to be an aesthetic idealism in which the teacher, especially the strong teacher, is a priest or rabbi of literary capital. This perspective creates not only an ideology of texts and of textual production, but an ideology of reading in which all things critical circulate through the classroom and stay there, unable to contend with society's bleak eloquence. If the world is imagined as a background for such detachment, it is represented as a place inhospitable to literature and criticism but needing their civilizing influence. The paradox of that irony is complete. Criticism is necessary but useless, an urgent inadequacy. Left out or obliterated in this defeat is the human agent, the teacher or student who is situated among many institutions (the school merely one) and must make sense of their corporate interaction. More than anything else, the unworldliness of the classroom obscures, if it does not deny altogether, the possibility that critical activity is (or might be) the one human force most committed to clarifying the world's structure in order to change it.

Thus the word *work* in the title of this chapter is deliberate and deliberately polemic. It points to the intimacy between the world of everyday labor and that other world of intellectual exercise which seeks an essentially theoretical clarity. These worlds are not divisible, but their entanglement is not apparent without some demonstration.[1] Whatever criticism amounts to in a world dominated by commercial and political rivalries that organize a distinctly aggressive order, a world in which the university plays the central role in the production of knowledge, it is a form of work. The question to be answered,

1

however, is what kind of work it is and for what goals and values, with what actual consequences for daily life. For me, one feature of this dilemma stands out. Criticism in the Western academic world is seldom thought of as work of any sort, a depreciation that is largely responsible for the confusion in textual studies today.

I do not want to exaggerate my point; every human activity has a component of labor. But academic criticism now tends more than ever toward a rarefied self-interest, as if writing and the critical act were severed from the institutional practices that define a capitalist society. The distance between criticism or theory and the world of daily labor has become a constant (though unconscious) feature of the professional study of texts. Today, as criticism enjoys its highest if also most internally contested moment of recognition, debate about the role and future of criticism is almost wholly self-referential. The cultural and institutional—which is to say the social and political—context of criticism in particular and of academic work in general has become a subject for serious theoretical concern within a select group of departments of literature across the United States as interest in Anglo-American Marxist writers (as well as in the Frankfurt critics and the work of such pragmatists as William James, John Dewey, and Charles Sanders Peirce) has extended the range of questions viable for text-centered practices. Disciplinary order has been preserved nonetheless. Where major critics and literary historians once put forth a putatively value-free assessment of textual knowledge, socially conscious contemporary readers now construct a political awareness inexplicably trapped or somehow forced to languish without concrete social usefulness. The social and political context of interpretive activity, a complex area deserving scrutiny, thereby remains separate from the texts and methods of reading that constitute criticism proper. This division perpetually reasserts itself as if critical writing and critical teaching were caught between an authorized "inside," a body of professional interpretive practices, and an unauthorized "outside" that is the world of institutions, of human uses.

No critical writer today can project a way out of this impasse without the risk of promoting a Utopian "solution" that ignores the fact that the political and social context of interpretive work defies a purely theoretical remedy but requires, instead, conscious political choices about the form and value of reading and writing within a society that first divides intellectual from physical labor and then redivides intellectual labor into separate areas of expertise. Any redemptive theory runs the risk of emphasizing the critic's plight at the expense of the general plight of human labor within the capitalist market. A book such as this one, concerned with the placement of criticism in its institutional setting, runs the added risk of announcing a problem it cannot fully describe—for much of the confusion among critics as a group and among humanists on the whole is self-inflicted, accentuated by the relative privacy of individual professional careers and by the semipublic nature of departments of literature. The professional identities and habits of group definition at work here are not wholly explained by such venerable sociological concepts as alienation, reification, anomie, and for that matter professionalism, although all of those terms direct our attention to the social and ideological causes of intellectual complaisance. Something else, an attitude that criticism stands or falls with, is involved. Even though academic writers seldom think of their work as courageous or pedestrian or even timid, such overt strength and weakness is in fact developed by critical activity. Certainly many people who have chosen to pursue intellectual work have done so because at some important moment in their lives they came across a teacher or writer who presented a conceptual clarity that was more than mere analytic elegance or explanatory brilliance but suggested, and perhaps demonstrated, the life-enhancing courage of passionate knowledge. That clarity undoubtedly comes with many kinds of unpredictable and irreducible difficulty.[2] It may prefer questions to answers and refuse conventional scholastic production. However it operates, intellectual passion is not a style. It is a form of warfare (in Nietzsche's sense), free of gloom, that converts aggression to self-conscious energy.

Such passion seeks to name and then to negotiate the tangible conditions of the real world's unsatisfactory options. Not everything human can be negotiated. But criticism, as an instance of organized intelligence, can oppose the enforcement of cultural domination by intellectual practices that obscure social reality and thereby advance capitalist hierarchies and the power of the state. Criticism can expose its own affiliations with the institutional and ideological organization of public space and use its considerable social leverage to promote the political solidarity of demoted cultures and disfranchised people.

The refusal to clarify the ways in which criticism and teaching are unavoidably political activities is not only the result of an insular professional ethos and the national political lassitude it feeds on (and in some degree creates) but a consequence just as much of a depoliticized critical identity fostered by academic consensus. The choice of an observational self-consciousness, enclosed by professional circumstances, is a political choice and a political attitude. For the teacher and critic working in the United States today, the possibility of evading the political repercussions of intellectual choices—such as the way texts will be taught in classrooms—is a self-indulgent fantasy. It amounts to intellectual immaturity. Lest I seem too urgent where others would rather find playful abandon, let me say that I see many problems in advertising the political function of the critic within an institution that prides itself on its transcendentalized irrelevance. To assert that criticism in North America inevitably serves a political role of one sort or another, and that the choice of roles needs to be clarified but also needs intellectual commitment of a fairly strenuous kind normally discouraged by traditional humanists, is to lose a large part of an already small audience.

Nonetheless, my position holds. Critical writing and critical training in the United States at present do not envision a social setting for the critical act, nor do they offer any truly sustained examination of the critic's political identity and of criticism's political force. Everything "critical" enhances Criticism, an institution within an institution, a subset of the essentially depoliticized pleasure of reading and teaching texts: an intellectual event without grounding in, and with no vocabulary for, the world of human work.[3] One wonders, of course, how this situation will resolve itself. Is criticism in the United States destined to define itself perpetually as a professional but impractical activity? There are reasons to think so, but I see signs of a growing awareness that such insulation is intolerable. For the immediate future I suspect the internal skirmish will continue. But it may continue alongside a sober reassessment of the institutional position of criticism and literary teaching in North American culture.

That reassessment can begin with an inquiry into the nature of critical authority. What authorizes the critic's work? What relation does critical writing have to the academy as a whole and to the society of which it is a part, a particularly self-conscious and somewhat paradoxically self-enabling and socially empowered part? Look for a moment at the kind of authority critics actually achieve both within the academy and within the cultural environment at large. Well-known critics are frequently asked to contribute to interdisciplinary journals that have a somewhat wider audience than conventionally segregated academic subspecialties attract. Some join the deliberations of research institutes as senior members with a certain measure of sway in setting agendas or redefining areas of inquiry. Others participate in public discussions concerned with the future of the humanities or similar topics related to educational and government policy. Still others have a crucial say in the publication of books and articles, in making and unmaking academic careers, and in fostering the kind of dialogue that influences curricular change. In all of these and related aspects of the critic's performance, the concrete authority that sanctions such work is seldom looked at or even recognized as a matter of considerable interest. Instead, habits of interpretive judgment remain safely unaccountable to everything except an extremely small realm, the self-contained area called Theory, a world that seems to have no political impact beyond its own professional realignments, little if any moral responsibility of the kind E. P. Thompson projects for historians,[4] and an almost thoroughly unexamined institutional context.

It should be obvious to anyone involved in this arrangement that the preservation of such authority most benefits those who hold academic positions. That is not a conclusion many critics want to draw. We arrive, therefore, at this stalemate: to look beyond the academy or, in reverse, to look at the academy's insistence on a neutralized, apolitical form of intellectual authority is to see that the cultural context of criticism calls for dissent and opposition of a sort that seems unattractive or illegitimate, out of bounds given the rules of critical writing. To write criticism today, much as always, is to follow fairly well-worn paths of critical respectability assuring the sanctity of various "great traditions," those of high literary master texts and the accompanying critical monuments that literally make critical writing a viable but unsituated practice. What is new here is that one must at the same time take into account the habits of undoing offered by overtly skeptical writers like Paul de Man, Jacques Derrida, and Michel Foucault, who appear to the entrenched conservative as nihilists and to the radical textualist as intellectual saviors, pathbreakers beyond the boundaries. For many who participate from either extreme, or from a position somewhere in between, the usefulness of dissent and opposition looks doubtful, since the actual conditions of professional textual study are geared to maintaining the status quo, to reproducing scholars and critics with no real thought about the place of scholarship and criticism in capitalist culture. Some find the critical quagmire so disabling that entering the field of critical debate is tantamount to suffocation.

Despite these and further drawbacks, criticism flourishes, perhaps because of its refusal to define its social function except in the most benign images of cultural affirmation. Dissent, in other words, for those who wish to gamble on the possibility of criticism's institutional rebirth, needs to be directed toward long-standing patterns of critical mystification—the way, for example, criticism appears as a "field" in its own right somehow attached to the formal study of texts but uninterested in making texts and interpretive practices more powerful democratizing agencies. Dissent and genuine political opposition of a kind that is not theoretically enclosed (though Theory, we should remember, is a means of collective action) need to show that the classroom is an extension of the world, not its antithesis. Oppositional criticism, specifically, needs to present alternatives to teaching practices that cannot or will not relate literary and philosophical expertise to the unfolding complexities of a society in which students find themselves asked to perform independently, critically, but, when the truth is known, obediently. In these efforts criticism is self-consciously a form of work.

I want to look at some of the difficulties of being a student of literature and criticism today. Anyone now at work as a professional critic might remember the self-discipline and intellectual indoctrination involved in acquiring the knowledge that goes into teaching and literary scholarship. Nothing about that process has changed much in the past forty years or so. Despite changes in society (the advent of television and now computers, the expansion of North America's material affluence and the rise of what has come to be called the narcissistic personality), despite shifts in national politics and in the critical fads that motivate professional writing, nothing has really altered the way students proceed through college and graduate school to become teachers of literature. Assumptions about the purpose of teaching, about the reasons for studying literary and critical texts, remain very much as they were at the end of World War II. Literature reveals the actual complexities of the human situation. It also voices higher aspirations for intelligence and imagination than any other human practice. And one more thing: literature provides the occasion to gain room for critical skills and critical insight neglected in the banal social routine. These things are the province of the teacher and critic. But the circumstances in which they can be imagined—and, more important, in which we can undertake the work of making criticism and literature useful in society—have changed even though the professional study of texts has not found a way to take those changes fully into account.

The difficulty of being a student of texts, of becoming a young literary intellectual today, is not that there are fewer jobs and more competition for them than there were ten or fifteen years ago. Though related to that, what I am pointing to is not directly and concretely a matter of job security. The problem facing the new or would-be humanist is that the United States, in the past forty years, has become an increasingly complex but also increasingly integrated institutional network of professions, corporations, and government bureaucracies. At the same time, the professional study of texts has become increasingly open to a variety of methodological and critical assumptions while simultaneously becoming more and more an institution closed by insular professional disputes unrelated to the possibility of creating human or social alternatives for a society whose technological homogeneity badly needs rejuvenation. In fact, criticism is increasingly unable to justify its work in terms of universal moral value and intellectual nobility, largely because the literary and scholarly profession (the teaching profession generally) is thought of by nearly everyone, and in fact defines itself, as one profession among others.

But this is just the first difficulty for anyone now beginning to advance through the profession of criticism and literary teaching. Anyone who has entered this line of work during the past two decades cannot fail to see that North American society is dominated by a market mentality. In each sector of its complicated organizational coherence, profit and efficiency rule. Those who should see this most clearly are people who are attracted to literature and philosophy, whose work derives from the humanistic tradition. The inability of professional textual study to address its own participation in the relentless commoditization of work and leisure—to incorporate the institutional and historical circumstances that breed cultural arrogance, economic inequality, and social injustice—undermines the possibility that teachers and critics could make the imaginative and analytic work of reading an agent of social change. American democratic capitalism is an economic and political system dominated by concentrated wealth and managed by a professional class striving for prestige and privilege, by people who pass through colleges and universities and on into the corporate structure of the professional marketplace. The way these people are educated, the degree to which they learn humane ideals and analytic skills that can be translated into professional behavior that resists cynical work routines and business practices, has everything to do with rejuvenating respect for individuals over profit, with creating a society that includes systematically outcast people (the poor, the sick, the elderly, the uneducated), and with promoting the dignity and even the safety of victimized people (women, children, minorities, and laborers of every kind). Or not.

That task is impeded by the profession as it stands. Young humanists who attempt to integrate the institutional context of criticism in particular and of culture in general with the work of teaching and writing about texts often find their way blocked. Until recently, the institution of textual study has been uninterested in its own institutional circumstances. Criticism's affiliation with society remains an unaddressed and in many ways uncongenial issue. This situation is not at all an abstract quandary but produces a deeply felt and often tormenting sense of placelessness and even uselessness for many people in the early phases of their humanistic careers. The choice facing most people starting out in the profession is abundantly clear. One can follow the numerous ways to teach and publish along well-mapped textually oriented and textually insulated lines. Or one can try to fight free of the tendency to keep everything critical and literary isolated by desocialized, ahistorical interpretive procedures. The first is the more prudent, less intellectually baffling choice. The second is not only difficult but perhaps foolish. Given such a choice, if it even appears to be a choice, one can hardly be surprised to find innovation stimulated by a few adventurous and established members of the profession and not, as in the sciences and especially in mathematics, by younger people. This state of events is related to the fact that humanistic knowledge and critical skill depend on a fairly wide range of learning that cannot be quickly gained, a process of reading and sorting through problems which has little or nothing to do with innate problem-solving intuition or analytic technique. As yet, however, the work of linking the critical "inside" with the institutional "outside" has few guides and fewer well-marked boundaries. For anyone who chooses the less-traveled route, the possibility of a game but futile effort to make sense of criticism as a socially productive, institutionally situated act (an act of political choices and political constraints) is real.

My point is that a major difficulty for the serious and committed student of criticism today is not the variety and confusion of interpretive positions so much as the fact that criticism is all but closed to the institutional basis and institutional consequences of its work. This is a restriction that graduate students at most universities become aware of quite early in their careers and that especially mature, professionally inclined undergraduates sometimes glimpse in their last semesters.[5] Such a closure has a stunning effect on intellectual give-and-take both in the classroom and in the individual pursuit of critical knowledge. A nearly tangible sense of induced accommodation, something short of coercion yet akin to it—call it doctrinal good sense or an unstated (but not unnoticed) regulation of intellectual behavior—develops here. It shows up in several ways. First, and most graphic of all, the study of texts does not have an apparent or clearly delineated relation to anything other than further mastery of texts. The student who works in textual interpretation generally sees two immediate careers ahead, teaching and the law, and in the absence of those finds at best a vague application of textual knowledge and interpretive skills. The uncertainty about translating humanist learning into immediately usable job skills or credentials is blamed sometimes on the shortsightedness of businesses and corporations, sometimes on the failure of the academy to "sell" its students and their employers on the general usefulness of critical reading abilities. Well-meaning advocates of the humanities point out how vital to any enterprise are the writing and analytic capacities uniquely produced by a literary education. This observation in itself admits, however unknowingly, the deficiency of the notion that criticism is a field or area in its own right. The argument implied in selling students and employers on the adaptability of critical training is that the analytic skill and conceptual knowledge generated by literary and critical texts are extremely malleable.[6] Such an education does not have instrinsic force or critical acumen; it is flexible and open to accommodation with any number of tasks.

I do not want to debate the merits of converting literary knowledge to occupational demands. My concern here is that the intrinsically critical function of a humanist education carries with it, or should carry, a resistant and immediately analytic force that cannot be thought of as easily adapted to commercial and capitalist practices, even if it can be (as I think it is) the best ally of anyone who ventures into a competitive environment. I am pointing to the vagueness surrounding what criticism is all about in the first place and why any student should want to learn to read texts well. As it stands now, criticism is a grossly academic enterprise that has no real vision of its relationship to and responsibilities within the corporate structure of North American (for that matter, international) life. It is simply a way of doing business with texts. It is in fact a series of ways, a multiplicity of methods that vie for attention and prestige within the semipublic, semiprivate professional critical domain. Thus, academic critics reproduce teachers and scholars and critics, reproduce a humanist but not a fully critical education. Academic critics train particularly able readers who move from literary texts as undergraduates to legal texts and law careers, leaving most of the others who pass through literature courses and the departmental major in a curiously unclarified situation.

This division reflects the radical separation that humanist critics have made for so long between the "literary" and "imaginative" on one side and the political and institutional world (the world of all other kinds of knowledge and of genuinely productive forces, the world of power) on the other. This separation draws the text—any text, the *New York Times* as much as *The Prelude*—away from the actual landscape of social and personal affiliations where people work and live, where literary and critical understanding takes hold to influence behavior and to construct humane ideas about what it means to live in a world of powerful, competing forces. Such understanding, the knowledge of texts and rhetorical strategies and historical events, *might* influence thought and behavior, that is, if reading and writing practices were seen to be inextricable elements of the world we live in.

Perhaps I should illustrate what I mean by pointing to my experience with graduate students. I have found almost without exception that graduate students—and now I am talking about generally well-educated, capable and committed readers—approach a seminar in, say, critical theory or Romantic texts with a combination of acquiescence and resistance. The most confident are neither impressionable nor combative but wary, interested, and skeptical. That is a healthy attitude, I think, but it is one that is often misunderstood as a sign of too much independence or of hostility to authority—to a particular teacher's authority or to the profession of which the student is now an initiate who must prove good faith and intellectual merit. The unseen content of the student's hesitancy is the academic framework itself, the professor's authority to discharge assignments and duties, to judge and help or stymie careers—an intellectual environment that for the most part has not given many of these students much sense of the social context of reading and teaching. The graduate student enters the career of critic and scholar as a devoted reader of texts who has very little grasp of the historical and political complications that speak through texts, complications that surround and in fact situate texts in a world of people and institutions, a limited and constructed world that at every point in human history is in the process of being built. This sense of historical process and of political energies that inform literary and critical (and all other) texts is not a standard feature of literary training in the United States, even though many departments of literature encourage their students to know as much as possible about history and about literary periods. In brief, graduate students come to be trained with almost no awareness of the social world in which texts are written and accomplish their effects. They have at best a dim sense that they have been led to divide texts from history and from the institutional reality surrounding texts (and, as I will note in a moment, inhabiting them as well). But they do not often know how to talk about that detachment, nor do they usually see it as a problem. On the whole, their education has worked fairly well. It persuades them that literature is something distinct from the world.

For some students, the initial consternation when they see how thoroughly texts have been isolated from everything else subsides. If they are shown how, a gradual awareness that texts can be read—with all their thematic density and stylistic complexity—as rhetorical events that respond to historical situations comes to replace frustration and literary enclosure. Texts then appear as provisional "solutions" or as strategies for coping with social and political problems, solutions and strategies that are themselves problematic. At this point the difficult job of putting texts together to clarify not only how they can be read strategically but also how they address historical dilemmas will probably cause a student to look for a critical vocabulary adequate to such a complex and even turbulent way of reading. This can induce intellectual crisis.

Less historically oriented, in any event, less critically restless (or politically conscious) teachers who encounter this struggle may misunderstand it as a challenge to their own authority. What begins as hesitant compliance or skeptical interest may turn to subservience in students who have no guidance in mapping a critical approach of their own. Or it may lead to burn out and frustration, simply dropping out, among those who cannot find a way to articulate a clear grasp of texts. These are often people who gravitate toward graduate school to find a focus they could not locate as undergraduates. Not always. But a third response, one that is unsettling to teachers who remain rigid in the face of questions that challenge the conventional boundaries separating texts from their contexts, is to seek the excitement that graduate study promises. The student who sees that texts speak *from the world* about definable and specific (and not "universal") problems, that texts speak *to the world* in which they are placed—a world distant historically yet available to comprehension with the help of such texts—such a student needs an intellectual community.[7]

Let me put this another way. I am saying that the work of criticism is unavoidably interrelated with a social and political context that cannot be siphoned off as so much bilge and that the work of making criticism a viable activity for students requires the teacher to show how that relationship works. It requires us to show that texts are strategies, that they carry values that exert a force in the social world. It requires us to deal with texts in a way that fosters intellectual ferment rather than making students' efforts conform to preexisting methods and critical dogmas. The one value I imagine should be held in the highest respect and honored genuinely as the legitimating motive of critical inquiry is the absolute necessity for the student and the teacher to pursue critical understanding wherever it leads. That is not what we find in literary scholarship today. More than anything else, we find men and women whose careers are founded upon small sections of knowledge defined by a fairly linear historical continuity. These literary and historical periods determine one way of building "fields" of textual inquiry. Another way is the deep respect individual "genres" elicit. Still another is the individual writer who acquires canonical status. A case can be made (and a new one needs to *be* made) for the serviceability of this routine. But within these rubrics, areas, and designations something else gets left out: the interpretive exchange.

Interpretation is not a purely academic activity. The kind of interpretation we call criticism—interpretations of texts and artifacts, of intellectual positions and historical events—resides in the academy. It takes place in classrooms and in professional academic organizations and as such forms the object of theoretical investigation. But that activity is not self-contained. The purpose of literary and theoretical teaching, of professional criticism, is to preserve the knowledge of texts and their traditions as well as to advance interpretive skills that allow students to become intelligent readers and writers. Most students, of course, do not become professional critics. They move into the world of business and the professions, where they interpret texts or documents relevant to their work. The training most of them receive in college as readers of poems and novels has at best an uncertain relation to their work as lawyers and doctors and business men and women. Seldom are students trained in college classrooms to read texts as if they related to the world of human choice and decision, to the interpretive dynamics of every rhetorical mode and moment.

Yet the preparation to read critically is a preparation to explore institutional conditions, not merely to decode. That exploration involves a somewhat intricate but by no means obscure placement of the interpretive act within historical boundaries (and historical conflicts) that define political roles, political identities, political limits. To students in North America in the late twentieth century such placement seems impossible or irrelevant. To those who wish to pursue a profession, grades are of extreme importance, and climbing through the undergraduate pack to enter medical school or some professional or graduate department, to secure the best school possible, is more urgent than considering the political, ethical, and epistemological value of various reading habits. More and more one finds students at every level compelled to "get ahead," and stiff competition leaves little room for deviance. They feel constrained to follow the teacher's lead rather than question it, to execute assignments as they are given instead of pausing to test one course and its outlook against another. This pausing and comparison, this invitation to analysis and evaluation, has to be encouraged. The stakes involved are nothing less than students' critical freedom as socially conscious interpreters aware of the circumstances and of the power of information they will be expected, as professionals, to serve.[8]

Careful readers and bright, enthusiastic students need sustained analytic contact with their lived environment if they are to activate a genuinely critical ability. And the less careful, uncertain reader absolutely demands it, or nothing very useful in the way of critical insight, critical questioning, will occur at all. That is the most reliable lesson I am able to draw from nineteen years of teaching. It is less a theoretical point than a pragmatic point, but it certainly has theoretical implications. Its force comes to this: all readers today stand between two cognitive worlds. The mostly visual, truly anticommunal world of advertising and commercial *entertainment,* controlled by giant corporate interests, opposes but also surrounds the world of literacy, the world of books and critical *thinking.* The outcome of that interaction is the world we live in, to some extent split between professional competence and cultural banality, to some extent integrated by the uneasy accommodation between corporate power (and state and military power) and intellectual work. The reader who wants to emerge from a dominating though ungovernable culture that quells resistance to its authoritative structure is a reader who deserves to be shown where critical intelligence stands in the world we live in. What must be looked at, then, is the role of the critic and the possibility of critical intervention in our culture at large.

Although there is no agreement about how to approach this task or about the predominant issues that constitute the theory of critical intervention, the chapters that follow attempt to sketch a preliminary movement through territories central to the work of making an enlarged political ethos for literary intellectuals. That attempt begins, in the next chapter, by looking at contrasting but not entirely unassimilable views of the critic's role in contemporary culture. The issue to be decided there is what, if any, political function critical intellectuals play in a diverse and open society. What role, in particular, do critical writers seek—or find given to them—in liberal democratic capitalist society? My view throughout this book is that Antonio Gramsci's writings on the importance of intellectuals in establishing and maintaining cultural order provide a useful, if incomplete, series of questions that open this area to an institutionally specific interrogation. Gramsci's presence extends across these pages, though some qualification of the directions he provides is necessary, most evidently in chapter 3, which discusses intellectual authority and the role of the humanities as a legitimating institution within the organization of capitalist state power. One of the issues at stake here is the debate, now emerging with new force within Marxist thinking, posing material and institutional forces against the relative autonomy of ideology and culture. It is worth noting that the consequences of bringing Gramsci's work together with that of other Marxist writers (the "capital logicians," for example—Ernest Mandel and Harry Braverman perhaps their two most powerful theorists) are not at all clear but nonetheless hold significant possibilities for the future of critical and pedagogical theory, for the future of Marxist theory as a whole. That significance resides, I believe, in two related areas:

1. To couple an investigation of the material, institutional, and economic grounds of our current historical situation with a critique of the reigning ideological and cultural structures is to engage (just possibly to invent) theoretical energies that promote the long-repressed analysis of *class struggle* as it approaches, and in extremely guarded or covert form circulates through, humanistic education. The form that class struggle takes in the humanities is most obvious in terms of its curriculum: a struggle concerning the representation of the dominant culture—of a "selective" tradition, as Raymond Williams calls it. That struggle embodies, above all, the inclusion of previously excluded cultures and peoples. Gramsci's notion of intellectual and cultural *hegemony* gives oppositional critics a way to situate themselves both within and alongside the texts and ideas that traditionally constitute humanistic activity. One of Gramsci's most powerful points was that hegemonic culture, dominant culture, is inherently contradictory. Hegemonic culture is that set of ideas and practices which reinforces social consensus. It is itself the product of class struggle, since it embodies the negotiated compromises that allow competing interests to transform potentially violent eruptions into agreements about larger "national" or general social interests that must be preserved for the "benefit" of all. Inescapably, within or underneath that putative coherence, disruptive forces remain with considerable volatility. Chapter 4 thus attempts to situate the critical act in the stratified but fractured institutional and cultural space that is its native turf. A materialist account of critical work, one might note here, reveals the implication of humanists and literary critics in the battle between classes and cultures, a battle that humanists frequently if somewhat naively impede.

2. The tendency of academic critics to forget (literally to overlook) disruptive or contradictory elements within the work they do as hu-

manists can be traced to more than the structural position of the humanities as the upholders of the great tradition of literary and philosophical classics. It can be seen also as an internal event. Intellectuals of every kind occupy professional workspace that discourages the critical consciousness required to evaluate the larger patterns of rationality that define professional reality. Chapter 5, therefore, examines Stanley Fish's argument for the serviceability of the existing professional order and moves to inspect Paul de Man's related political detachment as well as the extraordinary counterexample in the writing of R. P. Blackmur. Blackmur, I think, will eventually be seen as a critic whose practice probes well beyond the divisions that segment academic enclaves. The total body of his work is uniquely positioned to help others, young critics especially, gain a sense of place in a society where texts are instruments of information, frequently of oppression and obfuscation, but rarely of egalitarian combat. Blackmur's writing is passionately articulate about these things. This second potentiality of the antihegemonic work critics have before them—the making of *strategies* to educate professional and pre-professional people for explicitly democratic ends—may ultimately depend on the introduction of materialist analyses alongside ideological or antihegemonic critiques.[9]

That said, I should account for the limitations as well as the ambitions of my final two chapters. Chapter 6 is largely a critique of Fredric Jameson's description of a Marxist pedagogy. My critique of Jameson's position must be understood to depend on a debt that I owe (and that anyone else who pursues a Marxist reading of our culture also owes) to a critic whose writing and political engagement form a central model for socially alert intellectuals. The issue at hand in chapter 6 is the political uncertainty and the institutional embeddedness of a hermeneutic practice even as scrupulous, as critically conscious, and as culturally generous as Jameson's.

It is here that a materialistic reading of culture (which includes, of course, the critic's activity) supplements and raises potentially perplexing questions for a hermeneutic or textually centered analysis of culture. Let me approach this book as a whole, and my critique of Jameson in particular, by remembering Marx's useful admonitions against methodological analyses of any sort that fail to promote active, socially productive political awareness. Everything in Marx's tantalizing and somewhat contradictory conception of historical materialism, clearest in its nonetheless sketchy form in his theses on Feuerbach, leads to practical action or (to be more exact) to aligning the historian's and the critic's efforts alongside all other efforts to create social conditions favorable to working men and women.[10] Historical materialism is less a theory than a set of themes and guidelines for intellectual and political transformation. Its objective is to change political and cultural relationships, and eventually institutional and productive (economic) relationships, throughout society at large. The aim is to make a gentler, more diverse and interaffiliated humanity without rank and class divisions. Marx's materialism is founded on the belief that intellectuals have access to those ideas that most powerfully reinforce social life—that intellectuals can blunt or stimulate ideological coherence and the appearance of social unity—though this strain of analysis, at once materially and culturally oriented, was in effect dormant until Gramsci's clearer formulations in the first decades of this century gave it focus. The mature result of Marx's "materialism," in other words, is directly interconnected with educational institutions and with culture and ideology as a whole.

Marx's critique of ideology—what it consists of, how it operates, its specific institutional placement—has become a highly controversial topic. Marx's most extensive treatment, in *The German Ideology* (written 1845–46), was not published in his lifetime, although the word and the concept *ideology* circulate through his texts after 1846. There the term languished for the remainder of the nineteenth century. Largely because the term has both Leninist associations and a patchwork, essentially imported career, having woven its way to North America via the Frankfurt theorists (to a lesser extent via the "Western" Marxists, Lukács, Korsch, and Gramsci; Mannheim is another transporter), ideological analysis now appears to reside at some distance from the more entangled, thoroughly "material" and institutional field of economic, political, and necessarily cultural interactions. Jameson acknowledges this split in his preface to *The Political Unconscious* when he notes that he might "recast many of its findings in the form of a methodological handbook, but such a manual would have as its object *ideological analysis,* which remains, I believe, the appropriate designation for the critical 'method' specific to Marxism." His task, instead, is to focus on narrative embodiments of ideology: "to restructure the problematics of ideology, of the unconscious and of desire, of representation, of history, and of cultural production, around the all-informing process of narrative, which I take to be (here using the shorthand of philosophical idealism) the central function or instance of the human mind."[11]

Jameson's project in that text, therefore, is not "the path of the object," as he calls the first of the two trails leading toward materially conscious interpretive efforts. He is interested in "the path of the subject," in the interpretive maneuvers that constitute the pre-texts that give access to those seemingly more concrete texts that critics deal with. He divides that pursuit, for the sake of scholarly order, from the history and from the structural and institutional field of objects that constitute material reality. This is not an unhappy procedure. My point in following Jameson's project is to insist that the storytelling function of the critical teacher—that is, the mapmaking narrative that any activating (and activist) pedagogy must put in motion—has to avoid the neat cleavage between subject and object, between "mind" and its enabling contexts, which marks nearly all critical frameworks, even those devoted to social regeneration. Jameson is by no means a typical example, yet the issue his strategies raise relates not only to the authority of the critic's work, its specific institutional legitimacy, but to the writing and teaching practices such authority enables. In its baldest form this is the question of context. What "reality" do the texts that critics read and write about refer to or carry with them? What "reality" surrounds (and/or invades) critical and pedagogical acts? What cultural force resides within critical authority?[12]

About the first question Jameson is fairly clear and gives subsequent critics well-argued guidelines to challenge or to join him. A text, he argues, is an imaginary and symbolic response that contradictorily "resolves" (or finds a way of bridging) inexpungible contradictions at work in its own historical time and place. Any text, therefore, will both affirm and deny its own historical reality. And each of these evaluative intentions will exist on conscious or explicit levels of thematic complexity and on unconscious or latent levels of narrative encoding. The Gargantuan effort to sift the historical and ideological density that is sedimented problematically, in some sense invisibly, but always symbolically (and thus available to hermeneutic recovery) becomes an exercise in retrieving history from misreadings created in large part by professional readers—by scholars, critics, teachers.

This rereading of the narrative field, of a text as itself a field of competing forces, becomes a reading or rereading of history too. And Jameson's approach to that history, as far back as *Marxism and Form*, has been to assert "the anti-idealistic thrust of Marxism [which] aims at breaking the spell of the 'inverted world' of conceptual thought" as we find it suffused throughout capitalist and noncapitalist cultures alike. "The dialectic is designed," he writes, "to eject us from this illusory order, to project us in spite of ourselves out of our concepts into the world of genuine realities to which these concepts were to apply."[13]

The dialectical reading that Jameson brings to texts as miniature force fields and to culture as an ideological network producing and reproducing the conceptual conditions of specific material realms (a reading he has made significantly more complicated over the years) attends to a world deposited in, but also exceeding, texts and their academic treatments. Jameson's approach to this reality that texts and interpretations claim is provocative (I think laudable) but almost a paradigm of the blockage—here of course at a very high level of theoretical understanding—that first confuses and then disables any movement from ideological analysis and the interpretation of texts to a historical materialism made practical and politically productive. The question for Marxist analysis is this: How will such theoretical clarity help to redesign institutions? Typically, perhaps necessarily, the answer is something like this: as a preparation for a more enlightened culture, as a step on the long haul toward a more just society. Jameson's writing does not avoid this question. Nor does it promise more than it can deliver. It places us precisely, though with more energy and better equipped than most critical performances leave us, where criticism sits today: alert and politically stumped, culturally central and intellectually neutralized at once. It does so not because its cast of Marxism or its devotion to texts is inadequate, but because the theory of cultural logic and of antihegemonic work remains purely academic. In other words, the question of context to which Jameson gives a strong hermeneutic lift remains essentially unavailable for the passage from interpretive theory to the making of a body of critical intellectuals who know where they work, what they work for, and how they mean to achieve regenerative social goals.

Let me be quite clear about my focus, since these issues are complex and I am well aware how much my own text leaves out and has not, despite its aims, accomplished. I consider this book at best an opening statement toward a fuller account of an institutionally directed critical pedagogy. What I am saying is that Jameson's magnificently engaged work directs awareness outward, toward the capitalistic megastructure, but, not unlike the formalisms it supersedes, it leaves the internal solidarity and the creation of a critical community to one side as a later, more revolutionary moment of theory. I am not aware of any contemporary intellectual who could not profit from the one Marxist writer in North America who has found the energy and patience to revise the way texts are read. No longer can the old nostalgia for textual self-evidence or for referential uncertainty collapse with clear conscience into ahistorical thematizing. Jameson literally guides us through "the basic thesis of materialism," which, as Régis Debray notes, "is that any message exhausts all possible codes" (an understanding Jameson shares, somewhat at odds, with Jean Baudrillard).[14] But the historical materialism that might inform critical learning does not flow easily in our culture. The movement from a Gramscian concern with cultural domination to a more specific transformation of the cultural and social relationships—and here, most specifically, transformation of the *uses* of knowledge which uphold those relations and enable the increasingly information-based orientation of capitalist production to advance—will be blocked as long as critics do not contest (or inspect, at the very least) the insertion of their own authority within the divisions of labor that continue to define our economic and social world.

Literary critics need to ask how they are positioned within the culture and how they are used, how their work is used, and how they lend themselves to those uses. That is not an easy set of questions to pursue. They are no doubt more difficult to engage politically than intellectually (though the two are not so distinct here) because, once given legitimacy in institutions, many people find motivation to cross-examine their own authority either absent or faltering. Yet these questions persist. And they now have a force that cannot be ignored.

Jameson's strength is his clear sense of a world made of productive relationships, a class-divided and, for him, now "postmodernist" or "late capitalist" world that "assigns an increasingly essential structural function and position to aesthetic innovation and experimentation." The virtue of Jameson's recent writing on postmodern culture is its designation of a target, an antagonist, for critical energy. "If we do not achieve some general sense of a cultural dominant," he writes, "then we fall back into a view of present history as sheer heterogeneity, random difference, a coexistence of a host of distinct forces whose effectivity is undecidable. This has been at any rate the political spirit in which [Jameson's analysis of postmodernism] was devised: to project some conception of a new systematic cultural norm and its reproduction, in order to reflect more adequately on the most effective forms of any radical cultural politics today."[15] My argument with the designation of a "cultural dominant" as Jameson formulates it in some of his most interesting pages in *The Political Unconscious* (pp. 89–98) is not that it proposes "to homogenize the details of the contemporary landscape," as Mike Davis finds in the version offered three years later in *New Left Review*, from which I just quoted. Now and then Jameson does sweep contradictory and unassimilable phenomena together under the rubric "contradiction" (as it is theorized, for instance, as a structural event, an intersectional "variety of impulses from contradictory modes of cultural production all at once"). Rath-

er, the problem in targeting an immanent logic in culture itself, regardless of how contradictory and shot through with discrepancies
one considers it, is the tendency to deemphasize not so much the
economic dependencies of cultural forms and events (of culture's
reigning "logic") as productive logic—or, to be more precise, the
appropriation of labor of every kind. To stress the inherent logic of
the cultural field, contradictions notwithstanding, is to run the risk of
depreciating, by however little, the culturally manifested but not culturally determined exploitation of people and of work which maintains fundamental modes of production. We find these modes close
to us in the commoditization of knowledge that reinforces the cultural and economic logics we now live with.

Such a qualification can be applied to Gramsci's concept of cultural
hegemony, too. The problem there, a problem that a materialist account of culture and a Gramscian account of intellectuals might resolve if they were interrelated, is the tendency even within Marxist
analyses to separate social strata: to assign an indeterminate or contingent causal framework to a social "whole" of complexly interacting
"parts."[16] Such a solution is more tempting than ever as the proliferation of cultural vocabularies and the uncertainty of work relationships
within contemporary capitalism become more visible but less easy to
decode.[17] One notes in this regard that Jameson places his concern
with cultural logic squarely within the related logic of a constantly
evolving capitalist (and pre- and postcapitalist) mode of production,
which itself can be thought of as a homogenizing abstraction, since he
finds "that every social formation or historically existing society has in
fact consisted in the overlay and structural coexistence of several
modes of production at once."[18] What is left out in Jameson's trans-
umption of "the theoretical priority of the organizing concept of the
mode of production" (as he formulates a materialist basis for the
study of culture, appealing here to the decisive "concept of cultural
revolution") is an encounter with the *work relationships* that absorb
culture, drive the economy, and replicate the political and institutional orders of our time.[19] The problem literary criticism encounters
here, a problem that almost all academic work carries blindly, is the
productive and reproductive force that it creates by its own ordinary
efforts—and that it obscures by imagining itself somehow outside the
field of cultural, institutional, and economic logics that depend on
work and workers.

This dividing of labor from intellectual authority (as if the world
"out there" were essentially grist for theory) creates a dilemma for
critics in general and for radical cultural politics in particular. On one

side, it fosters the illusion that state power is autonomous and effectively unchallengeable. It does so by acting or speaking as if the appropriation of labor power and the generation of cultural authority (of noneconomic coercion) were separate realities, independent areas of the total movement of institutional power and its public and private control. As long as labor is not placed specifically and inextricably within the set of facts that constitute society, within the set of facts that critics interpret, the social network takes on a deterministic look—and not "from below," as a vulgar Marxism lurking in the shade to explain every deviance reductively. The failure to examine labor as a topic of intellectual respectability contributes to an even larger failure of criticism to understand its own effort as commitment, skill, and learning placed within (and in a sense to be grappled with, also contained by) our society. That oversight indicates the other side of criticism's continuing dilemma: abandonment of the knowledge by which it becomes culturally effective.

This emphasis anticipates my concern in the final pages of chapter 6 and in the last and longest chapter of this book, chapter 7. My argument turns from Jameson's instructive but I think truncated example of critical opposition to examine Foucault's writings on power and the state. I am concerned in particular with Foucault's understanding of our present strategic possibilities, with our capacity for strategic scholarship. That concern in turn leads me to examine Edward Said's powerful analysis of the critic's role in contemporary culture, an analysis that informs my position throughout this text. None of these writers deals as fully with the problem of class struggle (at present theoretically unfashionable) as does Nicos Poulantzas, whose analyses deserve more space than they receive here. My emphasis on labor power, its systematically demoted position within both classic wage labor and more recently expanded intellectual work arrangements, is a specifically Marxist emphasis. It is thus a topic less urgent for such a writer as Foucault, less central too for Said, but of the first importance for someone with Jameson's inclination and my own. This problem, nevertheless, cannot be summarized as an exclusively Marxist concern, since it is or should be a focal point for anyone who works to clarify the actual social forces and institutional structures that define contemporary human possibilities. It is also a topic that exposes major differences between competing Marxist positions. It is not only to Poulantzas's credit but to Ralph Miliband's, too, to have raised the issue of state hegemony, of the specific if also well-disguised authoritarian interests of the democratic nation-state, to the important though problematic place it deserves within critical discourse.[20] Though surely few things literary intellectuals do can be tied directly to the determining agencies of state power, enough of the impact of intellectual work is dependent upon or absorbed by the fundamental impingement of state policies on domestic and international events that critics can find concrete justification to ask about the role of the state, the shape of its power and complexity, in their lives and work.

Two elements of Poulantzas's position bear notice. The first is his understanding, similar to Foucault's, that individualization today— the room granted to people, to citizens, as "the subjects of certain freedoms" within the organization of political space where power operates—is limited by a series of mobile, more or less unapparent, but very real constraints upon political behavior. The emphasis here is on the state's contemporary organization. For Poulantzas, political life in Western Europe and North America excludes or at minimum depletes and counteracts popular mass political responses to state action. Such containment has not been perfect, by any means, but its significant accomplishment can be seen, in the United States, for example, in the alliance of labor unions with corporate management, an achievement that can be reckoned a step toward the widening and unification of state power. Such a fundamental change in the social landscape, dating perhaps most significantly from 1955 with the integration of the CIO with the AFL, has led to a declassing of the labor force as a traditional social element; and it has shifted the burden of political opposition to groups without long-standing political organization (blacks, women, antinuclear and ecological activists). But against this leakage of mass unrest, Poulantzas points to the fact that the state's coherence rests with the organization of knowledge that molds and constrains institutional and material life. Knowledge itself is seen to be a strategic force, an inherently technological and politically effective activity. To the extent that intellectuals are laborers who are not thoroughly absorbed within the managerial or administrative containment of creative energies, and to the extent that workers of every kind and increasing numbers of labor unions no longer find their interests accommodated within resurgent capital strategies (tactics of monopolistic takeover and noninfrastructural, or stock-appreciating, investment), very real affiliations between the two as uneasy allies mutually directed toward political change could be forged. This outlook projects a slow but steady commitment by large numbers of intellectuals to embrace the interests of laboring people, to advance those interests and thereby do their part to overcome the historic suspicion of the laboring class toward academic and other forms of intellectual authority.

Poulantzas's second emphasis worth noting is his stress on the openness of the state's dominating structure. That structure depends upon knowledge and the scientific information that a liberal society's free circulation of texts generates in enormous quantities. Knowledge and the ways it is formed and distributed, in turn, replicate the pervasive social division of labor that preserves the productive status quo. Although the state "is not a thing," as Ralph Miliband points out, but rather a constellation of loosely cooperating institutions—government agencies, judicial, military, and other instrumental apparatuses, alongside highly competitive but also cooperatively interacting businesses, schools, and foundations—the state is more than a notion, a mere theoretical blip. The state is the more rather than less ordered distribution of power and professional rationality which maintains existing relations of production.[21] Since those relations change for many reasons, the state must be thought of as a malleable and evolving set of operations, institutions, practices, and even traditions that create and recreate the fundamental relationships that preserve the productive order. In reverse, however, that coordination which constitutes the state as an active ensemble of human and material relations limits the degree as well as the kind of change possible in the structure of institutional coherence. Overtly, authoritatively, but also covertly as traditional intellectual influence, culture plays a crucial role in constructing the terms (the attitudes, the expectations, and most of all the vocabulary) of the permanence and change entangled there.

However abstract such an emphasis on the state may seem, it is not tangential to the self-consciousness a literary critic or philosopher or historian brings to the work of reading texts and teaching students. Poulantzas's thesis, a thesis central to debates both within and outside Marxism, projects what Jameson calls the "hard" rather than the "soft" vision of social domination. Poulantzas sees the state as a persistent political force in the economy, and thus he sees a form of political domination in "democratic" arrangements. He envisions power as "a series of relations among the various social classes" whereby, ultimately, "power is concentrated in the State" as the institutional embodiment of that inequity.[22] In opposition, we find the vision of cultural (rather than political) domination presented by Herbert Marcuse, Jean Baudrillard, Jean-François Lyotard, and others who stress varieties of depreciation in the critical impact of rational analysis. The remarkable feature of liberal democratic capitalism in this century, for Marcuse, has been its cultural flexibility—endlessly replaceable and consumable but, finally, discarded messages, a world without memory, repressively unleashing momentary intensities, devoted to the denial of historical depth and understanding. Such a culture industry, in the darker view of Baudrillard, presents "a type of absolute liberty" in which the sign, with its referential value emptied and without public access to rationally verifiable meanings and uses, becomes an object of "pure circulation" that not only expresses but reproduces the commoditization of all acts and artifacts.[23] Lyotard believes that this replication of economic logic within the organization of symbolic exchange culminates as a postmodern "incredulity toward metanarratives" which "entails a certain level of terror, whether soft or hard: be operational (that is, commensurable) or disappear."[24]

Each of these views unwittingly illuminates the linkage between writers and workers, between the writer-as-worker and everyone who is excluded from the authority and power that drives our society. The commoditization of symbolic exchange, of knowledge, asserts itself as a systematic operation—a state-legitimated, state-protected mode of extracting value from human energy—which in one phase discourages and in another prohibits any alteration of the material field that is built upon a class structure rendered obscure, accidental, lamentable (frequently deniable), but of course firmly in place. That noted, Poulantzas's emphasis has a further implication. The view he presents of the state's institutional materiality carries forward a debate in Marxist and non-Marxist accounts of culture which pits a systematic and in some sense totalitarian (more accurately, authoritarian) bureaucratic control against a potentially no less sytematic but more perverse arational (or countercultural) indoctrination. Recent debate about the shape and the influence of contemporary capitalist culture has focused on varieties of these alternative readings. We live, it seems, in a society controlled from above by the enormous strength of abstract capital and its not so abstract effects; or we live in a society induced to cooperate with existing realities (not all of them pernicious) by the sheer seductiveness of images that turn human and communal possibilities into the dead stuff of consumer packaging.

These certainly are not our only options for instructing students, for constructing intellectual and political alliances. Nonetheless, Poulantzas's formulation of the state's imbrication in the making and employment of knowledge calls attention to the all-but-overlooked class struggle. Poulantzas urges intellectuals to know more about the formative power of the division of labor that defines all work in our society. That focus offers hope of reviving our somewhat lagging awareness of the power intellectuals possess as the givers of names, the makers of categories and viewpoints and readings. Despite the sad retreat in his position in the last year or so of his life, Poulantzas did what many fail to do. He marked out where intellectual work stands and what it might stand for.[25]

These considerations call attention to the present difficulty of locating the specific force and contours of criticism's context. On which culture, for instance, should critics focus—the contemporary world of popular art forms, mass media, varieties of spectacle, and so on, or the traditional academic and intellectual practices with their accumulated bodies of knowledge? Can they be so neatly separated after all? And what is the relation between them? How, for example, do numerous ethnic cultures, at once unrepresented (or misrepresented) in mass culture and underrepresented in academic culture, fit into the social and cultural whole? In other words, what is criticism's specific object? Can it be thought to have one, or will criticism continue to disperse across textual fields and problems? Perhaps it is now necessary, if uncomfortable, to pursue a conflict-laden track that attempts to straddle disciplines, to link previously adjacent or discontinuous bodies of research, in order to locate the tactical advantages as well as the purely theoretical clarity of doing critical work. The mild form of this reconstruction might be "a novel system of discourse, a new way of talking" among intellectuals which Clifford Geertz sees as beginning with the task of "redescribing the describer as it [he or she] redescribes the described."[26] A much harsher, more skeptical form would begin (and end) with Georges Bataille's belief that "there is nothing" in capitalist and noncapitalist cultures "that permits one to define what is useful to man."[27]

I am neither as sanguine as Geertz nor as pessimistic as Bataille. My argument in this text is that North American critics have amassed the knowledge to move beyond positive and negative assessments of literary study (and of the role of knowledge in promoting social change). Critical awareness has achieved sufficient intellectual sophistication to undo its professional self-encasement by constructing both the conceptual and the institutional means for evaluating the ways in which research of every kind gains legitimacy, mainly in the university, to enforce its technical or professional authority within society as a whole. Our own research as literary specialists and theorists is not excluded. It "is impossible, now more than ever, to dissociate the work we do, within one discipline or several, from a reflection on the political and institutional conditions of that work," Jacques Derrida reminds us. His remarks in the Andrew Dickson White lecture at Cornell in 1983 carry recent critiques of professionalization and academic segmentation to a full realization of what is now at stake for critical writing. The "double question of 'professions'" in general, as a frame for the intellectual work that has been building our civilization throughout this century, marks out a distinct obligation that is at the same time a kind of privilege. The critical writer (deconstructor, dialectician, narrative tactician) writes from an institutional position whose authority, while limited not only by interinstitutional relations but by ideological and methodological disputes, nonetheless intersects with every conceivable interpretive community. That authority—its risks and rhythms, the ground it stands on—must be called into question or the critical act dies. Such questioning is criticism's enabling condition. It is troublesome if not just paradoxical. A writer can operate critically only from the self-undermining position that interrogates everything that stands "in front" as its ordinary field of interests and everything, also, that "grounds" or situates its own capacities. Derrida is right: "It is this double gesture that appears unsuitable and thus unbearable to certain university professionals in every country who join ranks to foreclose or censure it by all available means, simultaneously denouncing the 'professionalism' and the 'antiprofessionalism' of those who are calling others to these new responsibilities."[28]

The "double question" Derrida poses is the question of the professionalization of the university itself, of the work done by and within universities. It is, first, a question of the professional norms that "regulate university life according to the supply and demand of the marketplace and according to a purely technical idea of competence." It is, second, a question of which professional competencies (and what goals) the university has structured itself to pursue. This two-pronged question situates the university's raison d'être both historically and ideally (that is, in relation to its own founding principles). Derrida finds "the possibility of the modern university," restructured as it was in the last part of the nineteenth century, to be grounded on the principle of reason—that most Kantian of all themes and horizons. The university as we live and work with it today thus carries, unconsciously, a curious connection to a somewhat nostalgic era of intellectual enlightenment, an era whose ideals persevere as noble remnants of a faith that rationality can comprehend its own movements. That faith, of course, extended outward to all things. And so the principle of reason once seemed sufficient to "ground" itself even as it inspected, analyzed, catalogued, and dissected every material and conceptual element.

But, Derrida notes, reason may be "something that gives rise to exchange, circulation, borrowing, debt, donation, restitution." Reason, Derrida imagines (after Nietzsche and Bataille), is problematically and complexly interwoven with mechanisms or habits of guilt and punishment, on one side, and with consumption and its unproductive expenditures (with waste, luxury, and excess) on the other. This is a large and important topic that Derrida in this lecture only skims in passing as he moves to take stock of the responsibility that intellectual work is always enjoined to uphold. It is, however, a topic that he explores in several places and that, confronted here, if only allusively, stakes out limits on (and in) the principle of reason.[29] "Are we obeying the principle of reason when we ask what grounds this principle which is itself a principle of grounding?"

We are not, Derrida points out, but he does not mean to say that we disobey the principle of reason when we pursue its foundations or contexts. In other words, reason, that great justifying ideal of academic effort (of university operations), is the agent of all those formal interrogations that question the self-sufficiency of reason and provide the means to inspect the university's "autonomy." The university today, Derrida sees, is increasingly an "institution of modern technoscience . . . built both on the principle of reason and what remains hidden in that principle." It is for this reason, for reasons of rational insufficiency, or at any rate of reason's embeddedness in operations that resist reason's ideal and suspicious clarity, that Derrida argues in "Le Parergon" (1978) that deconstructive readings of texts (in every sense, of every sort) must also pursue their own institutional contexts. Such writing is "rational" but not unproblematically, immediately, and solely rational. It cannot, for one thing, effortlessly separate "the reassuring reality of what is outside the text" from what is "within" a text or "inside" thought and conceptual activity.[30] The question of reading and of critical writing thereby leads to the question of their place or grounding, which is, unavoidably, the university and its academic and professional practices. Thus to pursue reason is to pursue texts. And to pursue either is to come under the obligation to interrogate "what is generally, and wrongly, considered as philosophy's external habitat," what seems to be

the extrinsic conditions of its exercise—that is, the historical forms of its pedagogy, the social, economic or political structures of this pedagogical institution. It is by touching solid structures, 'material' institutions, and not merely discourses or significant representations, that deconstruction distinguishes itself from analysis or 'criticism'. And to be pertinent, it works, in the most rigorous manner possible, in just the place where the so-called 'internal' operation of philosophy articulates itself necessarily (that is, internally *and* externally) with the institutional conditions and forms of teaching and learning. And it drives this to the point where the concept of institution itself would be submitted to the same deconstructive treatment.[31]

This is, I think, the moment to verify the significance of the Marxist concept of "the mode of production," that set of complicated interrelations of the economic structures that initially call into existence and then limit everything we refer to as the institutional framework of any social formation. The notion of an overall "mode of production," Etienne Balibar asserts, introduces a theoretical awareness of the discontinuity, of the specific and concrete institutional embodiments, that particular societies impose upon what can too easily seem to be a natural or inevitable historical context (our current capitalist environment, for example). Within each society's mode of production two forms of opposition or contradiction can be found. One is situated essentially within the social and cultural networks: the struggle that manifests class divisions, overt and immediately human entanglements that legal and cultural institutions often obscure, rendering their contradictoriness anything but overt. The other antagonism resides primarily in the economic sphere. It is the antagonistic structure that divides workers from their labor, a chasm (institutional, ideological, but mostly relational, as in the practice known as "selling one's labor") between forces of production and the relations of production which define an economic order.

I return to this somewhat technical notion of the mode of production on the heels of Derrida's comment about the specific rigor of deconstruction because it seems to me that we need to pursue not only the *concept* of institution but the *conditions* of thought and writing (of making concepts) and the conditions that *generate institutions* as well.[32] Derrida has seen deconstruction as "an investigation which questions the codes inherited from ethics and politics."[33] But not until recently, and even then somewhat obliquely, has he moved further toward embracing the necessity of investigating the political and institutional conditions of that work, of the writer's placement in a material and cultural context. A number of things need to be said in this regard.

First of all, Derrida's claim in the passage from "Le Parergon" is that the "inside" and the "outside" of a concept or text are not unrelated to each other and not separate (or stratified) in the work of deconstructive reading. This claim follows the long-standing and essentially foundational aim in Derrida's work of unlocking static classifications, dual oppositions, inert and merely programmatic third terms that appear to "resolve" antagonisms with yet more general or abstract conceptual sublimations (transcendences, etc.). Derrida is always alert to forms of conflict which maintain themselves in new guises that assert a higher movement or perspective and falsely claim resolution. He is no less alert to conceptual embeddedness and overlapping, to the way terms imply their own complements, demand supplementation, call for a variety of differential terms and operations in their putative singularity. Since intellectual effort is always attached to a conceptual play that is systematically inserted within the tradition of Western hierarchical oppositions, attached also to the institutions that employ those linguistic structures authoritatively, it follows that a rigorous undoing of metaphysical assumptions (and operations) will have to confront the institutional conditions that ground its tasks and movements.

And so we see Derrida in his moving and I think powerful lecture at Cornell grappling with the institutionalization of reason. That institutionalization is extremely concrete, with extreme and altogether substantial consequences, and Derrida's pursuit in fact approaches its concreteness. The major embodiment of the "obscurantist and nihilist effects" of the present institutional order on the principle of reason resides precisely in the professional compartmentalizing that undermines everything in reason that is common, nontechnical, and irreducible to specialized uses. Derrida decries, in particular, the "new 'censorship,'" which, more subtle than its official royal counterpart in Kant's day, does not prohibit so much as it constrains by "orienting" research—that is, by forcing all intellectual endeavor funded within the university to succumb to a logistics of "application," of end-oriented or "bottom-line" rationality. "A state power or the forces that it represents no longer need to prohibit research or to censor discourse, especially in the West. It is enough that they can limit the means, regulate support for production, transmission, and diffusion." In sum, the bureaucratic machinery of normal university functions acts as a conduit for inventing and maintaining certain forms of surplus value while diminishing others. But the skewing and repression of the dominant ideal of "fundamental" and "disinterested" research does not take place only there:

> We can no longer dissociate the principle of reason from the very idea of technology in the realm of their modernity. Never before has so-called basic scientific research been so deeply committed to aims that are at the same time military aims. The very essence of the military, the limits of military technology and even the limits of its accountability are no longer

definable. . . . At the service of war, of national and international security, research programs have to encompass the entire field of information, the·stockpiling of knowledge, the workings and thus also the essence of language and of all semiotic systems, translation, coding and
decoding, the play of presence and absence, hermeneutics, semantics,
structural and generative linguistics, pragmatics, rhetoric. I am ac-
cumulating all these disciplines in a haphazard way, on purpose, but I
shall end with literature, poetry, the arts and fiction in general: the
theory that has these disciplines as its object may be just as useful in
ideological warfare as it is in experimentation with variables in all-too-
familiar perversions of the referential function. Such a theory may always be put to work in communications strategy, the theory of com-
mands. . . . From now on, so long as it has the means, a military budget
can invest in anything at all, in view of deferred profits: "basic" scientific
theory, the humanities, literary theory and philosophy. . . . What is produced in this field can always be used. And even if it should remain
useless in its results, in its productions, it can always serve to keep the
masters of discourse busy: the experts, professionals of rhetoric, logic or
philosophy who might otherwise by applying their energy elsewhere.[34]

There, as clearly stated as it ought to be, is the field of forces in
which critics and students of textual study now work. This last possibility, the humanist's distraction, can be posed against the emerging
political relevance of scientific dissent. One cannot fail to comprehend the importance of such efforts as those of the Union of
Concerned Scientists and the more recent collective action of scientists involved with United Campuses to Prevent Nuclear War (an organization aimed at persuading scientists and engineers throughout
the United States to refuse government funds for "Star Wars" or
Strategic Defense Initiative research). The critic's institutional context, no less than the physicist's, is saturated with a militaristic purpose
that, Derrida suggests, draws intellectual work into its ever-widening
scope. Most at stake immediately is the will to resist, to make dissent
collective and highly public. Whether or not it is appropriate to bring
the concept of a current or predominant mode of production to bear
on Derrida's remarks—whether he is smuggling in, unknowingly perhaps, the disaccumulation theory that sees the capitalist state as simultaneously an investor in and a consumer of large capital programs
(military buildups serving as the most efficient way to promote established capital interests while creating profits that do not "trickle
down," thereby prompting renewed demand for large social programs by an emboldened proletariat)[35]—Derrida is doing more than
posing a theoretical issue here. He is, of course, certainly doing that.

For example, the issue at work in particular is the question of the-oretical foregrounding: of the cognitive and material or social space before (at the threshold of) the intellectual work that generates mod-els—models of texts, of interpretive practices, of institutions and in-stitutional framing, and of theoretical structures (such as Kant's "in-stitution of the principle of reason"; such as the Marxian "mode of production"; such as the Derridean "deconstructive" project). Yet Derrida has moved well beyond textually centered theory without sacrificing his characteristic antifoundational concerns. Here, accept-ing his Andrew Dickson White professorship-at-large, mulling aloud the significance of the Cornell landscape, poised as it is between two ravines, Derrida offers what amounts to his most decisive judgment on the political and institutional landscape of intellectual work:

> A major debate is under way today on the subject of the politics of research and teaching, and on the role that the university may play in this arena: whether this role is central or marginal, progressive or dec-adent, collaborative with or independent of that of other research in-stitutions sometimes considered better suited to certain ends. . . .
>
> Such a problematics cannot always—cannot any longer—be reduced to a problematics centered on the nation-state: it is now centered instead on multinational military-industrial complexes or techno-economic net-works, or rather international technomilitary networks that are appar-ently multi- or trans-national in form.[36]

These statements, and his Cornell lecture in its entirety, clarify a confusion that has crippled North American deconstructive practices even though Derrida himself has not been confused (Perry Ander-son's view to the contrary notwithstanding).[37] Since *De la gram-matologie* (1967), the relation between texts and interpretive opera-tions, on one hand, and the violence and coercive power of material institutions, on the other, has been marked out if also kept to one side in Derrida's writing. Deconstructive literary criticism on the whole has misunderstood Derrida's concern with groundings and foundations, with texts and their contexts, most specifically with the generative context of Western writing, which he has looked at not as a series of texts (a collection of cultural events) but as a signifying practice imme-diately linked to clerical and state bureaucratic (as well as military) power. Without question Derrida's almost exclusive emphasis on sig-nification, to the detriment of a better delineated culturally material set of conceptual and writing practices, has given that misunderstand-ing room. But Derrida has always presented the notion of *text* in a larger sense than it has been accorded by most of his academic followers. It is this larger, more troublesome notion of text and context that inhabits Derrida's concern with the principle of reason as a foundational concept, an institution, in fact, within an academy now more than ever devoting its resources to a grotesquely irrational application of that principle. Writing and its empirical or institutional "outside," as Derrida insists, are never dissociated. Each is sedimented inside the other as the contradictory and inevitably self-fracturing discourse, virtually infinite in its embodiments, which can be arrested as a document of knowledge, authority, or power.

One of the most trenchant criticisms of Derrida's project has been that it has not been specific enough in designating the way writing, as an organized operation of metaphysical assumptions and signifying habits, carries or embodies force.[38] The particular insertion of *archi-écriture* (of the primordial foundation of sense and meaning, of time, of presence) in Western culture, a historical structure with determinate boundaries, in large measure remains vague in Derrida's work and to that degree has encouraged methodological reductions of his texts for a variety of essentially antiseptic academic projects. In his lecture at Cornell, however, Derrida moves away from small pedagogies of textual uncertainty. He has placed the terminological reversals and eccentric vocabulary of his remarkable anti-ontotheological enterprise within recognizable institutional and historical space. With referential clarity undiminished by unwarranted technical sophistication, Derrida calls for a commitment among all intellectually engaged people "to define new responsibilities in the face of the university's total subjection to the technologies of informatization." This enterprise necessitates, Derrida reckons, "a new way of educating students that will prepare them to undertake new analyses in order to evaluate these ends and to choose, when possible, among them." That imperative, in particular, embraces a much more deliberate focus on the political aims of education at every level—a topic that thrusts criticism and theory into the least resolvable disputes in our culture. It demands, for example, that the curriculum be looked at as a transmission of values that simultaneously challenge and uphold existing social constructs. The object of such pedagogical renovation would be to activate the critical skills of students currently trained to professionalize (to channel, narrow, and depoliticize) their intellects. For critics this "new way" means a much greater role for the intricate demands of instructing. It goes considerably beyond the traditional task of teaching students to read and write. It implies, in sum, the need for group efforts to change institutional processes of creating, implementing, and evaluating courses so that students may be put on the troubling path of learning how to imagine society as a structure of contradictory and competing elements. Institutions, political forces, economic relations, ideologies, historical conjunctures, transitional moments *can be named* even as students and teachers grapple with the complexities of argumentation and representation which divide varying accounts of the issues at stake and of the social ensemble itself. The least realized and possibly most necessary job within that effort is the clarification, both historical and theoretical, of social reality as an institutional whole without final shape or outcome: a network of institutional relationships held together by traditions and practices objectified (made available, authoritative, and rational) by institutional means.

One of the outstanding features of this task, one that Derrida helps to frame, is the recognition of unconscious but wholly "naturalized" oppositions in the social process suffused, and one might say rigidified, throughout language. The whole matter, of course, could be put in reverse, oppositions in linguistic structures, metaphysical pressures, and discursive actions invading and effectively contaminating social events. Such flexibility amounts to an indeterminism akin to indeterminisms that Derrida has seemed to champion, a textual world, as Said has noted, surprisingly unconcerned with "the role of information" in the reading of texts. The point of noting this reversal is to admit Derrida's point that interpretation, theory, and teaching itself are all vulnerable to a latent ideological invasion that can be constituted at a level of generality vast enough to throw into ever-receding arguments and problems any analysis that means to discriminate the precise place of ideological force or gestation. But the principle of reason, on which intellect and academy both ground their actions, operates in institutionally specific circumstances that are historically specific as well. They are not unattached to practices that can be determined and more or less clearly designated. The will to make such determinations and designations shows signs of gaining entry into Derrida's writing. The new pedagogy Derrida calls for can come into being only if exceedingly particular descriptions of pedagogical action and equally specific examinations of institutional consensus become important features of the humanities curriculum.

Because Derrida's work has assumed such central importance for just those literary critics and teachers most concerned with the dynamics of texts and language, a concern that leads to analyses of the role of language in everyday practices of social and cultural domination, his turn toward concrete historical and institutional circumstances is more than a token gesture of momentary interest. Derrida has, in effect, opened the concept of text and of intellectual work to an "outside" that simultaneously transverses what we read and how we read as well as where we read. For those who have followed a deconstructive track in order to stay within a safe textual haven (an intertextual maelstrom, perhaps), this more explicit doubling and re-doubling of reading and teaching practices alongside the problematic subjection of all intellectual activity to technologies of information control poses a challenge: to work through the genuinely troublesome issue of "text" and "context" as mutually implicating, interrelational networks of authority, force, meaning, and cultural density (what Marshall Berman has dubbed "the signs in the street").[39] Dominick LaCapra warns us not to grasp some form of manifest context as an immediate horizon, a fixed and stable frame for reading. "For the historian, the very reconstruction of a 'context' or a 'reality' takes place on the basis of 'textualized' remainders of the past" which plunge the wary reader, the historically acute reader, into a difficult series of choices about which texts provide adequate access to the traditions, cultures, institutions, and issues that pose the "site" of knowledge (at once historical and critical) to be retrieved from forget-fulness and postulated without reduction. LaCapra's "point is that in treating the relation of texts to contexts, what is often taken as a solution to the problem should be reformulated and investigated as a real problem itself."[40]

The virtue of Derrida's more graphic opening onto institutional conflict is, first of all, its promise of initiating reading habits that, less compromised by the ordinarily conservative access to traditions that hold knowledge (its "difference"), allow writing room to investigate the present in order to imagine alternative futures. LaCapra's notion that "interpretation is a form of political intervention that engages the historian in a critical process that relates past, present, and future through complex modes of interaction involving both continuities and discontinuities" is one way to frame this Derridean promise. That process involves, in addition to the "rigor" with which texts may be read, a very specific interrogation of the *placement* of reading prac-tices. And here LaCapra's warning makes greatest sense: "It is mis-leading to pose the problem of understanding in terms of either of two extremes: the purely documentary representation of the past and the 'presentist' quest for liberation from the 'burden' of history through unrestrained fictionalizing and mythologizing."[41] In other words, besides the diachronic movement of texts, traditions, and in-terpretive practices which must be read as a never-ceasing transfor-mation of culture, people, materials, and modes of production into texts-and-contexts where knowledge actually lives, we find a more momentary synchronic structure that is the projection (or the understanding) of a cultural and institutional formation in which writers write, readers read, and events take place. This transformative "context" is invented by any imaginative reader as a historical frame for (and in) the work of interpretation. It is continuous with the present as traditions, themes, problems—as texts and the enduring process of social change—carried from the past and ultimately invading the interpretive act. This historical context makes a constructed and not a discovered or recovered and intact horizon. As a context emerging through change of many kinds, stable enough in these delineations to seem continuous within discontinuities, it frames the act of critical interrogation and the pedagogical circumstance as the historical depth and thickness that have placed us where we read and write. This framing, then, appears both "here" and "over there" some way. Much of the difficulty of avoiding false extremes—reified "documentary representation" and "presentist" self-evidence or immanence—resides in grounding the study of texts so that our students recognize how much our situation as we live it is enmeshed in a history of material and cultural forces erupting through our acts.

If the "move" Derrida has made foreshadows a radicalizing of attention and commitment to investigate the emergence of history in our own institutional actions, it will do so by increasing interest in three interrelated issues: the question of *domination* (framed now, most often, as the problem of "postmodern" culture); the question of *audience* (who, precisely, critical discourse means to reach); and the question of intellectual *responsibility,* which is at once an issue of the goals and purposes of intellectual work and of their strategies (discursive, institutional, and more generally though problematically political). All of these issues bear directly on the way intellectuals define themselves professionally. They bear just as insistently on teaching practices. The virtue of looking at our cultural and institutional contexts, then, appears most forcefully as a strengthened exploration of the material consequences of discourse.

This is where Marxist thought and writing are most helpful, but two features of Marxist scholarship must be taken into account. First, despite the recent emergence of a deep and multilevel Marxist efflorescence in the English-speaking academic world, an event Perry Anderson regards as a "nascent Anglo-American hegemony in historical materialism," very little of its substance collides with the day-to-day work of the universities where it is produced.[42] Such extraordinary analytic competence sits in uneasy relation to the more comfortable nonmaterialist and undialectical practices that structure teaching and research. Theory, perhaps historical materialism most of all, is institutionally rootless—a sort of nomadic interloper on foreign soil. That rootlessness is not exclusively a cultural matter but reflects the way knowledge is generated and used in our time. Knowledge is a materially bounded, materially reproductive realm that more and more links technological innovation to a central cultural matrix that for some time has taken its defining models and images from scientific discourse. Such models, of course, have helped to legitimize a social order that is dissolving traditional grounds for class confrontation and reorganizing itself along bureaucratic and technocratic lines. Jameson, I should add, has commented in this regard about "the difficulty of articulating cultural and informational commodities with the labor theory of value."[13] But one of the elements in that difficulty is the marketplace affiliation between intellectuals (teachers, critics, writers) and the world of corporate capitalism. To the extent that intellectuals consider themselves experts who should fashion their work on exclusively specialized paths, the commoditization of intellect and information will continue, and they will continue in their social and political affiliation with huge capitalist interests instead of with ordinary human interests, with those who own and manage capital rather than those who are used by it.

The last circumstance acceptable to university managers would be a coordinated curriculum motivated by its critical zeal to change the way knowledge functions. It may be in this sense that LaCapra's caution about dividing texts from contexts makes its best point. The critic's texts are part of a larger text that opens and closes lines of access to the social whole surrounding the critic's work. Since that work at present is stymied as an effective political force in our culture, the choice of deconstruction or historical materialism matters only as a preparatory move—as a strategic choice of interpretive perspective for explicitly concrete social goals. Thus the first thing to note about Derrida's turn toward institutional contexts, on one hand, and about the growing strength of Marxist studies in England and North America, on the other, is their mutual availability in an academic structure that restricts their intrinsic ambitions to revitalize resistance to a culture that makes possible an expanding, dehumanizing, and persistently abstracting mode of commoditized knowledge production. The second feature to be noted—and here I share Anderson's political and intellectual sympathies—is the absence of properly Marxist strategies that could generate pedagogical and critical practices "for directly confronting the problem of the overthrow of the authority of capital."[44]

If one turned back, then, to seek the defining facts of the contemporary modes of production we live with—or to seek their concept for the purpose of analyzing humanistic education and the political reason deposited in our knowledge-bearing institutions—one would need to confront a certain degree of irrationality. This irrationality can be looked at, from Jameson's perspective, as a specifically political form of unconscious but concrete forces: a political unconscious that is not an aggregate of psyches and individualities, not a collection of images or competing ideologies, but a much less malleable structure of material reality which shapes the institutional organizations that give life meaning as well as social limits. Therefore, even to pose the notion of a determinable mode, or set of modes, of production is to open up all the trickiest issues critical intellectuals now face.

When we do so we see, after Foucault, that in some real sense the institutional conditions of culture are already deposited within discursive formations—for example, within the writing activity of critics. The question here, as we will notice in looking at Foucault later, is not what funds or originates meaning and its practices; it is what position intellectuals can occupy if they are to carry out a transformative and not a reproductive, legitimating role in society. What limits constrain writers in advance of any attempt to make sense or nonsense? The idea of a mode of production is not directly embraced by Foucault, but it haunts his work as an unstated issue he skirts by projecting institutional forces within instead of without or around the writer's work. Derrida, too, denies the antagonistic opposition of inside and outside, of text and context. The concept of an active, targetable mode of production has been maneuvered in his work (most graphically perhaps in his Cornell lecture) to constitute the principle of reason itself, a principle that contains traditional intellectual legitimacy and an ever-evolving set of uses that ratify productive energies. It is here, at the heart of the university's claim to be above and beyond political and economic determinations, that scientific and professional disciplines enforce modes of production that are simultaneously cultural, legal, logical, economic, and ultimately institution-making and institution-breaking—political in essence, derived from the material and ideological fields they inhabit. To probe the political responsibility of the critic's work, then, takes us everywhere intellectuals manifest their socially significant self-consciousness.

2

The Role of the
Critical Intellectual

In the context of international influence that North American culture enjoys, the failure of the humanities to sustain interest in the function of intellectual authority suggests that the intellectual's role may be troublesome.[1] It is not insignificant, then, to find intense if indirect debate about the intellectual's present position in our society. That is what we find when we read Alvin Gouldner's studies of Western intellectual elites alongside Noam Chomsky's essays on the interaction of intellectuals and the state. The debate is joined by Gouldner, who examines Chomsky's Huizinga lecture, "Intellectuals and the State," given in Leiden in December 1977, although the full extent of disagreement between their positions emerges only when we compare the ways they define the nature of intellectual authority. The central texts in Gouldner's distinguished list of publications (in a career cut short by his death, at sixty-two, in 1982) are the three volumes of his trilogy *The Dark Side of the Dialectic* and his essay "Prologue to a Theory of Revolutionary Intellectuals." Chomsky's important texts are too numerous to mention, but his essays "Objectivity and Liberal Scholarship" and "The Responsibility of Intellectuals," in *American Power and the New Mandarins,* are among them, as is the lecture Gouldner looks at. That piece and another strong statement, "Foreign Policy and the Intelligentsia," are collected in *Towards a New Cold War.*[2]

Gouldner is interested in clarifying both the limits and the possibilities of critical discourse in its attempt to further a "revolution-in-permanence" that, in his estimation, intellectual elites since the French Revolution have sought. That notion meets a great deal of resistance on both the left and the right, since, on one side, scholarly activity in its conventional forms appears to be strongly attached to national identities and state agencies while, on the other side, critical discourse is viewed as a subordinate partner to the essentially conservative function of protecting and dispensing literary or philosophical, not "revolutionary," values. Gouldner sympathizes with each side of this resistance and accounts for both positions in his "left Hegelian sociology," as he calls his work, by defining intellectuals as historical agents in the international class struggle. As a group shaped by varied disciplines, motives, and projects, intellectuals constitute "a New Class" which is, he insists, "a flawed universal class":

> The New Class is elitist and self-seeking and uses its special knowledge to advance its own interests and power, and to control its own work situation. Yet the New Class may also be the best card that history has presently given us to play. The power of the New Class is growing. . . . It is a class internally divided with tensions between (technical) intelligentsia and (humanistic) intellectuals. No celebration, mine is a critique of the New Class which does not view its growing power as inevitable, which sees it as morally ambivalent, embodying the collective interest but partially and transiently, while simultaneously cultivating its own guild advantage.[3]

Borrowing legitimacy for this use of the concept of class from Marx's ascription of the term to economic and cultural differences that divide one group from another, Gouldner sees intellectuals to be united by class interests because for the most part (and despite ideological divisions) they stand in a similar relation to power. They share among themselves what Gouldner calls "cultural capital." In other words, intellectuals—teachers, scholars, writers, theorists—construct the ideological bases for any society to accomplish its economic tasks and national purposes. Managers of private and public institutions employ technocratic and linguistic skills. And so, Gouldner reminds us, every society depends on various sorts of expert knowledge and interpretive ability to accomplish its routine functions. The service intellectuals perform in society is somewhat ambiguous, however. They occupy the always contested role of symbol creators and managers; they help to define each area of culture. But most of all they reproduce and modify the course of society by controlling knowledge. As teachers, intellectuals train critical readers and writers and prepare those who will move into positions of power and authority throughout society. Inevitably, the authority intellectuals assume within the culture depends on the way they are perceived by society as a whole. But, and this is one of Gouldner's central points, since intellectuals themselves have considerable control over the way they are judged, their authority is primarily self-generated and depends on the active reformulation of culture by theoretical and scholarly production.

The authority of intellectual work thus turns out to be both paradoxical and ambivalent. Those who control the economic infrastructure are forced to accommodate an intellectual class whose activity at once legitimates and undermines what Gouldner calls "old" capitalist values and status.[4] To put this another way, Gouldner argues that "all the specific traditions constituting the *cultural* formation of (Western) intellectuals spark rebellion against the tradition and authority in being."[5] But his further emphasis points to the contradictory nature of intellectual activity, since intellectuals themselves rarely think of their work as *historically* grounded but see it as *self*-grounded and autonomous: "The basic ideology of discourse, as the ideology of intellectuals and intelligentsia, premises a sphere of autonomy in which speech and action are rule-oriented rather than causally controlled by external force; where conclusions are reflectively *selected* and constructed in the light of certain rules, rather than being imposed by force, tradition, impulse, or the imperative 'laws' of science."[6]

In brief, intellectual elites are language elites who depend on market conditions for the kind and stability of their employment. They occupy not only the theoretical and pedagogical positions within society but managerial positions in technological organizations as well. Their linguistic expertise, however, in large measure blinds intellectuals to the functional and pragmatic nature of their work, Gouldner tells us. Instead of defining themselves as historical agents of change whose constant renovation of cultural and professional discourses extends beyond the rule-oriented circulation of knowledge, intellectuals see themselves as executing a kind of work unattached to anything except their own writing. In other words, intellectuals may identify with the general human interest, but in fact their identity derives from their work routine as people who stand somewhat outside the ordinary commerce of society.

This perspective opens up the privileged area in which scholarly authority and critical knowledge reside. Since intellectual activity cannot be validated in methodologically unambiguous ways, and since intellectuals tend to identify themselves as distinguished from those who do not write (who are not scholars and theorists), "intellectuals can be conceptualized rigorously only in terms of the 'language game' they play, in Wittgenstein's sense."[7] Gouldner's point here admits the extent to which intellectual work is founded on a carefully nurtured sense of cultural detachment and on professional disagreements. At the heart of the intellectual enterprise is a fundamental uneasiness about what constitutes critical authority and scholarly expertise. In some sense one could say that authority itself is the central topic of concern for writers in every branch of knowledge, humanistic knowledge perhaps most of all, since the canonical docoments and scholarly procedures that establish an academic discipline are always open to challenge. Underneath the contests that generate scholarship, a set of rules and assumptions—all of those conventions and practices that embody a field of study—regulates the norms of discourse that allow someone to enter a particular intellectual community. The crucial factor in organized intellectual work thus is the "normalizing" of routines and questions, eventually of the texts and disciplinary standards, that collect into a recognizable rationality with its own rules and special languages. These are the habits that allow intellectuals to perceive themselves as historically "free" agents whose self-defined activity is not attached to any vested authority or power beyond their own professional competence.

The positive aspects of this position should be obvious. Intellectuals, because of their self-regulating rationality, have been able to adopt positions as "representatives" of society as a whole. They have not emphasized their own class status to the exclusion of those larger perspectives that alone are capable of weighing local interests against human welfare generally. The specific form this position has taken, as Gouldner goes to considerable lengths to make clear, is theory in all its varieties.[8] Intellectual culture, Gouldner notes, is a "culture of critical discourse" that conceives itself to be *"relatively* more *situation-free"* than ordinary speech and writing. In essence, critical discourse proceeds "not by invoking authorities" but by advancing arguments that seek to authorize themselves without recourse to external social arrangements. This, at any rate, is the scholarly ideal. Just this "wish to be free to re-examine the standpoint of the common sense and of everyday life,"[9] however, generates a new dilemma that Gouldner articulates in a lucid passage in his "Prologue to a Theory of Revolutionary Intellectuals."

> The real crux of the historical problem of intellectuals and intelligentsia . . . [is] that they are *both* elitist and the bearers of an emancipatory rationality; their rationality enables a critique of the institutionalized forms of domination, but it also contains the seeds of a *new*

form of domination. Their new rationality entails an escape from the constraints of tradition but imposes new constraints on expressivity, imagination, play, and insists on control rather than openness as the key to truth, on a certain domination of nature, including the self, rather than on a surrender to it.

The intellectuals' culture of careful and critical discourse implies that it is now possible for anyone, however rich or powerful, to speak wrongly. It implies that whatever is *may* be wrong or made better. . . . Yet, in setting themselves up as judges of established systems of stratification, the speakers of the new grammar, the intellectuals, not only undermine *traditional* inequities, but they tacitly affirm a method which is itself the standard of a new inequality. To speak well and live with reflexive self-examination is better than living an unexamined life, they affirm. Philosophy is better than art, they hold. Thus even as the traditional inequities are subverted, a new hierarchy of the knowing, the knowledgeable, the reflexive, and insightful is silently inaugurated. This is a central contradiction of emancipatory intellectuals—the new universal class in embryo—that brings a new darkness at noon.[10]

This culminating figure of portentous intellectual gloom suggests the political emphasis implicit everywhere in Gouldner's outlook. We have here, as Chomsky makes clear, the theme of "the god that failed," always accompanied by distress about the violence of Marxist "vanguard" politics—the violence of revolutionary intellectuals—and by a corresponding belief in the more passive role of intellectuals in the politics of Western state capitalism.[11] Without question such distress has often been appropriate. The history of the various twentieth-century Marxisms has been brutal and bloody. For that reason, Gouldner points out, "the community of Marxist and socialist revolutionaries has tended increasingly to expand the importance of violence as an agency of social change."[12] But this misuse of intelligence, the demise of sober reflection in the exercise of force, cannot be attributed solely to Marxist intellectuals. In fact, the theme of violence and its relation to intellectuals—the ways in which, and the degrees to which, intellectuals accommodate their work to state power and to the logistics of its force—is not only one of the most controversial topics imaginable for intellectuals in non-Marxist societies but an issue that exposes political differences between otherwise compatible viewpoints. Gouldner and Chomsky share a disrespect for the technocratic rationality of modern societies; each promotes political, not cultural, solutions to the economic and social illness all but accepted as an unchangeable reality by conventional humanist scholarship. Yet the targets they select for their writing, and thus their subsequent definitions of the intellectuals' role in society, diverge precisely at the point where violence—or the actual impact of intellectual work on state power—arises as a topic for critical debate.

That the difference here is not superficial can be seen in Gouldner's disagreement with Chomsky's critique of "moderate American scholarship," that "process of 'counterrevolutionary subordination,'" Chomsky tells us, "which poses a threat to scholarly integrity in our own counterrevolutionary society, just as 'revolutionary subordination,' a phenomenon often noted and rightly deplored, has undermined scholarly integrity in revolutionary and postrevolutionary situations."[13] Chomsky is concerned with scholarship that serves the power of the American state, legitimating, protecting, and often obscuring the violence of its foreign policy. Gouldner, on the contrary, worries about the exploitation of intellectuals, whose influence in revolutionary movements is "greater *prior* to the time that the movement succeeds in capturing state power."[14] This concern leads him to consider the revolutionary intellectual's position in peasant uprisings in the Third World and in the cultural revolutions in China under Mao Tse-tung. More startling yet, it leads him to speculate on the need for "a theory that focuses on the social character of intellectuals and intelligentsia as involved in the domination of Soviet society *and* in the *resistance* to that domination."[15]

We see here two fundamentally opposed projects. Chomsky seeks to clarify the body of knowledge that determines the public perception of our government and its decisions, while Gouldner turns away from the revolutionary or counterrevolutionary possibilities of North American scholarship in order to reckon fundamental contradictions in Western intellectuals, contradictions that doubtless account for the failure of humanists in the United States to make the systematic abuses of government authority a central pedagogical and scholarly concern. Chomsky's aim, as Gouldner laments, is clearly moral. He wants to shed light on the workings of the society we live in. That is the society most open to the influence of North American critical intellectuals; certainly the Soviety empire will not be altered by that scholarship. And so a strange but somewhat familiar ambivalence shows up in Gouldner's examination of Chomsky's position:

> [Chomsky's] recitation of the often shameless behavior of the New Class is convincing. Its toadying for favor, advancement, awards, and notice; its eagerness to provide (paid) services and arguments for both industry and the state; its readiness to be the "servant of power" (in Loren Baritz's apt phrase), are among the New Class's more unloveable traits. I can think of no epithet Chomsky uses that is altogether unjust.

Yet from another perspective it may be that these are simply characteristics common to rising groups before they take power. One wonders
why Chomsky thinks the New Class should set a new historical standard
of morality? In most societies most classes at most times serve the powers
that be. Why shouldn't the New Class at first be the "servant of power"?
The bourgeoisie, for example, was the servant of the court and crown
for as long as it had to be. And the working class today is everywhere the
servant of some power.[16]

Apparently Chomsky is right about Western intellectuals but wrong
to call such strict attention to their cooperation with capitalist interests. The reason for this skewed assessment is not hard to find.
Gouldner sees that intellectuals as a group are already secure within
the structure of privilege and cultural authority. They are at once
"elitist" and "emancipatory," he tells us, a "contradictory" class that
undermines "*traditional* inequities" while becoming "itself the standard of a new inequality." In other words, intellectuals are well inside
the hierarchy of social power. The warning he offers, that "the New
Class is hardly the end of domination," that it "is also the nucleus of a
new hierarchy and the elite of a new form of cultural capital,"[17] becomes as much an excuse for the counterrevolutionary habits of intellectuals as it is a meek indictment. Nowhere in his writing does
Gouldner define precisely the way "domination" by intellectual elites
might work. We find instead enormous optimism about the future of
intellectuals, since, in a society that depends upon ideological justifica-
tions to contain tensions generated by its own contradictions, intellectuals control the means of ideological production. This is the "revolutionary" outcome of the rise of the new class within postindustrial
capitalism. Three elements, therefore, characterize the role and the
place of intellectuals in contemporary reality and will, from Gouldner's point of view, determine the future of capitalism: (1) intellectuals own or manage "cultural capital" and, especially, foster a disruptive critical discourse that challenges the status quo; (2) as a result, the
intellectual class is fighting a complex and often obscured "guerrilla
warfare against the old class" to wrest the means of social control away
from capitalist interests and place them firmly with "new class" professional expertise; and so (3) the battle seems winnable because the
class of humanist intellectuals and technocratic intelligentsia "is reproducing itself faster than any other class in society."[18]
  Clearly Gouldner's view is not lacking a concept of struggle, an idea
all but extinct in North American scholarship. But if intellectuals as a
group exercise their own kind of "domination" alongside or within

the workings of power throughout society as a whole, we need to know how that works. Is it essentially benign enforcement of their particular authority as teachers and scholars and critics? Or is this domination oppressive in ways that Michel Foucault illuminates, a power of observation and judgment "ensuring a surveillance which would be both global and individualizing"?[19] Finally, how does Gouldner reconcile his optimism and his awareness of intellectual complicity with state power? The answer seems to be that "critical discourse" is inherently disruptive, eroding "old class" capitalist influences throughout society.

But is that true? Is it the case that most or, at any rate, a significant amount of critical discourse is antagonistic to vested capitalist interests? Gouldner's thesis operates on the assumption that intellectuals (especially humanist intellectuals) define their work as specifically against the reigning social order. He seems to believe, credulously, that the federal government is radically at odds with corporate interests, so that as "universities and colleges receive increasing funding from governments, the influence of the old class on them weakens."[20] David F. Noble's *America by Design,* Leonard Silk and Mark Silk's *The American Establishment,* and Herbert I. Schiller's *Who Knows: Information in the Age of the Fortune 500* provide conspicuous dissenting voices. "The corporation," Christopher Lasch notes, has "shifted to the university, an institution partly or wholly financed by the state," especially for large and expensive scientific research projects. And so "engineers regarded the First World War not as a disaster for civilization but as a 'unique opportunity' to put their ideas into practice—to bring the corporations, the universities, and the state into closer partnership."[21] In such a climate it should be clear that the humanist "intellectuals' culture of careful and critical discourse," which is the instrument of their leverage in society, providing whatever "domination" academic writing is capable of, is not (and never has been) the monolithic "emancipator" Gouldner suggests it is.

We move a good deal closer to accounting for the varieties as well as the consequences of critical activity when we look at changes in the history of critical discourse and assess its fads and biases. Richard Rorty, for instance, surely comes nearer to the self-arresting pluralism of contemporary intellectual reality in the United States when he notes the changes in North American philosophy in this century:

> The period between the World Wars was one of prophecy and moral leadership—the heroic period of Deweyan pragmatism. . . . The period since the Second World War has been one of professionalization, in

which philosophers have quite deliberately and self-consciously abdi-
cated such a role. In the pre–World War I period . . . philosophy defined itself by its relation to the social sciences. At the beginning of the
professionalizing period, philosophers attempted half-heartedly to define their activity in relation to mathematics and the natural sciences. In
fact, however, this period has been marked by a withdrawal from the rest
of the academy and from culture—an insistence on philosophy's autonomy.[22]

I will defer my objection to Rorty's "heroic" Deweyan period of philosophical "moral leadership" for a moment in order to underline the
turbulent nature of critical discourse that emerges, albeit somewhat
unconsciously, in this quick survey of shifting loyalties and emphases
within academic philosophy. While Rorty is right to understand the
evolution of interpretive positions within a historical context, he leaves
the relationship between academic change and social reality undefined. In effect he provides an appearance of historical explanation
without any real account of the extra-academic political and cultural
pressures that intersect with (and to some degree create the conditions for) intellectual battles. This swerve away from the institutional
framework of philosophy marks the transcendentalist ambition of the
humanities generally, not merely a withdrawal "from the rest of the
academy and from culture" by philosophy and by literary criticism,
but a growing inability throughout the "professionalizing period"
since the end of World War II to believe that critical intellectuals have
a role within society. The result is a sustained vagueness about the
critic's identity. In the absence of a definition of the social role of
criticism and philosophy, the critical writer is left with a relatively
sterile career: comfortable work conditions, a constantly renegotiated
professional field (the fight for superiority among critical positions),
and a lack of any social or theoretical basis for building the kind of
cooperative interaction that would allow humanists to address one
another and their students as citizens of the world.

The self-deceptive search for intellectual "autonomy" varies from
time to time, and the openness or generosity of academic debate
certainly varies, depending not only on internal professional pressures (fads, judgments, ideological choices) but on external pressures
generated through the whole of society as it calls on or turns away
from informed "expertise." Gouldner is not unaware of these shifts.
He is also capable of a humorous sneer at "the sobriety and prudence
of the 'professionalism' claimed by a technical intelligentsia" whose
"communism of the modest," as he dubs it, extends just as much to hu-

manist intellectuals. The reason Gouldner finally excuses the collaboration of the intellectual class with corporate and government power has everything to do with his confidence that intellectuals are gaining stature and authority that can result only in the extinction of traditional capitalist power. In a revealing passage at the end of *The Future of Intellectuals and the Rise of the New Class*, we find the source of that optimism:

> Any class aspiring to rule must establish its hegemony in society and this means it must have itself defined as a *legitimate authority*. The universal requirement for legitimacy is that the class must be trusted to rule in a *non-partisan* way on behalf of the *collectivity*. Who now trusts the old class as non-partisan and legitimate? The opinion polls do not show that the large corporations in the United States evoke public confidence. The old class has failed to capture the symbols of legitimacy: i.e., science, morality, technology, professionalism. As it explores *détente* with the USSR, and as its multinational character becomes known, even its nationalist credentials may become suspect.
>
> The principal factor now maintaining the old class's social power is its economic *productivity:* consumerism. Much of what maintains the old class today is neither brute force *nor legitimacy* but, rather, the masses' sheer experience of consumer gratifications and their association of these with the *status quo*.[23]

These words were written in the latter half of the 1970s, before the resurgence of the political right and Ronald Reagan's reassertion of "old class" values and power. Not only do they fail to anticipate political shifts that can disrupt a policy as fragile as "détente"; they underestimate the power of consumerism, of the "brute force" of commodity logic and its underlying economic structure. It may be that capitalist interests are not exactly legitimated by most of the culture (though I believe they are). But every day those interests are obscured and rendered benign by advertisements that plead the case for big business, images that put a human face on profit and capitalist power. Each day, without exception, television and the national news media reaffirm the greed, the competition, the objects of desirable wealth that offer false transcendence. In addition, the ensemble of military power, permanent unemployment, and political confusion reinforces the fundamental (if nonetheless subliminal) reality that the "coherence" of American society resides in the dominating power of massive accumulations of capital—hoarded in international banks and in multinational corporations—and in the willingness of North American culture to accept and even to justify what it cannot change.

Gouldner's analysis of the superior legitimacy of intellectuals over unpopular capitalists ignores the fact that large monetary interests do not have to be "legitimated" if they control just about all of the technology and most of the flow of information and images and define general human interests (morality, in short) in terms of professional expertise that is fractured into well-contained areas and disciplines without independent political organization or a tradition of opposition to capitalist power. In other words, Gouldner makes the habitual mistake liberal intellectuals indulge in to fight off despair or unhappy conclusions. He underestimates the cultural affiliation and economic cooperation among business, government, and private professional interests.[24]

North American institutional reality does not offer much room for subversion of the kind that Gouldner imagines to be the special contribution of the intellectual class. Certainly the intellectual production of critical writers is politically unaffiliated with any segment of American society. It is an academic event, a matter of book writing and competition for academic jobs. Critical culture, in the whole of its variety, complexity, and extraordinary analytic capacity, is a professional enclave without dialogue with any other strata of the population. Instead, as Regis Debray has shown, the "information apparatus" of the national and international press and broadcasting media has "subordinated and restructured the pedagogic, religious, trade-union and political apparatuses—and a fortiori, the cultural apparatuses." It has also "had the side effect of shattering the coordinates of the intellectual field."[25] The publicly disseminated (but privately controlled) information system has grown so vast that it has "broken down the closure of the traditional intelligentsia." In fact, contrary to Gouldner's notion of an intellectual *class* that can be thought of as a relatively coherent collection of diverse conceptual activities, Debray insists that such a group is not a class at all, since it "cannot be defined by its position in the material process of production" but instead "functions on the institutional model." Intellectuals, he asserts, are "representatives of the qualitative" who are now, along with all other people and occupations, increasingly contained within the logic of marketplace operations and values.[26]

Nonetheless, to be a professional reader and writer in North America is to choose, to be able to choose, an intellectual position. Such a choice is not reducible to one's "method" or "hermeneutic" sophistication. It is a matter of one's fundamental relationship to the possibility of knowing—of seeing or finding connections among meanings, texts, problems, and the actual world we live in. The useful result of such a recognition for humanists is, or could be, fresh intellectual agility and revived commitment to pursue knowledge as a value-making occupation that enables critics to name the institutional conditions of their work. Such a commitment may seem crassly idealistic, yet such idealism is exactly what Gouldner assures us drives intellectuals toward revolutionary involvement in the first place. It approaches his essay's principal educational vision, which is concerned with "historical mechanisms that contribute to the radicalization of Western intellectuals."

The crucial factor in this radicalizing process, although Gouldner indicates several contributing influences, is the "grammar of critical rationality," as he calls the humanist base from which educated elites receive their analytic and linguistic expertise. The decisive impact of that education can be considered to be a sort of humanist zeal, a view of the world through the kaleidoscope of history and its multiple perspectives. From one point of view this way of looking at the world could be thought of as negating ethnocentric provincialisms; from another point of view it might mean an enlarged concept of "the whole." At any rate, as Gouldner puts it, the culture of critical discourse means a change in the viewer's standpoint:

> Historically effective elites are commonly trained, as well as positioned, to take the standpoint of the totality, even if seeing it only from the top down.
>
> There is little doubt that some, and perhaps many, intellectuals become revolutionary or support revolutionary programs, in part because it is in their *material* interests to do so. It is not just "material" interests, however, that govern intellectuals' conduct, but their interests both *material and ideal:* it is also their special vested interest in their education, knowledge, language and culture of critical discourse, and in these as such, and not only in the incomes or prestige they may produce.[27]

This is precisely the standpoint of the unsituated viewer, "free" and unaffiliated with anything but scholarship or theory. The view "from the top down" is the perspective that founds "the remarkable ideological homogeneity of the American intelligentsia in general," as Chomsky notes, a coherence that reflects the "most important postwar development in academic politics," according to Leo Braudy: "The increasingly strong allegiance of the professor to his field rather than to his university."[28]

We might pause to ask about the professor's allegiance. The conflict that has marked criticism for the past several decades reveals a considerable inability to create institutional or intellectual coherence.[29] And yet until recently criticism has avoided the question of power almost completely. It still overlooks the critic's institutional placement in society, settling for a less specific image of the critic as a bemused onlooker, a relatively unimportant adjunct to the general business of society's economic logic. The allegiance of the scholar to a field or to a profession, and not to the university or to any project or struggle outside (or for that matter within) the university, attests to the habit of maintaining scholarly autonomy against threatening involvements, against social upheavals that appear to compromise intellectual sobriety.

Is it surprising, then, that intellectual work in the United States and much of the Anglo-European community plays down its relation to the institutional environment surrounding it? Certainly it is controversial to assert that criticism and textual studies are somehow affiliated with overall patterns of cultural management and, though perhaps remotely, with the institutional management of state capitalism. Frederick Crews's address to the Modern Language Association in 1969 was very certain of this connection: "Capitalist scholarship that deals with the contemporary world is distinguished by its mistaking of an ideological consensus for neutrality, its reluctance to question capitalism itself . . . its embarrassment about recognizing power, and its penchant for isolating phenomena from their structural causes."[30] Crews has since recanted, but in a passage as appropriate to the 1980s as it was for the considerably different moment of its birth, Crews points to underlying causes of such disengagement. "What bears investigation," he writes, "is our remarkable political innocence rather than our guilt" as critics and teachers: "We are dealing rather with a congruency between ideologically useful attitudes and what scholars already believe, and the question to be asked is whether ideology has helped to shape those beliefs without the scholars' conscious awareness. This would be a relatively undramatic but quite serious politicization of learning, for someone who does not even know he is thinking propagandistically is farther from objectivity than one who decides to suppress his real views."[31] That is one way to make sense of the "cautious politeness and orderliness" of intellectual life in the United States at present—a politeness (despite squabbling now and then) that accepts the disciplinary divisions of scholarship while overlooking the effect of predominant academic values on the organization of social forces. The commoditization of knowledge that Derrida, Lyotard, Baudrillard, and others have addressed within the past few years is an event in our culture that is carried, made both possible and portable, by the thoroughgoing professionalism of academic work.

The blow that event deals to political consciousness can be felt in most literary departments no less than in their philosophical and historical counterparts on the same campus. Intellectual production for its own sake has created a "substitute world," to borrow Crews's incisive and now ironic term, a world that is situated squarely in the reproductive heart of Western economic life (the university) but that locates its force elsewhere, in the transcendental realm of professional competence.

Richard Rorty, whom we saw a moment ago lamenting the loss of Dewey's "moral leadership" and who, more passionately, laments the failure of philosophers in the post–World War II period to match literary teachers in protecting "the presentness of the past," captures that contradiction:

> Mild chauvinism was in vogue during the Deweyan period, and occasionally we still feel nostalgia for it. . . . Its attitude was best expressed by Sidney Hook in an essay called "Pragmatism and the Tragic Sense of Life," which closes by saying "Pragmatism . . . is the theory and practice of enlarging human freedom in a precarious and tragic world by the arts of intelligent social control. It may be a lost cause. I do not know of a better one." There is indeed no better cause, and the nostalgia which philosophers in the professionalizing period have felt for the prophetic Deweyan period comes from their sense that they are not doing as much for this cause as they would like. But the defense of this cause is only incidentally a matter of formulating moral principles, and moral education is only incidentally a matter of choosing and defending a cause.[32]

Who could quarrel with "enlarging human freedom," although that is the ambition of right-wing writers who seek to consolidate the power of those who already enjoy considerable privilege? The ascription of "mild chauvinism" to the years between the two major wars completely understates both Dewey's commitment to national military belligerence and the ferocity of debate about the forms and affiliations of radical dissent during and after World War I. Dewey's intellectual leadership at the start of the war, Randolph Bourne reminds us, helped to create "a younger intelligentsia, trained up in the pragmatic dispensation, immensely ready for the executive ordering of events, pitifully unprepared for the intellectual interpretation or the idealistic focusing of ends."[33] "What concerns us here," he goes on, "is the relative ease with which the pragmatist intellectuals, with Professor Dewey at the head, have moved out their philosophy, bag and baggage, from education to war. So abrupt a change in the direction of the national enterprise, one would have expected to cause more emotion, to demand more apologetics."³⁴ The revisionary purpose in Rorty's passage, which emerges in the light of these statements, quite obviously carries a large burden of nostalgia itself, nostalgia for the sort of prophecy Rorty finds in Dewey's liberal pragmatism, which, in Sidney Hook's telling phrase, sought "the arts of intelligent social control."

I am not certain precisely what "art" is involved in such activity unless it is the art of manipulation we normally call propaganda or surveillance. Indeed, Rorty's essay (delivered as a lecture at the Bicentennial Symposium of Philosophy in New York City, October 10, 1976) is marked by a curious vagueness that finally declares its overt political intentions. If "the defense of this cause [enlarging freedom by the arts of intelligent social control] is only incidentally a matter of formulating moral principles," then it must be, he asserts, a matter of professional philosophical expertise of a certain kind, a technical or intellectual rather than a moral activity. In itself such division between the realm of values and the realm of knowledge, analysis, and intellect is worrisome. But Rorty's closing celebration of American pragmatic reasonableness carries more than bicentennial cheer:

> Although America will go down in history as having done more for this cause than any of the great empires so far, there is no particular reason why a nation's philosophers, or indeed its intellectuals, need be identified in the eyes of history with the same virtues as its political and social institutions. There is no reason to think that the promise of American democracy will find its final fulfillment in America, any more than Roman law reached its fulfillment in the Roman Empire or literary culture its fulfillment in Alexandria. Nor is there much reason to think that the highbrow culture of whatever empire does achieve that fulfillment will resemble our own, or that the professors of moral philosophy then will build on principles being formulated now. Even if, through some unbelievable stroke of fortune, America survives with its freedoms intact and becomes a rallying point for the nations, the high culture of an unfragmented world need not center around anything specifically American.³⁵

Apparently Rorty has decided to overlook the actual consequences of North American power. Although he is careful not to nominate the United States as the champion of a future worldwide integration, he leaves no doubt that its culture would form a central component of such an arrangement, as it surely would, as it is in fact now doing throughout its sphere of influence. But a very disturbing, and characteristic, habit asserts itself in this way of assessing "highbrow culture." The genre of writing Rorty is alluding to is literary criticism, which, he insists quite accurately, defines itself against more technical disciplines (such as professionalized philosophy of the post-Deweyan period) by employing a "transcendentalist point of view," an "attitude that there is no point in raising questions of truth, goodness, or beauty, because between ourselves and the thing judged there always intervenes mind, language, a perspective chosen among dozens, one description chosen out of thousands."[36] There is little use in berating Rorty for his joyful embrace of contemporary academic values. The particular virtue of such transcendentalist highbrows, in his estimation, is their ability to tell the story of the past to young people in college classrooms. They keep the "presentness of the past" alive against technical specialists.

Rorty stands on the side of literary education against careerist self-interest. But look at the cost of his patriotic celebration. America becomes the more or less benign empire that unproblematically furthers the cause of freedom and democracy while allowing its intellectuals to quarrel among themselves in search of ways to divide high culture into manageable parcels. Culture in this model is something inadvertent, marginal, and unaffiliated with the political and social institutions that create policies and markets for international military mercantilism.[37] In fact the division between transcendentalized culture and the rest of a society given over to capitalist resources of every sort, including the very book culture Rorty means to protect, is so great that one is unable to imagine how to move from one world (daily reality) to the other (the humanities) as long as such separation continues. Such a decontaminated, nonpolitical view of culture distances the critic and the literary intellectual from any taint of involvement with power and politics. We could consider this isolation a charming desire for freedom from outside interference, a hope of maintaining untroubled knowledge of the past in a world that allows too little room for intellectual lucidity. We could also think of it as an example of the "political innocence" Crews once lamented. Alternatively, we might see it as the willingness of the serious humanist to affirm, perhaps reluctantly, the stratifications and institutional divisions that maintain culture. Rorty joins Gouldner here by acceding to "a new hierarchy of the knowing," distant from but somehow on the side of the democratic process.

Another look reveals Rorty's purpose. His bicentennial lecture defends cultural relativism from the philosophical technicians on one side and the bad reputation of the academic entrepreneur on the other. "The public no longer associates our profession with epicene delicacy, but either with political violence and sexual licence or with hard-nosed Presidential advisors."[38] The remedy for such negative identity is retreat: to embrace a transcendental role, to refurbish the good image of the humanist as a blissfully uninvolved custodian of the past, someone whose value to society is more general than that of the scholarly drudge or academic specialist, someone who affirms the cultural heritage and thereby helps to preserve the nation. That strategy, however, passes over two problems. First, the negative identity that attached itself to humanists during the campus protests against the Vietnam War was largely, though not wholly, a construction of liberals and conservatives within and without the academy who fed upon the always lively anti-intellectualism of American culture. The excesses of a few theatrical faculty rebels provided a convenient target despite the indifference of many more and the genuinely mild response, the muffled anguish, of the majority. Second, a return to the reassuring relativity of a transcendentalized culture can only replicate the intellectual conditions that prevailed before the United States' disastrous invasion of Indochina. In what way, one must ask, will the "presentness of the past," as Rorty imagines it, work against similar lapses of moral will and political judgment in the future? Rorty's model of the nonintervening culture critic—a writer and teacher happily advancing the best of the intellectual tradition with little concern for the institutional context of that knowledge—defines the humanist's traditional role. But culture is both a product and an environment. Among other things, it is what intellectuals practice and the way those practices are distributed through institutions that stimulate, engender, limit, and finally ground communication. Culture enables people to talk with one another, to do specific things, and to prevent other things from happening. Culture is not relative, benign, abstract, compactible, or removed from the immediate context of a people's thought and behavior.

Against the current intellectual confusion that wavers from one interpretive program to another, Noam Chomsky has persevered since 1965, unseduced by fad or pretense, to clarify the distribution and consequences of power—political power, economic power, intellectual power. Most of all, Chomsky has focused on the role of academic writers in contemporary state capitalism. His central concern may well be the discrepancy he finds between the ordinary decency of the majority of people and the arrogance of those who accumulate power, a discrepancy that could be lessened by intellectuals if they resisted similar temptations in their own work and opposed institutionalized arrogance of every sort. That, of course, is a large hope. Chomsky's audacity may in part account for his anomalous status in the intellectual world. His scholarship has achieved the highest level of clarity, passion, and intellectual integrity; nonetheless it stands outside the cloisters of respectable humanist scholarship: read by nearly everyone with an ounce of intellectual curiosity yet ignored in the traffic of normal critical debate. This duality is startling for its ability to reveal the academic decorum scholarship thrives on, as if even those who admire Chomsky's work are embarrassed by the scope of his observations.

I do not find it strange, although it is disheartening, that in an era of humanistic perplexity as the United States rebuilds the ideological consensus lost in the Johnson-Nixon years, Chomsky's work has not been taken up as a means of reviving the political consciousness of critical thinking (John Carlos Rowe's issue of *Cultural Critique,* on the Vietnam War, is a lonely exception). Chomsky's writing leads away from theoretical insularity to pose immediately accessible questions. What, for example, is the political function of criticism in a time of expanding military readiness, when the national government has declared an all-out cold war against the Soviet Union and begun a rearmament commitment more massive than any ever before attempted in peacetime? Surely many humanists frustrated by the vague political consciousness and overwrought technical dexterity of deconstruction, by the detached elegance of old humanist pieties, by the failure of Marxism to develop as a broadly accepted alternative to structuralist, poststructuralist, and traditional close readings that deprive texts and concepts of historical significance, of historical *force*—surely many teachers and critics struggling to regain a sense of mission or usefulness for the work they do could find in Chomsky's writing a clarification of the interaction between culture and those economic and political interests that perpetuate the aggression of the powerful few against the distracted or impoverished many. As members of a cultural elite, critics may find this way of talking about the world too dramatic or too incriminating. Critics are trained to pride themselves on the understated dispassion of intellectual sobriety. Articulate without urgency, lucid without ethical designs or overt political agendas, criticism and the teaching of literature in North America have been captured by the myth of intellectual neutrality, of the role of intellect as witness. But fine as intelligent witness is, and crucial to the purpose of criticism, it cannot transform the pervasive impotence one sees in students today and hears in the conversations of one's colleagues.

Chomsky's importance is not limited to his politics, to the particular stand he takes against his country's omnivorous militarism, but derives from the conscious fire he brings to the act of institutional analysis. What writer in North America has so frequently and so well called attention to the invidious consequences of our eroded democracy and so thoroughly demystified its causes?

> We expect to find—and do find—that those who accommodate to the needs of domestic power and serve its interests will tend to dominate the system of communication, education, and indoctrination. We find it particularly easy to adopt this quite rational stance in the case of official enemies. . . .
>
> It is more difficult, and far more important, to adopt the same rational stance with regard to one's own society or its close allies or dependencies. In modern state capitalist societies such as our own, domestic decision-making is dominated by the private business sector in the political as well as the strictly economic arena. . . . Furthermore, those who have a dominant position in the domestic economy command substantial means to influence public opinion. It would be surprising indeed if this power were not reflected in the mass media—themselves major corporations—and the schools and universities; if it did not, in short, shape the prevailing ideology to a considerable extent. What we should expect to find is (1) that foreign policy is guided by the primary commitment to improving the climate for business operations in a global system that is open to exploitation of human and material resources by those who dominate the domestic economy, and (2) that this commitment is portrayed as guided by the highest ideals and by deep concern for human welfare.[39]

Underlying Chomsky's analysis of domestic policymaking is a recognition, therapeutic to the degree it can motivate intellectuals to examine the institutional bases of their work, that "the level of culture that can be achieved in the United States is a life-and-death matter for large masses of suffering humanity."[40] The flow of discourse in this country determines the allocation and control of resources throughout the world. This is Chomsky's particular concern: the impact of American values on the majority of the earth's inhabitants. Consider for a moment his primary argument. "Under capitalist democracy . . . [the] press and the intellectuals are held to be fiercely independent, hypercritical, antagonistic to the 'establishment,' in an adversary relation to the state."[41] In fact, the vast majority of journalists and intellectuals keep their criticism "within narrow bounds." More or less unknowingly, as Chomsky assesses it, they succumb to a "democratic system of thought control."

> The basic principles of the state propaganda system are assumed by the critics. In contrast to the totalitarian system, the propaganda apparatus does not merely stake out a position to which all must conform—or

which they may privately oppose. Rather, it seeks to determine and to limit the entire spectrum of thought: the official doctrine at one extreme, and the position of its most vocal adversaries at the other. Over the entire spectrum, the same fundamental assumptions are insinuated, though rarely expressed. They are presupposed, but not asserted.[42]

Here we find the germ of the position that prompts Gouldner's mistaken judgment that Chomsky "breeds political pessimism, social quietism and acquiescence to the *status quo,*" a position in which "no rational change is possible."[43] Dozens of passages in Chomsky's writing as well as entire essays disprove that notion. One might even find Chomsky unduly optimistic (or at any rate sublimely hopeful) when in his 1969 essay, "Some Tasks for the Left," he asserts "a fundamental human need to take an active part in the democratic control of social institutions."[44] But the appearance of untarnished enthusiasm is certainly dispelled by his warning that "a movement of the left condemns itself to failure and irrelevance if it does not create an intellectual culture that becomes dominant by virtue of its excellence and that is meaningful to the masses of people who, in an advanced industrial society, can participate in creating and deepening it."[45]

A moment ago I suggested that an analysis of the institutional bases of culture and of intellectual activity might be "therapeutic" for the current impoverishment of the humanities. In fact I narrowed my assertion even further by saying that the specific awareness Chomsky seeks to promote—an awareness of the dynastic superiorty of American culture in world affairs—could be therapeutic for the kind of work teachers, critics, and scholars do. My statement contains a belief much like Chomsky's, that an examination of the institutional arrangements binding intellectuals to society as a whole is necessary (in truth the only way) to break the impacted stratification that keeps critical intelligence circulating harmlessly within the insular debates on critical theory and within traditional scholastic idealism. I do not mean to impugn theory or scholarship. Each has a powerful place in North American intellectual life, and each is an ally of the imperturbable critical energy that turns intelligence and knowledge against anti-intellectual forces. Such faith is certainly open to dispute, but unlike Gouldner's faith in the growing power of intellectuals, it does not promise any victory. On the contrary, I find Chomsky's clarity about the purpose of intellectual activity to be the kind of reminder, serving as a motivation, that dissolves both premature optimism and premature pessimism. Intellectuals, in this view, rationalize the state and its dominant culture by upholding assumptions and values that contain the limits of debate (especially, in the humanities, about the entanglement of culture and the economy in the shaping of national policies and educational goals), or they intentionally oppose and question the authority of the state and everything that contributes to its cultural and ideological hegemony.[46] In other words, intellectuals either ratify or challenge the existing social order from whatever position of authority and persuasion they hold, or else they exercise some form of ameliorating revision (part conservator, part debunker) in between. But the point is, regardless, that intellectuals exercise a political function. They transmit standards of conceptual behavior, supply information that is never "neutral" in its uses, construct or modify categories of analysis and judgment, and manage all the terminologies of differentiation that allow choices to be made within an acceptable framework of status and reference.

One fact becomes evident in the clarity of Chomsky's uncompromising focus. Every writer is situated in the midst of power—political power, institutional power, financial power, cultural power—which offers distinct and limited choices. Such choices taken and emphasized, overtly or covertly, define a strategy for dealing with power. Every writer finds or makes a strategy or does not write at all, and the choice is inevitably between a greater and a lesser degree of consciousness of the actual forces that constitute social reality. These are economic forces and ideological forces, sometimes legal and military forces, but they are always namable just as they are always capable of being repressed or overlooked in silence. Chomsky's achievement is that he names, more than most, the forces he contends with. On the whole his writing pursues "the question of how private economic power functions in American society," a question that leads to "the universities, the scholarly professions, the mass media, and society at large [which] are carefully insulated" from recognizing the systematic aggressiveness of United States national agendas and their protection of capitalist power.[47] At the heart of Chomsky's vision is an unflinching horror at the magnitude of American militarization. This, above any other, is the power against which Chomsky writes.

A concerned humanist may feel this is a noble effort but fail to see its relevance to the teaching of literature or the manufacturing of articles. Chomsky, however, has provided a way to situate the humanist's work. Perhaps the main context he offers is derived from Antonio Gramsci's concept of ideological hegemony, the systematic indoctrination of a society by means of cultural values and institutional practices (in particular *educational* practices) mediated by the state.[48] Everywhere in his studies of media journalism, of government policy

and propaganda, of historical scholarship and technical research habits, Chomsky is concerned with the subtle and not so subtle adjustments that comply with the tacit assumptions and reigning presuppositions of the state's ideological apparatus. The point of Chomsky's
analyses is to separate the facts of an event—the Vietnam War, for
example—from the reports and perceptions that grow up around
that event and surround it, bit by bit, with a generally accepted framework of interpretation which resists all but the smallest, least significant deviations from the prevailing outlook. I should say immediately
that Chomsky has worked extremely hard to reveal facts that underlie
well-circulated historical myths and political images. One of the most
illuminating results of that effort is his demonstration of just how
hard it is to find the "facts" even in an event as large and as public as
the Vietnam War.

"Even" there is naive, of course. Precisely *because* government policy was first hidden and then regularly distorted, the "facts" as well as
the ruling assumptions about the purpose of such a venture continued to be directed by a small handful of men whose self-serving
deceptions were looked on as truthful, even honorable, instead of
vicious or, at minimum, stupid. Lest this reminder of the central event
in North American history for those now in the middle of their personal and professional maturity seem too much like a bothersome
digression, let me point out how costly it is that the lessons that could
be learned from that war have not yet filtered into the humanities
curriculum; nor (and this is where one would expect to find them)
have they penetrated into the critical consciousness of teachers who
are always hard pressed to make connections between the "real
world" and the less immediate but no less inviolable world of history
and of texts. In fact, one finds active resistance to such assimilation—
fear of (or contempt for) joining the humanities to an immediate
historical awareness.[49]

Chomsky's concern with the ideological control that makes manipulation of public opinion not so much a concerted act of fabrication
and repression as an already established system of assumptions goes a
long way toward completing Gouldner's unfinished notion of the intellectuals' "cultural capital" that exerts some unspecified form of
"domination." It also provides the framing concept sorely lacking in
the humanities as they are at present constituted, theory divided from
historical research, interpretation of texts by and large unrelated to
the explication of those contemporary assumptions that situate the act
of reading in the first place. The notion of ideological hegemony that
Chomsky borrows from Gramsci derives from Marx's analysis of the

"ruling ideas of the ruling class" in *The German Ideology*. Just as Gramsci extends Marx's vision of society as a structure determined by productive relationships so that civil society now can be seen to include, and to be molded by, cultural and ideological relationships, I think we may find that Chomsky has extended Gramsci's understanding of the importance of intellectuals in the exercise of state power. Like Marx and Gramsci before him, Chomsky sees that the liberal democratic state is organized to serve those with wealth and privilege, that it uses the whole of its resources—material, legal, military, and cultural—to enforce its power and to repress those who resist or seem to threaten its rule.[50] "Insofar as the technique of management and control exists, it can be used to consolidate the authority of those who exercise it and to diminish spontaneous and free experimentation with new social forms," he tells us. "Where the techniques fail, they will be supplemented by all of the methods of coercion that modern technology provides, to preserve order and stability."[51] The role of the intellectual in consolidating political authority, therefore, lies primarily in justifying the "fairness" of the system, its "openness" and "rationality," and thereby in diminishing the need for coercive social controls. In essence, the intellectual's role is political because it either reinforces belief in dominant values that "contain" popular consciousness or it opposes those beliefs. (We might remember here that the concept of "the state," absent from North American critical vocabularies, raises the issue of the various means by which social coherence is achieved—some economic, such as the building of a transportation system and the maintenance of welfare, medical, and retirement benefits, some ideological and cultural. Education and the state school system are the most powerful of those means. In short, we might remember that the function of the state in the first place is to legitimate and stabilize the whole social order.)[52]

Gramsci's response to the subordination of intellectuals to state power, to all of those apparatuses of ideological and bureaucratic control which permeate social life, posits "a long war of position" in which revolutionary (his term is "organic") intellectuals are able to wear down the dominant class by invalidating its cultural and ideological hegemony. If enough teachers and writers resist the assumptions that support the ruling class, Gramsci thought, it will be forced to rely increasingly on repressive means to enforce its rule, and the ensuing crises not only will expose the bankruptcy of capitalist values but will foster the conditions for change. Chomsky's America is considerably more elaborate than Gramsci's Italy. However we account for the differences, revolution in the sense Gramsci envisioned is impossible today. Chomsky cannot assert, as Gramsci did, that there are "two powers" locked in battle for control of civil life—"the power of the bourgeois State and the power of the working class: the second is gradually destroying the first."[53] This last optimistic note exceeds Chomsky's position (which extends Gramsci's work by exposing the relation of intellectuals to counterrevolutionary violence), but their agreement about the role of the teacher and critic in preserving order and fomenting change makes the points of contact between them a topic worth further examination. It also suggests why Chomsky is a writer who might clarify the political function of criticism for many who at present labor without any sense of immediate historical affiliation or sustaining intellectual solidarity. I want to outline in conclusion, what I mean by that statement.

While Gramsci looked toward workers and the workers' party as natural allies, Chomsky has no such concentrated constituency to address or, for that matter, to draw upon as a national cadre of vanguard workers and intellectuals. North American culture is so intricate and the strength of its dominant institutions so great—the scope of its economic and military power so vast—that intellectual authority, as it is currently constituted, is overwhelmed. Peter Nettl once noted that the "unitary area of culture within which intellectuals operate and from which they obtain their validation has itself been cut up into different, increasingly unrelated sectors."

> As high culture and mass culture become differentiated and as specific efforts are made to rescue minority cultures from the lethal encroachments of the mass media (by providing them with mass media of their own), the cultural arena of intellectual concerns has shrunk to a narrow island of inbred reverberation surrounded by indifference and commercialization. . . . Instead of legitimating themselves for society as a whole, intellectuals merely legitimate each other. They have become each other's reciprocal articulators and audience, no more. Groups speak to each other across a cultural gulf, if at all, and then only on the assumption that each is the acknowledged authority in its own area.
>
> In short, the intellectual's role in society has been undermined primarily by increasing specialization, by different but professional groundings of authority, by separation between culture and politics, and by the breakup of unitary cultures—or at least the hierarchy of better as opposed to worse culture. The intellectual is forced into precisely the position which [Raymond] Aron characterizes with such scorn: "Radical criticism has abandoned the attempt to reshape the world or to change it, it is simply content to condemn."[54]

Nettl's comments reflect the general sense that the political relevance of intellectual work has been obliterated by bureaucratic organization, that intellectuals are left to affirm the status quo or to snipe at it unproductively. Better, therefore, to stay within the safe confines of professional specialization and ignore the difficult or impossible task of reanimating political consciousness. We can see, then, why Chomsky does not address his writing to academic intellectuals. Instead he means to reach anyone who has not yet sought haven from the shock of concepts and analysis. The basis of his thinking, Carlos Otero has suggested, is a strenuous exploration of contradictions that flourish between the self-affirmation of cooperative individuals and the selfish acquisition of competitive exploitation.[55] Chomsky wants to revive not just the moral authority of intellectual energy but a particularly political form of moral criticism that can inhabit, and interrogate, theoretical and critical writing.

Here we return to the points of contact between Chomsky and Gramsci and to the way Chomsky extends Gramsci's notion of ideological hegemony. No revolutionary intellectual exists for long without a highly developed moral intelligence, but no effective critical writer succeeds without a well-developed conceptual framework. Gramsci's virtue as a thinker was to see the limitation in Marx's view of the state as fundamentally repressive, the source of organized violence and military readiness. Such intimidation is not enough by itself to maintain social stability, nor can it motivate economic output. Gramsci saw how vital culture is in every facet of social life, that culture elaborates and inserts the role of the state in maintaining order into every sphere of human activity. Wherever ideas can go, the state's ruling values go also. This is Gramsci's crucial departure from Marx's cruder formulation. Cultural hegemony, in other words, is the ability of common-sense assumptions and routine expectations, of all those normal practices that make up ordinary existence, to saturate consciousness (including the thinking of intellectuals) and thereby promote a genuinely dominant view of reality: an ideological matrix, a selective tradition; in short, a culture.

The stunning plasticity of a culture evolves from its differentiation, from its variety of expressions, and from the multiple forms of its incorporation in distinctly divergent institutions. Can anyone doubt that the purposes and values of universities and of banks are easily distinguishable? Yet would anyone really doubt that shared assumptions about economic and social reality—for instance, about the nature of professional life (that it is defined by one's value in a particular job market and that it expresses itself in the form of a "career")—

joins the two within the web of a common and altogether prevalent culture? Gramsci's insight can be galvanized by the formulation Nicos Poulantzas gives it: "the system of the State is composed of *several apparatuses or institutions* of which certain have a principally repressive role . . . and others a principally ideological role."[56] Culture constitutes the divergent and extraordinarily heterogeneous mix of values and practices that circulate around and through mostly unnoticed presuppositions about what is desirable, about what is necessary or possible—what the limits of choice really are, given things as they are. Gramsci recognized that culture is relatively autonomous and not at all homogenized. Chomsky, however, extends Gramsci's realization that culture serves the power of the state by demonstrating that ideological hegemony and international (imperialistic) hegemony are two aspects of the same structure. Chomsky's writing shows anyone who cares not to miss it that militarism, a systematic belligerence and ceaseless preparation for large wars and smaller-scale interventions, is the central tenet of United States domestic and foreign policy.[57] The constantly rehearsed violence of commercial entertainment (television, movies, professional sports) forms a part of what Chomsky calls "the Cold War system along with its domestic counterpart, militarization of the economy."[58] Surely it is to Chomsky's credit that he reveals how thoroughly the militarization of the economy, of the culture, and of public policy provides the terms of consensus (including room for dissent and even mild civil disobedience) by which this country is organized.

Seventy years after Randolph Bourne found the intellectuals of his time mostly "apologists for the 'gigantic irrelevance' of war,"[59] the United States is poised decisively for every imaginable aggression, including the final unimaginable strike. My sense is that humanists today are not so much apologists for the state's irrational authority as they are onlookers frustrated by professional indifference to material and ideological combat. If the humanities are to become a force of persuasive dissent within our culture, they will have to manufacture moral commitment and political energy that relieve their embarrassed privilege as civilized but silent witnesses. The role of a value-oriented writer need not be only to condemn. It may be to create the anomalous arguments that widen and deepen the critic's responsibility. This is a task Chomsky has begun.

3

Intellectual Authority
and State Power

Chomsky's critique does not undermine the conventional order of scholarship in the way that, for example, deconstruction seems to.[1] Chomsky attacks the assumption that intellectual work lies outside the reach of power, that the scholar and critic are detached from the political consequences of their cultural influence. His target is the authority of North American intellectuals.

What is the authority of humanist scholarship in the United States today?[2] What do we mean when we speak of intellectual authority, of the critic's or the theorist's authority as a writer? For the most part we mean a definitively institutionalized and thoroughly professional activity, writing, lecturing, publishing within a circuit of universities and publishing houses (journals, presses, reviews), work that is normalized by a variety of professional expectations and directed almost solely to a small group of similarly trained, similarly placed readers. One of the most striking features of this activity is the steady state of the knowledge involved and the stability of its audience. "Whatever authority the critic possesses," Hayden White declares, "is a function not only of conventions which legitimate the particular judgments he may render in a given act of criticism but also of the prior authority which convention itself appeals to in order to know what is proper and what improper in any social action whatsoever."[3]

We can hardly overlook the internal regulation and control that take place in that situation. The consensus that underlies scholarly routines exerts itself in conventional assumptions and conventional practices, as protocols about what is "proper" or "improper." In the world of scholarship such things do not change very quickly or very

64

easily. We can see why. Intellectual authority and the authority of scholars and critics are first of all guild creations, products of the credentials conferred by schools that exercise their norms of judgment in order to reproduce themselves. The first rule of professional institutions is to maintain their own stability, to perpetuate themselves and recreate the maximum circumstances for survival and legitimacy. This priority makes all professional organizations procedurally conservative if not necessarily politically conservative. It is not surprising, therefore, that such concern for institutional stability makes any organization, especially one with a long-held dedication to preserving tradition, somewhat dynastic and open to challenge only by someone well established in the hierarchy of rank and privilege.

Such a challenge is offered by Richard Ohmann's *English in America: A Radical View of the Profession.* Ohmann's position to the left of the tightly bunched center of academic discourse is permanently assured by that text, but more important, Ohmann has pursued the question of intellectual authority with rare clarity. Like Chomsky (and Gramsci), he sees that the predominant interest among literary intellectuals is pacification: to reconcile academic work to political reality by an emphasis upon the structural complexity of texts and by a depoliticizing insistence upon the adequacy of formalistic analytic competence. As Ohmann points out,

> a critic and teacher of literature whose work is fun and respectable, but who sees little evidence that he is helping to ameliorate social ills, or indeed serving any but those destined to assume their own positions in the ruling class—a teacher in this dubious spot will welcome a system of ideas and values that tells him that politics and ideology are at an end, that a pluralistic society is best for all, that individual freedom is the proper social goal for rich and poor alike, and that the perfection of self can best be attained through humanistic intellectual endeavor. And this is what the New Criticism and its rival theories had to offer. The tacit ideology [of that consensus] has its proper place in bourgeois culture; its main features are practically inevitable, given the position of critics and teachers in this capitalist society.[4]

Ohmann's point is that the post–World War II literary intellectual has avoided looking at historical and political forces, forces that are economic and material and not at all reducible to spirtual or literary values. His point is that the "critical spirit," as he calls it, has been eviscerated by false boundaries placed around the literary and critical act and by the disingenuous application of a nonideological outlook that conducts literature away from the grubby facts of a world professors feel powerless to grapple with. This elevation of "literary" over "ideological" values is itself ideological. The "tacit ideology" of the humanities is "the idea of freedom," the dominant concept in American culture, a concept that can be found nauseatingly over-worked in patriotic rhetoric. That inner freedom is possible for every-one who learns to read well, that beyond the "freedom" of the mar-ketplace another freedom is available, the artist's and intellectual's contemplative freedom (free from action of any sort, free to experi-ment without political consequences): such is the tacit ideology of literary study in the United States. It is worth noticing because the central thrust of a literary education not only separates texts from the systems of reading by which they are taught; it assumes that the end product of textual study is personal and critical self-enhancement for the development of individual careers.

Ohmann's book raises the troubling question of critical purpose. What can literary study accomplish, what useful role can the educated person play, as long as the idea of book culture and of the humanities as a civilizing force is kept separate from the student's and the teach-er's relationship to the cultural environment, an institutional and so-cial environment in which the state is the least noticed, least adver-tised element in an apparently unregulated yet well-coordinated professional market? Ohmann does not have an answer. But he sees that the "emergence of the technostructure and the new reliance on planned control of markets has made organizational abilities" in-creasingly important. It has stimulated the "ideology of value-free inquiry, which academic intellectuals have been a century in develop-ing," and it erodes the skeptical critical consciousness literary intellec-tuals are proud of.[5] One reason for these effects is close at hand. English departments "have been full participants in the development of the new American university" that has risen into prominence in the past twelve decades. They have shared "its growth, its prosperity (slightly less than the share of scientists, economists, and the like), its professional pride, and its mystifications." They have also, Ohmann finds, contributed powerfully to the strengthening of the corporate state: "both the skills (fluency, organization, analysis) and the at-titudes (caution, detachment, cooperation) that we encourage in the young are essential to the technostructure and to the smooth func-tioning of liberal (not liberated) society."[6]

Ohmann does not say that English departments and freshman En-glish programs are in thrall to the state. But to the extent that the teaching of literature and writing remains devoted to the preparation of individual careers over collective interaction and the application of critical knowledge to correcting the waste and structural abuses of our economic system, the humanist curriculum can only work in the service of private political and capitalist power. This insight leads Ohmann to a highly controversial conclusion:

> To stand apart from the industrial system and its menacing uses of knowledge, universities would have to be much *more* political—less pure—than they are. They would have to relinquish the flattering ideology of the ivory tower, the dodge of academic freedom, the false security of professionalism, and all the trappings of neutrality, which conceal a subtler partisanship. They would have to shape academic policy to expressly political ends, asking not "how can we best transmit and improve the knowledge that exists?" but "what knowledge do we and our students most need for liberation?" They would have to seek out ways of making knowledge serve the powerless. They would have to dispense with the barrier between thought and action, and find ways to ensure that the *uses* of their research and teaching weighed against the present rule of corporations and the Pentagon. In short, they would have to act as allies of socialist revolution.[7]

Nothing in North American society at present is hospitable to this vision of a politically active education. Everything in the culture and the economy stands armed to oppose the first step toward a revolutionary university. Only a few scattered theorists, a loose collection of anomalous radicals in the vast minority in universities, will take Ohmann's challenge seriously. The situation in reality is so antagonistic that anyone who would want not merely intellectual space but social or political affiliation for such a change would need to create the conditions of revolution. And yet Ohmann's position is not only lucid but sane, optimistic in the one way that could give the humanities a genuinely critical and adversarial (no longer instrumental and amoral) purpose.

Its optimism resides in the effort to challenge the literary establishment. Ohmann is well aware that his book will seem excessively radical to many humanists. Yet the whole point of critical thinking is to challenge accepted wisdom, to confront those attitudes and perspectives that have long dominated significant institutions. Ohmann's "radical" analysis is therefore not so radical, especially when one looks at injustices innate to our social logic, at the organized distractions of North American culture, its consumer idiocy and bloated arms production. These things have been scorned though not fully analyzed by literary teachers, and yet the cornerstone of United States foreign policy since World War II (a policy that antedated that war, in truth) has been an assault on foreign territories and populations with "economic assistance" (loans, credit, sometimes covert "gifts") granted to encourage or require our "allies" to buy weapons. It should now be common knowledge that, as Stanley Karnow writes, "impoverished Asian, African and Latin American nations that lack the means to feed their people, not to mention providing them with education or medical care," are driven into outrageous debt to United States banks to acquire "weapons to settle border disputes that otherwise could have been negotiated."[8] Ohmann's position embraces this awareness. It moves literary education into contact with historical and political reality. In sum, it gives the humanities a concrete context to develop critical consciousness. Ohmann would have us see that language is a material force in culture and that culture creates the terms for decisions that determine social and political reality.

The outcome of a critique such as Ohmann's is difficult to project, though its success or failure will count heavily in molding literary education. Perhaps conflict in the humanities will continue to follow the lines Ohmann describes. Yet anyone who takes contemporary reality in its present cultural and institutional forms as a model of the future distribution of knowledge, wealth, and global political influence fails to imagine the incalculable impact of economic instability now at work in the world. An accelerating world population and the emergence of increased political consciousness and political participation among previously apathetic or suppressed minorities (as one sees today in South Africa) can have unforeseen consequences. It is also impossible to predict the impact in North America of aroused public consciousness of the financial stress of an endless arms race. Nor can anyone say categorically that the major television networks that follow rather than lead dramatic events (nonetheless creating an extraordinarily powerful but often distorted spectacle) will not be captured at some point by a growing protest against nuclear weapons. I am not predicting such events but suggesting, first, that Ohmann's challenge to traditional humanist indifference gives us a way out of intellectual demoralization and, second, that events in the world (what Marx in the *Grundrisse* calls the "world market and crises")[9] exceed the capacity of any administration or managerial control to produce outcomes wholly favorable to vested capitalist interests.

This may be, then, an appropriate moment to revive the idea of a "cultural dominant" at work in apparently disjunctive realms, in high academic print culture as much as in commercial media or "popular" culture, in most forms of organized political life as much as in marketplace economics. The point of doing so would be, first, to resist any temptation to engage in denunciation which a critique of humanist indifference might arouse, and second, to appreciate the analytic strength of Jameson's formulation of a logic in the evolution of capitalism in our era. In chapter 1 I stressed the tendency to underplay the appropriation (and the creation) of surplus value, of exploited labor, which the term "cultural dominant" brings with it. The warning exerted there errs on the side of emphasizing, polemically but cautiously, the reductive misapplications possible when a term or critical concept with a uniquely totalizing energy appears on the scene. I will return to the issue of Jameson's totalizing momentum in chapter 6. Such reduction in this instance, however, would move away from traditional Marxist reductions to place explanation and interpretive understanding in the superstructure rather than the infrastructure. Culture, seen as pervasive and now "dominant" as a semiautonomous realm transcribing and also delivering the "meaning" of (i.e., the imagery and common public access to) every social event, thus disperses into random yet highly systematic formative acts. Culture then appears as if it were a wholly reified collection of language games that express the commodity logic of late international capitalism while simultaneously intensifying the conversion of all things human and natural into abstract exchanges. Not only have economic forces, once thought distinct from cultural energies, thereby been subsumed by spectacle, sign, image, language, advertisement, and media ubiquity, but human agency, the critic's work, all intellectual effort at collective oppositional strategies seem blocked in advance because absorbed by the superior force of a culture in the service of the desocializing commodity logic that "controls" public space without any specific institutional residence that could be held accountable by critique and by political action.[10]

The hazard, in sum, attached to the concept of a cultural dominant is that it could leave obscure both the economic sphere and the political realm (the place of democratic transformation and revolutionary change). A perspective such as Ohmann's would seem defeated before it starts, before it can gain whatever strength it deserves in helping teachers and critics set a new pedagogical agenda. My caution has the effect of holding on to not so fully outmoded Marxist analyses, *Capital* III for one, as a frame for the point of view Jameson offers in order to establish "the context of a general mutation of culture throughout this period [our own], a context in which 'theory' will come to be grasped as a specific (or semi-autonomous) form of what must be called postmodernism generally."[11] Although it should be obvious that theory is no more certain of achieving worthwhile social or political results than would some lonely anticapitalist jeremiad, the closure Jameson constructs here does not entirely rule out the possibility of making or enlarging openings within the contemporary institutional field.

And this is what Jameson's full treatment of his notion of a cultural dominant is intended to promote. Postmodernism, as he maps it, "is precisely the waning" of the once traditional opposition between high modernism and mass culture. This "new conflation of the forms of high and mass culture" leads critical analysis toward "the social functionality of culture itself"[12]—that is, toward culture's putative "autonomy," which is the corrupted form of an Enlightenment ideal that expressly focused intellect and public knowledge (rational analysis and education generally) on social transformation and political intervention. If one were to shorten the complex issue of postmodernism, the one emblematic change most linked to other transformations at work in postmodernist culture might well be the flattening of historical perspectives in both academic and commercial discourse. That result can be seen in critiques of representation associated with structuralist and poststructuralist innovations that attempt to escape from the hegemony of some tangible cultural dominance within intellectual practices. The loss of historical perspective is now well documented and familiar to everyone laboring on these issues (see especially *The Anti-Aesthetic: Essays on Postmodern Culture,* edited by Hal Foster, and *The Structural Allegory,* edited by John Fekete).[13] The emptying of authorial and, finally, historical "content" from signs and sign systems requires renewed historical transcription. Jameson, for his part, has taken a number of routes across the dehistoricizing field now common to both high and mass culture. Alongside his readings of novels as ideological constructs providing formal access to historical events and submerged class energies, we find a commitment to diagram as much of the "common objective situation" as possible without overstepping the fact of our own embeddedness in circumstances still undergoing clarification and convulsion.

This effort to "periodize" our historical moment draws upon the notion of a cultural dominant and helps, I think, give substance to Ohmann's project to make scholarship useful.[14] The idea of a cultural dominant as Jameson frames it updates the way materiality can be looked at. "Matter," facticity, the brute boundedness of an altogether circumscribed field of forces and interests—the order of "the real" that divides social life into classes so that the barrio and the shantytown speak the system's planned indifference to the misery it creates—now must be thought about in terms of "the opacity of the

Institution itself as the radically transindividual, with its own inner dynamic and laws, which are not those of individual human action or intention."[15] This "new" realm of matter suffusing individuality, institution, and society is a culture saturated by information and media: a process of image making and information swapping which touches everyone because it not only "mediates" but establishes the operative terms of negotiable existence. No one can make do in the world today without coming into contact with and somehow internalizing North American and Western European advertising culture, its big-business logic. Culture, in short, has become homogenized, ever more public and present. It alters the way institutions as well as ideas intersect.

Here we can understand the fall of culture into the world, the loss of an autonomy it seems to have when looked at as an industry (mere commercial ventures) in its own right. By the logic of cultural dominance, selfhood is dissolved within the field of competing institutions—that is, individuals become an effect of the roles they are given to play—and the concept of institution itself is dissolved in the dialectical swirl of marketplace intrusions upon formerly precapitalist regions (Brazil, Alaska, Borneo, Kenya) and upon previously detached or incompletely absorbed roles and functions. Jameson thus sees the crisis of capitalism in its self-redeeming advance to be a crisis of Marxist understanding also, since our era for the past quarter-century has been "a period whose active political categories no longer seemed to be those of social class"[16] and since Marxist analysis has been strained to cope with the concrete results of this expansion of capitalism's postmodern "cultural" colonialism. Jameson's hero in the attempt to find a route out of that impasse is Ernest Mandel, whose *Late Capitalism* provides "the link between the neocolonialist transformation of the third world during the 60s and the emergence of that seemingly very different thing in the first world, variously termed consumer society, postindustrial society, media society, and the like."[17] The logic here, a logic specific to a refurbished notion of materialist critique, the logic of cultural dominance, weaves together (*a*) the acculturation of First World populations by the subtle adjustment or accommodation induced by spectator perspectives (everyone is constantly a target for commercial seductions); (*b*) the expansion of capitalist markets by international corporate networks; (*c*) the containment of opposing political energies within "democratic" institutions; and (*d*) the latent "utopian" necessity of exposing state power—that is, revealing the political consequences of present economic formations—to the future professionals as well as to the current victims of capitalist development (a topic I will return to later).

The idea of a "cultural dominant" thus can be taken as an ally of intellectual practices devoted to curricular change of the sort Ohmann seeks. It need not be a globalizing, abstract, and monolithic category that overwhelms minute analysis of social territories and work regimes. Indeed, Jameson's recent work in plotting the "long decade" of the sixties is careful to situate itself in relation to the economic and political breaks that once shaped and now characterize the sixties as a historical moment of social and cultural transition.[18] But if this notion is to be of use for critical work with transformational social goals, it will need efforts similar to the one Ohmann has made in *English in America* to extend its otherwise technical precision into broad circulation. We also might bring Edward Said's well-known commitment to account for the institutional and social "force of statements in texts" to bear on this issue.[19] Such efforts might lead a great many more humanists to see that they are in a position to ground their work in the actual cultural space they occupy. If that grounding were to become a source of intellectual solidarity, critics would need to examine the several ways their knowledge moves away from them into society's competitive environments. The alternative is to hold to the image of a steadfast protector of a literary past too fragile, too precious, too otherworldly for critical ends.

On the strength of Jameson's vision and Said's suspicion, with the help of Chomsky's and Ohmann's examples, criticism can be seen as something to use as a goad against professional, cultural, and political distortions (against numbing proprieties). My point here is that the civic function of criticism is not merely an ideal if it creates clearly defined public controversies or if it contributes to awakening public consciousness. This is certainly one way to measure Ohmann's achievement—as yet incomplete but unique among literary professionals who prefer order to provocation, polite regard to intellectual energy. In 1968, at the plenary meeting of the Modern Language Association standing committees, amid civilizational disruption in North America and Indochina, Ohmann thought out loud

that the MLA should seriously consider taking public stands whose social and political content is entirely manifest—stands on repression and censorship, the Selective Service system and its social effects, the war, race and inequality in the schools, and so on. Without question each of these affects both the pursuit of scholarship and the interests of teachers. For instance, the Vietnamese War is in direct conflict with whatever benign internationalism the Foreign Language Program implies. It diverts resources from education of all kinds, and our kind in particular. It is about to remove our graduate students from the scene. It is destroying

the ability of all students to think about books and languages in a disinterested way. It has led thousands of our members and their colleagues
to station themselves outside the boundaries of law. It carries with it the
threat of a repression of intellectuals which could far outstrip the per-
secutions of the early fifties. . . . By remaining silent, we say loudly that
we do not see a connection between our professional interests and "the
love of our neighbor, the impulses toward action, help, and beneficience,
the desire for . . . diminishing human misery." I wonder if this consequence is what our members intend.[20]

The strange appearance of such words in our postpolitical maturity
attests to the distance we have come from that fleeting interruption.
For a moment it seemed permissible, even necessary, to speak passionately, forthrightly, about the brotherhood of intellectuals and victimized peoples. Of course subsequent turmoil in the MLA created
wounds that still cause very real ideological and personal divisions.
This is something Ohmann in part foresaw and tried to mitigate,
recognizing that some "questions would sufficiently divide the membership that any declaration would be hollow" or worse.

I revive these relics of a now-lost moment of political resolve, a wish
left unfulfilled, because the forces grown from that time have become
more massive and less certain.[21] Few intelligent people can be confident about the computerized technological enhancement of war now
being implemented by two governments locked year after year in a
fatal marriage. I think the lesson to be gained by listening again to
Ohmann, this time more closely than before, is that the critic's job
must *lead* and not merely react to adversity. By now literary intellectuals should see that they have the information needed to insert their
analytic intelligence and their literary and philosophical training
more forcefully into the "normal" operations of the university. By the
same commitment, they have license to interrupt or intersect (to
speak and be heard within) their own professional organizations as
readers and writers who are citizens before they are "professionals,"
people incapable of being muzzled by academic protocols and the
rules of tacit consensus.

Many humanists would argue that the public role of the critical
intellectual and of the professional literary establishment is incidental
or inadevertent. That argument would point out, no doubt, that the
airing of such political concerns has caused more harm than good.
The legacy of bitter debates and lingering frustrations has produced
not a strengthened critical education but (and I believe many who
disagree with my outlook would agree here) an insistently retreating

academy, a professional organization suspicious of any move to commandeer its work. And so high culture as we find it now is looked at once again by humanists as an autonomous realm of knowledge whose authority must be protected from invasions or perversions. It is treated thus because that authority is the source of the humanist's own legitimacy in a world more than ever driven by competition, distrust of authority of any kind, and just plain disbelief in the possibility of cooperative human community. Given that mind-set, any erosion of professional stability becomes a threat to humanist identity, to humanist authority, and therefore to the critic's position. Eugene Goodheart's *Culture and the Radical Conscience* argues that an outlook such as Ohmann's may very well be dangerous, since "the work of the 'radical conscience' in literary studies has been largely destructive." Against political and intellectual radicalism of the sort Ohmann proposes, Goodheart holds out "radical disinterestedness" or what he calls "the project of sustaining independent thought"—in short, "radical criticism" instead of radical politics.[22]

The issue that most divides Goodheart's radicalism of "a constructive dissenting clerisy" from Ohmann's radicalizing of the university curriculum is the possibility of maintaining "the integrity of the cultural life and consequently the vitality and health of a free society."[23] These terms, however, are problematic. For example, the difference here evolves from disagreement about the kind and scope of "freedom" that North American society permits the democratic process and the cultural marketplace to generate. From Ohmann's point of view, Goodheart's notion of "radical disinterestedness" is an unusually mystified ideal meant to separate literary study from politics—or, more accurately, to depoliticize literary teaching in a moment of cultural retrenchment. The unusual quality of this mystification seems to be its willfulness, for Goodheart is aware of the economic and cultural contradictions of American life. His attempt to heighten critical self-consciousness without questioning the institutional context of intellectual authority encourages professional reform of a radically truncated sort. To overlook the situated interaction of university and capitalist interests, to assume that humanist critics stand outside the material and social field where intellectual work takes place, is to imagine a spiritual freedom unattached to the conflicts that generate our political history. To do so is also to postulate a kind of dialogue or critical analysis that cannot address the world we live in because it refuses to name the situated interests and the movement of knowledge in a society that gives the critic room to theorize or dissent as long as the material and political structures are not altered.

In short, humanist reform, if it increases the detached unconcern of intellectuals with their immediate social reality, can only reproduce the intellectual conditions of capitalism as we have it. That is an intellectual landscape that denies social leadership. It admits moral leadership of a distinctly vague sort, one kept distant from emerging political opportunities. Unquestionably, for me at least, even this diluted notion of intellectual or critical "leadership" cannot be put forth credibly unless it is understood as concerted action to create the educational framework to inform students about the world they live in, a world in which their own opportunities and responsibilities as educated citizens of the one society capable of global improvement *and* destruction must be argued in each public and professional area.

My sense is that Goodheart believes that liberal democracy is deeply flawed but that it nonetheless constitutes the only available space for constructive change. It is difficult to quarrel with that assessment because it offers the common-sense virtue of acknowledgeing real social limits. The question, however, is what the concrete position of the intellectual really is. How closed within the instrumental appropriation of all intellectual effort, of all knowledge, is humanist teaching? Is it essentially an academic offering, another disciplinary routine that the student has to hurdle on the way to a professional career? What, in brief, is the scope of critical effort? What role does it play within and outside the university? Are some roles, or is the radical one Ohmann works for, destructive? That is the threat Goodheart is concerned with:

> The radical case for politicizing the university rests on the premise that the universities are political already. If the work of political science, sociology, and engineering is conducted not only under government auspices, but in the interest of formulating and executing government policy, it is disingenuous, so the radicals argue, for defenders of "academic freedom" to insist that the university remain free of politics. Many radicals do not argue for a university that is free of politics because they are committed to a view that all thought is ideologically motivated and that the problem is to choose the right ideology, that is, one that fosters human values. . . .
>
> The radical case rests largely on the character of the social sciences (in particular, political science). The evidence of subordination of the intellectual enterprise to government purposes is extensive. One must, however, distinguish among disciplines—for example, between political science on the one hand, and the study of literature or philosophy or mathematics on the other hand. There is doubtless an ideological component in all fields of study, but the ideological component does not necessarily make for servile scholarship, as any Marxist historian, for

instance, would be quick to agree. It is an important distinction to make, because the issue is as much the extent and character of the politicization as the fact that the university is already politicized. If one can cite a long list of academic departments that are insubordinate to the political purposes of the American government, the argument about the inevitability of a politicized university becomes more difficult to make.[24]

Goodheart's confidence in his profession's ability to clarify its own activity, a confidence in what Gouldner calls the "intellectuals' culture of careful and critical discourse" (a faith endemic to the nature of scholarship and criticism), leads him to "battle against the political vulgarization of the literary process . . . in the interest of aesthetic and intellectual freedom, but [also] in the interest of the democratic experience itself."[25] And yet what precisely "the democratic experience" actually is in the particular complex of institutional interactions that make up American capitalism not only remains a cherished but unexamined ideal here, as in the bulk of North American scholarship, but stands, along with "intellectual freedom," as the sort of god-term that lures even wary critics from their own analytic vigilance.[26]

More disturbing and more useful in assessing where the threat to intellectual inquiry resides is the viewpoint taken within the government itself. The confusion about intellectual roles and targets for critical scrutiny—the dispute between literary radicals and literary moderates or conservatives about the culpability of professional textual study in the imperialism of American power—reflects a muddle that is certainly not devised by humanists, or able to be solved by them, but is an objective condition of international political and cultural warfare. The humanities may dissent from United States government policies; yet anyone who believes in the innately "insubordinate character of the intellectual process" needs to look at the institutional nature of intellectual activity.[27] To do so is to find, as Hayden White says, that "the profession of criticism in general tends to gravitate toward the liberal and conservative bands of the ideological spectrum, rather than toward the extremes of either radicalism or reactionism. And this because the critic's authority unlike that of the artist and scientist or, for that matter, the politician, is purely conventional in nature."[28] Within this broad middle range of critical styles and critical attitudes, the ideal of radical disinterestedness holds something like a privileged place providing not so much encouragement for intellectual insubordination of any kind as an excuse for a variety of accommodations to the critic's disempowerment.

It is instructive, therefore, to read what those in the policy making arena write about humanists. Here is Zbigniew Brzezinski, nine years before he joined the Carter administration as national security adviser, while he was directing the Research Institute on Communist Affairs at Columbia University. The occasion for his comments is the paradoxical emergence of a national political crisis alongside what he sees to be strengthened governmental and intellectual authority at local levels:

> Today, the university is the creative eye of the massive communications complex, the source of much strategic planning, domestic and international. Its engagement in the world is encouraging the appearance of a new breed of politicians-intellectuals, men who make it a point to mobilize and draw on the most expert scientific and academic advice in the development of their political programs. This, in turn, stimulates public awareness of the value of expertise—and, again in turn, greater political competition in exploiting it.
>
> A profound change in the intellectual community itself is inherent in this development. The largely humanist-oriented, occasionally ideologically-minded intellectual dissenter, who saw his role largely in terms of proffering social critiques, is rapidly being displaced either by experts and specialists, who become involved in special governmental undertakings, or by the generalists-integrators, who become in effect house-ideologues for those in power, providing overall intellectual integration for disparate actions. A community of organization-oriented, application-minded intellectuals, relating itself more effectively to the political system than their predecessors, serves to introduce into the political system concerns broader than those likely to be generated by that system itself and perhaps more relevant than those articulated by outside critics.[29]

This displacement of the dissenting humanist by specialist-experts or generalists-integrators who are moving from the university into government and the bureaucratic management of large corporations depicts the now-classic scene of critical disfranchisement and humanist pathos. What I find interesting is the unconscious agreement between Brzezinski and Goodheart that our "meritocratic democracy" has effectively separated humanist work from policymaking and from useful public roles—the roles of social scrutiny and of setting educational agendas that might rehabilitate both intellectual and moral skills. Instead the world is seen to be systematized. Government is divided into agencies, each with particular tasks and expert managerial knowledge. Universities are divided into departments and intellectual areas, each with different portions of knowledge to adjudicate with disinterest and dispassion. Both government and business rely on university expertise (raid it, fund it, and so on), but nowhere in the exchange do we find a model for humanist intervention, for critical insurgency to rival or offset the relentless technologization and bureaucratization of North American society. How can critical intelligence have a meaningful function in redirecting society if humanist dissent stays peacefully trapped within its ever more irrelevant margin? And in what way could the ideal of radical disinterestedness accomplish genuinely productive critical results unless it began to trouble itself by finding points of interest between intellectual fields that could be joined to resist the instrumentalizing of all knowledge? If we say that knowledge is inherently instrumental (or ultimately so) because it eventually serves the human community or has no claim to wisdom, truth, or accuracy, then what interaction of intellectual skills will generate a life-enhancing use of knowledge? In sum, where can dissent take hold if not in the university itself by calling attention to the subordination of knowledge to expedience and commoditization? To say that such work is disinterested and not political is to miss the point of that work. *Because* knowledge can enhance or reduce human life, *because* it can enlighten or distort social reality, it is never disinterested in any of its forms but, on the contrary, is interested either in private or in public affiliations, in specialized or in general purposes, in demoting human cooperation or in promoting it. Where knowledge goes, interests are at stake. The question is, *whose* interests? For *what* uses? At what *costs* to the overall integrity of human possibilities?

I am, in other words, wondering how dissent of the kind Goodheart distinguishes from radical politics, radical criticism instead of radical action, can revitalize intellectual purpose in a nation so given to the cult of expertise and the dissociation of intellect from questions of value. The difficulty with any position within the humanities today, whether overtly political or otherwise, is its lack of contact with the rest of institutional reality. Humanists talk with humanists, but seldom strategically, with an interest in enhancing the pedagogical or critical force of the humanities. Since the university budget process stacks department against department and often individual interests against one another—a process that mirrors the capitalist marketplace precisely—how can dissent of any kind (interested or disinterested) be turned into commitment strong enough to recapture, or invent anew, the institutional authority of criticism? Naive as they may seem, the questions I ask are hardly illicit when the uses of intellectual freedom are necessarily for some redeeming or productive purpose beyond the gratification of a reader's self-absorbed enthusiasm. I take it that Ohmann and Goodheart, despite their significant differences, both want a way to deal with texts so the subversive power of alternative vision could challenge what Brzezinski calls, with apparent glee, "the increasingly cultivated and programmed American society" we now live in.[30]

None of my questions catches the institutional perplexity of literary studies as well as this report by Armand Mattelart:

> The group of strategic researchers of the Pentagon's National School of War, after conducting a study which came to the conclusion that "the phenomenon of the growth of multinational enterprises, mostly North American, can play a major role in the amelioration of our political, military and economic global strength," underlined the need for the civil and military apparatuses to draw closer together . . . in order effectively to guarantee the security of the Empire. This document recognized the importance of ideological battle, considering how important it was to preserve North American values and assure the propagation of the transatlantic mode of life: "on this ever-smaller globe of ours, all societies, all cultures are engaged in an inevitable competition for predominance and survival. Those who will fashion tomorrow's world are those who are able to project their image (to exercise the predominant influence and a long range influence). . . . If we want our values and our life style to be triumphant we are forced to enter a competition with other cultures and other centres of power. For this purpose, the multinational company offers considerable leverage. Its growing business arsenal with its foreign bases works for us 24 hours a day. It is a fact of osmosis which does not only transmit and implant entrepreneurial methods, banking techniques and North American commercial relations, but also our judicial systems and concepts, our political philosophy, our mode of communication, our ideas of mobility, and a way of contemplating literature and art appropriate to our civilization."[31]

This final statement is sobering. What "appropriate" mode of study or contemplation could members of the Pentagon research group have in mind? Clearly what they mean is the kind of apolitical, value-neutral pretense to objectivity that we find currently in a methodological death grip with the recent theoretical complications that have invaded literary criticism. The harshest irony here is not that such an innocent contemplative model still persists, as it does, somewhat harried, years after those statements were written for the Kennedy-McNamara administration, which expanded America's disastrous incursion into Indochina in an attempt to enforce its own political superiority. The most troubling realization of all is how very little the underlying social and cultural conformation has changed in the intervening years, despite all the social protest, the anguish of curricular reforms, and the divisive misunderstandings within criticism itself. Almost everything called "theory" in higher intellectual circles contributes to the small, well-marked, and politically extrinsic growth of criticism as an industry rather than to efforts to define the contexts and conditions in which intellectual production actually takes place. I say "almost" because some writers seriously engaged in theoretical debate have not been sterilized by the self-protective, self-affirming rarefication of literary and critical professionalism. To this point, however, critical authority has been viewed for the most part as the institutional privilege of insiders content to let multinational corporations define democratic globalism.

Recently Wayne Booth, "as a liberal who has reluctantly been driven to give up dogmas of autonomy," has found that he and other critics "can now question, without too much anxiety, the 'natural' opposition of the aesthetic order and the political order. We can now look at the ethics and politics that were concealed in the professedly anti-ethical and apolitical stances of modern aesthetic movements. We can question the notion, implicit in certain of those movements, that art is more important than people."[32] The reason for this shift seems to be, for him, the emergence of feminist criticism, which is attempting "to break through the hegemony of male voices." Significantly, he seeks to treat that change of critical perspective not as a question of power and of the wresting of a major cultural discourse from entrenched interests and institutionally established writers or discursive practices, but as an instance of critical freedom—freedom *to*, he avers, instead of freedom *from:* the kind of creative freedom "gained only by those who surrender to disciplines and codes invented by others, giving up certain *freedoms from.*"

This is an invitation to explore Foucault's (and Nietzsche's) thesis that writers who succumb to codes and disciplines are in a distinctly unfree or operationally limited, institutionally mandated situation that does not leave them free *to* commit any particular inventive act except within rigorous conceptual, procedural, and even political boundaries. From there one may notice the idealistic discrimination still at work in Booth's conversion to feminism. Booth imagines critical and creative freedom as something no longer isolated from ethical and political choices (perhaps from their impact and social setting also, but this is not clear), yet he understands his own freedom as a critic to be enabled, as it is, by an essentially professional discipline whose codes and routines allow him room, motivation, and vocabulary to do his work. His fear or worry is that he may project a "self-privileging" discourse outside the bounds of group consensus or group expression. The sort of freedom he has in mind for a critic projects commitment to those who will listen to him, whose work joins his and that of writers before him in making an intelligible but wholly professionalized ethical reality.

That this collegial discourse (criticism, philosophy, the community of academic writers) cannot be overwhelmed, no matter how much any writer immodestly attempts the personal or critical sublime, escapes Booth's logic because he does not see that every possible intellectual position takes place in an already deidealized realm, the corporate interaction of particular institutional regimes, each with "disciplines" and "codes" constrained by interactions in the inter-institutional world. In sum, no one can step out of the borders of intellectual understanding and still make sense, that is, command attention and exert force or influence. This fear of self-privileging which dogs Booth's cautious critical freedom appears as a final figure of "threatening chaos" about to envelop us now that politics and the claims of new voices have entered the intellectual world.

What makes this stance so utterly problematic is that Booth celebrates a belated appreciation of feminist writing, which deserves more than appreciation, but in doing so he reerects the old barriers that exclude criticism from an insurrectionary role as an ethically and politically disruptive effort that no longer serves as the confirming voice of social consolidation. He inscribes himself, and all who follow him, within another version of the separation between intellectual "freedom" and human reality so congenial to conventional academic practices. That he does so is seen most graphically in his assertion of "a permanent irreconcilability of a fully historical and a fully critical view," since he cannot shake "the plain fact that nobody ever manages fully to enter an alien period or culture."[33]

Foucault, as we will see, is also concerned with this problem, but he resolves the apparent "irreconcilability" of history and critical knowledge by showing how critical discourse constitutes what is *there* in the world, what can be known. Foucault insists upon a viewpoint that, in turn, comprehends critical discourse itself as constituted in history. Criticism and intellectual understanding are ways of forming reality, ways of knowing that exclude and include themes and whole discursive regions. So the way we know the past is by understanding its own ways of postulating reality within peculiar discourses. Thus, between critical discourses and intellectual practices, alien periods and cultures reveal themselves—not as a series of essential meanings, but as a series of discursive maneuvers (and limits) that create the conditions of social, cultural, and political power. History is the way things get done in specific places at specific times. That fact can be reconstituted theoretically, critically, as an interaction between intellectual authority and institutional power.

The point of looking ahead to Foucault right here is to see the distortion that takes place in Booth's swerve away from power toward freedom to do professional things idealistically cut off from the historical social world.[34] The constraint upon the critic's freedom as a writer is not, as Booth thinks, the privacy or eccentricity of cognitive subjectivity. It is the consensual nature of discursive relationships (the limitations, blindnesses, ideologies at work in particular "disciplines"), which itself is situated in an actual relationship of authority and power—a relation between authority and power—which is manifested in the institutional structures and ways of addressing others in our professional and personal, socially grounded lives. One of the questions we can explore that cuts against subjectivity is this: what kind of authority does intellectual effort uphold right here, under these immediate conditions, where criticism and teaching are at work?

We can face that question by recalling Max Weber's discrimination among three forms of authority: traditional, rational (or legal), and charismatic authority, three "publicly advanced types of reasons or 'grounds' for obeying," Steven Lukes tells us, "each of which, according to Weber, tends to prevail under certain conditions and is in turn associated with and explanatory of power relations and forms of administration."[35] This formulation echoes Gramsci's observation that every kind of society generates its own sort of intellectuals. Thus "the ecclesiastics can be considered as the intellectual category tied to the landed aristocracy: legally it was on a level with the aristocracy, with whom it shared the exercise of feudal landownership and the enjoyment of the State privileges bound up with property." Gramsci thus accounts for the rise and formation of intellectuals as a group:

> Just as these various categories of traditional intellectuals have a sense of their own uninterrupted historical continuity, of their "qualifications" and of *esprit de corps,* so they see themselves as autonomous and independent of the ruling social group. This view of themselves is not without consequences in the ideological and political field, consequences of vast importance: the whole of idealist philosophy can easily be connected with this assumed position of the social complex of intellectuals, and may be defined as the expression of this social utopia through which intellectuals believe themselves to be "independent," autonomous, clothed in their own characters.[36]

Similarly, for Weber, the kind of authority intellectuals can draw on for their work varies with the social conditions (with the relations of production and with the political structure of a particular civil society): "traditional" authority is indigenous to feudal societies, "charismatic" authority occurs in disruptive periods of social transition and political upheaval, and "rational-legal" authority predominates in modern bureaucratic states. Underneath all of these forms of authority Weber posits an operation of power, "based upon constellations of interest," which dominates but does not overwhelm authority. In fact, for Weber authority provides "the ultimate grounds of the validity of a domination."[37] Authority is the way power justifies itself and validates its threat of force as well as its exercise of force.

We can see why intellectuals deny their actual affiliation with power. On one hand, intellectuals give respectability even to the coarsest organization of state power by operating rationally within its systematic order, by not openly rebelling or seeking to confront its aggression. On the other hand, intellectuals enjoy privilege and status under the protection of state power. On the whole, the relation between intellectuals and the state is mutually beneficial—as long as the state does not threaten the well-being of the intellectual class or, in reverse, as long as intellectuals do not undermine the efficient operation of the state. Almost any dispute or tension between the two can be tolerated by either side as long as political stability is maintained and allows the manipulation of cultural and economic policies to continue unopposed for the benefit of those in power. And yet, as Lukes says, "Weber stressed the ultimate role of power, in the form of coercion, or the threat of force, as an indispensable underpinning for the exercise of authority: for 'the political community, even more than other institutionally organized communities, is so constituted that it imposes obligations on the individual which many of them fulfill only because they are aware of the probability of physical coercion backing up such obligations.' "[38]

The term that Weber offers to improve upon the relatively ambiguous notion of "power" is *Herrschaft*, domination. He uses that concept in a more and in a less restricted sense. First, in the wider application, domination follows from structural inequities of influence or of any kind of social leverage (from what Weber calls "a position of monopoly" in the marketplace or anywhere else a monopoly of force or persuasion can result in the ability to command people to one focused will). Second, in the more restricted application, domination follows from a delegated or assumed authority to create rules obligating others to obey. The central feature of the concept of *Herrschaft*, as Weber uses it, is that structural domination, the assemblage of interests and forces that ensure compliance within a state, can be converted to forms of domination by the exercise of authority.

Now in Gramsci's notion of cultural hegemony and Weber's concept of domination we can find a great deal in common and also a certain, and important, degree of dissonance. For both, authority of various kinds at once exerts power and serves to mask or mute its overt presence. Equally, both see that power tends to seek out, and finally to culminate in, authoritative people, roles, institutions, and discourses. Power and authority, in other words, are in some measure interchangeable—up to a point. Exactly where that separation takes place is not always clear in either writer, since each has many and sometimes divergent things to say about the exchange between authority and power. But while both writers are deeply skeptical about the possibilities and claims of democracy as the rule of freely consenting people bound together in an open political process, Gramsci reserves a larger role for intellectuals in the managing and production of consent that a democratic system depends on. If for Weber domination is the partner of every form of authority, a systematic operation of the *administrative organization* in each society, distinct from its hierarchical structure, for Gramsci the persuasive force of a society's ideological order is an unannounced controlling agency that occupies a dominant position prompting consent through the *legitimizing function* of its intellectuals and their acknowledged authority as "knowers," "specialists," and "experts." But, Gramsci cautions,

> the relationship between intellectuals and the world of production is not immediate, as is the case for fundamental social groups; it is "mediated," in different levels, by the whole social fabric, and by the complex of the superstructure of which the intellectuals are in fact the "officials." . . . For the moment we can fix two great "floors" of the superstructure: that which can be called "civil society," i.e., all the organizations which are commonly called "private," and that of "political society or the State," which corresponds to the function of hegemony which the ruling class exercises over the whole of society.[39]

Gramsci makes it clear that intellectuals derive their authority in part from the existence and operation of the state, a claim that erodes the fiction of disinterested and autonomous critical consciousness, and he presses his insight to comprehend the service intellectuals render (structurally, innately) in the maintenance of the state:

> Intellectuals are "officers" of the ruling class for the exercise of the subordinate functions of social hegemony and political government, i.e. (1) of the "spontaneous" consent given by the great masses of the population to the direction imprinted on social life by the fundamental ruling class,

a consent which comes into existence "historically" from the "prestige" (and hence from the trust) accruing to the ruling class from its position and its function in the world of production; (2) of the apparatus of State coercion, which "legally" ensures the discipline of those groups which do not "consent" either actively or passively, but is constituted for the whole of society in anticipation of moments of crisis in command and direction when spontaneous consent diminishes.[40]

I think it should be obvious that Gramsci's Italy is not contemporary North America. The resistance Gramsci continued to generate from prison against Mussolini's Fascist state acknowledged both a civil and a political organization considerably simpler—more easily captured, more thoroughly opposed—than a society "unified" by a high degree of political and religious tolerance, coordinated by legal and cultural institutions with genuinely diverse and divergent outlooks, functions, and traditions. Yet Gramsci was well aware of the cultural and intellectual diversity within his native state. As Edward Said has shown in a series of essays that skillfully draw upon Gramsci's historical and critical awareness, culture (in the sense that Gramsci used the term) "has a density, a complexity, and historical-semantic value that is so strong as to make politics possible." In sum, "culture—elaboration—is what gives the State something to govern and yet, as Gramsci is everywhere careful to note, cultural activity is neither uniform nor mindlessly homogeneous."[41] Gramsci's position demystifies the separation between humanists and the state, since social and political "authority is maintained by virtue of the cultural process" which is verified, modified, and elaborated by humanists.[42]

The point here is that cultural authority, humanist authority, and the authority of Western institutions, of Western commercial values, tend to be mutually reaffirming. Not absolutely, but the opposition between the humanities and "democratic" state power as it exists not so invisibly in our time is limited by the role the humanities play in preserving traditional values, in upholding a view of the past which confirms the fairness and the predominant orderliness of the present state of things. Yet the appearance of rationality, of the fairness and institutional stability confirmed by a scholarly world that is allowed to dissent and even to expose the social system's flaws, shows up less in themes and topics debated outright than in the organization of knowledge. Not the conclusions of humanist scholarship but the apparent open give-and-take among concerned people, among critics, ensures belief throughout the professional world that reason and justice are possible. In reverse, by the exercise of just such reason, those beliefs preserve whatever real possibilities for justice exist—possibilities that have gained significant ground for once alien groups and interests.

The trouble plaguing radical critics no less than traditional critics is that the audience for sophisticated interpretations and theories is a subset of a larger audience, the academy, which on the whole reduces the world to specialized disciplines and languages. Give-and-take essentially propounds the rationality of existing academic divisions, of separate intellectual fields. Bringing these fields together at the level of their greatest precision and inventiveness is a challenging task even when we are dealing with such closely related areas as philosophy and critical theory or anthropology and linguistics. Though North Americans have greater access to information about the world's cultural, political, and economic realities than any professional or private citizens in history, the intellectual skill (and the theoretical will) to pursue relations between literary knowledge and all other kinds of knowledge that reveal complex and sometimes grim facts of social organization is by and large lacking. One obstacle here, not the only one, is the guild consciousness of scholarship, which has failed to develop the concept of a general, indivisible intellectual interest.[43]

That this narrow focus may be part of what Gramsci calls "ideological hegemony" seldom dawns on anyone, since in the first place the notion of ideological and cultural hegemony is still outside the mainstream thinking of humanist scholarship and criticism, and second, even among those who are aware of the Marxist tradition of reading texts (somewhat clumsily) as events situated within the ensemble of social facts, many yet find such terms at odds with the prevailing norms and vocabularies of liberal academic writing. Nevertheless, Gramsci's concept cannot go unchallenged as a self-evident fact of social life. For Marxists who see material production and the production of capital as the innermost core of contemporary capitalism—placing emphasis upon the labor process as the basis of surplus value (the basis of profit and expansion)—social or cultural organization is a *consequence* and not a determining cause of institutional reality. This interpretation (the "capital-logic" theory associated primarily with the work of Paul Mattick, Michel Aglietta, Ernest Mandel, Roman Rosdolsky, and, in the United States, mostly with Harry Braverman)[44] stresses the accumulation of financial power by monopolistic interests that direct the major structural changes of a society dependent upon the flow of capital. This emphasis has the virtue of explaining the rise of labor unions and their erosion by capitalist strategies to buy off and blunt labor militancy. It explains, first, the integration of labor into the fixed production costs of industry by means of long-term labor contracts and, second, the replacement of labor-intensive work by machines—an event that coincides with a movement to a service-oriented society and increased control by management over engineers, scientists, technicians, and specialists of every sort within the evolving knowledge-intensive work force. From this materialist viewpoint we can comprehend the permanent military economy, which began with large-scale state intervention in the economy during the Civil War (a process boosted with each subsequent war) and continues to serve as a constant source of jobs for a large segment of the population while pumping enormous amounts of money directly into numerous large corporations. This is capital that is not vulnerable to shifts of competition in the market, that does not produce commodities that compete with already overproduced consumer goods. A militarized economy has the added benefit of legitimating the appearance of an autonomous and "neutral" state organization, since the same governmental apparatus that creates public welfare programs, builds highways, and supports public schools, that at times ensures some vestige of access to the legal system for everyone, is the consumer of last resort for farmers and weapons makers alike. In that practice we find there is an extra "benefit." The purchase of military equipment reinforces the hysteria about foreign threats to civilian well-being.[45]

From the materialist perspective the state helps both to accumulate capital and to disaccumulate it, to consume both unused raw materials and idle plant capacity, and in doing so to generate consumption by an otherwise unemployed part of the population. The net result is to stave off the endemic crisis of capitalism, unemployment. The anti-Gramscian thrust of this view resides in its understanding of capitalist contradiction in terms of the exploitation of workers rather than as the falsification of consciousness. Labor is seen to be a consumable item for the production of profit; workers are hired, trained, shifted, and kept in jeopardy of temporary or permanent layoff by corporate decisions that fulfill the logic of capital—that is, by the effort to increase capital's leverage in endlessly turbulent domestic and international markets. From this perspective, Gramsci's emphasis on cultural domination and the ideological determination of social reality (the regulation of behavior, the creation of values) appears to be idealistic, shorn of the calculations of capital's self-interest and its planned waste, its intentional irrationality. But the relation between capital and the state is clearly not direct and unmediated, without intervening forms of resistance, judgment, and even "democratic" decision making. Multinational capitalism is not subordinate to the state, and in reverse, only a crude mechanistic formula would view the state as completely subsumed by capitalist interests. In other words, the relation between capitalism and social consciousness—the way various institutions within the general economic framework create an identity, assert themselves—is not unproblematic. Or to put this positively, it is problematic in just the ways that knowledge is vexed and not at all an immediately self-revealing body of statements or numbers that explain reality. Since all explanation, all knowledge, is interpreted and interpretive, institutionalized practices that generate information and knowledge exert an ineradicable influence on what a society wants to "know" to begin with. Not only that. The topics to be pursued, those areas of research that create knowledge of some interesting or usable kind, are themselves open to judgment and interpretation.

I am suggesting that Gramsci's concept of cultural hegemony has an important place in critical activity because it allows interpreters to account for the selection of topics and research areas within capitalist institutions. It allows critical readers and writers to make more explicit sense not only of their own relation to the cultural and institutional (and inevitably economic) whole, but of the creation, use, and distortion that follow from prevailing interpretive perspectives. In other words, from the standpoint of cultural hegemony we can begin to debate the linkage between intellectual work and the complex interaction between state policies and capitalist interests in an economic and cultural environment increasingly dominated by the creation of knowledge-intensive industries. Part of that linkage (a deliberately vague term), but only part, is to be found right here: in the investment of big business and big government in the production of new forms of knowledge, investment in research institutes and both private and public universities. This linkage does not so much "buy" intellectual labor, although it sometimes does that, as it supports research and commits intellectuals, including humanists, to operate within a well-controlled institutional order in which they are free (in fact, compelled by standards of intellectual honesty) to exercise deviant or dissenting opinions.[46]

The question for literary or critical intellectuals within this interplay of opposition and confirmation can be put in two forms. Negatively it is: Given the functional position of the humanities in their role as validators of cultural and even political authority—as that official area in which dissent is allowed as a relatively harmless alternative to an unjust social order—how can anyone exert an oppositional position that is not compromised or absorbed utterly by the self-verifying antagonisms of capitalist society? Put more positively, we have this: Given the structural logic of capitalism which can be plotted as a target for resistance, whether we view it from a materialistic or an idealistic perspective, how can criticism increase its unmasking and debunking activity in ways that expose capitalist contradictions to a wider audience so that the inherently political function of culture (its ability to create group identities) might become part of informed awareness at both national and neighborhood levels? In other words, how can humanists turn the rather elegant and complicated readings of cherished texts into politically productive knowledge for a society immersed in consumer junk and drowning in images of false liberation? In all its forms, the question is how criticism can become practical without losing clarity and analytic skill, become democratic (or democratically useful) and not evasive.

4

Intellectual Territories

The answer to the question just posed is unclear for a number of reasons but one of the strongest is this one: most critical writing is politically blind and will remain so as long as critics refuse to find room for the concept of "the state." Instead, the idea of "the nation" or of "culture" or the even more amorphous notion of "society" (without any sense of its intellectual and political organization) locates the field of forces where texts and values operate. The advantage of the concept of a "state" with its economic and cultural apparatus is immediate once we see that most writers cannot specify, except in vague, idealistic terms, the way their work fits into the ongoing clash of rival interests.[1] The idea of the state opens the otherwise buried class struggle. It points to the coordination of ruling values and allows us to investigate the forms of political and conceptual integration that depend upon power, both economic and military, and that legitimize power. It also allows us to clarify contradictions that hold the concrete possibilities of revolutionary change.

The distinction between the terms *nation* and *state* amounts to the difference between an abstract and essentially "natural" social order based on tradition and custom (nation) and another, in opposition, that embodies the artful, altogether constructed policies and images supervised by a ruling class or a dominant group (state). A state is an assemblage of laws, institutions, and material resources which creates the complicated coherence of a social and economic system. Out of this coherence evolve cultural and intellectual behaviors. In the absence of this concept we can hardly wonder why our intellectual life is so naive about its political capacities. One of the predominant myths of North American scholarship is the rigorously combative nature of democratic consensus. Our political reality is thought to be based on agreement about the essential attributes of a desirable human existence. Thus only the means to achieving it, small adjustments made by harmonious rival parties, are worth disputing. In a democratic consensus, in short, there are no "ruled" and no "rulers"; opposition to the dominant culture is already at work in the system itself.[2] Therefore the critic need not be concerned about the political consequences of his or her work. It is absorbed (happily, necessarily) by democracy.

For those who hold to the notion of democratic consensus, Gramsci's explanation of the intellectual as an "officer" of the ruling class will seem mistaken if not preposterous. That intellectual authority in our time does derive from the state in some significant way can be seen, nonetheless, when we look at the scholar's or the critic's relation to culture. This is a work relationship, a relation to labor as much as to knowledge. Few people are "intellectuals" without being *employed* as intellectuals. To be an active writer is usually to have ties with institutions where intellectual work takes place: schools, journals, research institutes, and the like. These affiliations allow some measure of evaluative detachment from social norms and the political process, but they all exist within the sphere of legal, moral, and economic regulation. The work of humanists in particular—the work of supervising cultural values—circulates through the value system as a whole, forming, re-forming, constraining, and, by all the ways that ideas and attitudes can qualify decisions, helping to mold the principal models of behavior that construct a national ethos, a state regime.

This much should be obvious. No matter how radical a critical position may seem, unless it arouses popular political energies, unless it takes hold in public consciousness or influences public awareness, the most it can achieve is to assume its place in the spectrum of professional debate. It is the *institutional* nature of intellectual activity, the *institutional* nature of conceptual and moral energy, the *institutional* nature of schools and professional affiliations that together allow reading and writing to exert influence. These institutions prosper as the state system succeeds; they also experience the moral apathy and political chicanery of the state in their own routines, since they produce information and specialists to fit the system as it operates.[3]

The university's work funnels into a society now organized by technological knowledge that, throughout this century, has increasingly militarized the culture and the economy.[4] Paul Fussell's study of the literary and artistic background to that transition, *The Great War and Modern Memory*, insists that this "primal scene" of intellectual effort constructs "a virtual allegory of political and social cognition . . . one dominant form of understanding" which is "essentially ironic" and which "originates largely in the application of mind and memory to the events of the Great War."[5] In sum, "war itself," as Robert Anchor writes, has "become the moral equivalent for civilization." To "speak of the priority of war-making potential as the principal structuring force in society, to maintain that economic systems and political philosophies serve and extend the war system rather than curtail or moderate it, to believe that the unstable peace of our time is due more to a reckless balance of terror than to political wisdom or voluntary restraint, and to conclude, therefore, that war itself is *the* basic social system within which other secondary modes of social organization conflict or conspire" is to confront the grisly truth of our institutional order.[6] No writer moves outside of it. All intellectual authority is compromised by it.

Richard Falk takes us one step further. "The state system is tied to war-making and to territorial notions of economic, social, and political well-being." Two related facts here orient our grasp on the institutional framework of intellectual authority. First, "the logic of state sovereignty continues to be the prevailing mode of [international] political organization." Second, "the central political challenge of our time involves the capacities of the state system to cope with the major problems confronting humankind. We have taken the state system for granted for so long that alternatives to it strike us as 'utopian.'"[7] In fact, this organization of the world into state sovereignties fighting over territory has continued, Falk notes, since the Peace of Westphalia in 1648. We cannot expect it to change easily. Few politically conscious people expect it to change at all.[8] For the literary intellectual who is engaged primarily with artistic events in the Western cultural heritage, this wider focus is crucial if criticism is to have a social impact. "The intellectual, if his values are not to petrify," Philip Rahv points out, "must join with the new, and in that very union he will redeem the old."[9]

One of the things critics must learn to do is to situate texts in the field of institutional forces in which they are historically conceived, in which they continue to operate, albeit differentially, as extentions (symbolic, conceptual, and social) of a world that employs texts, including literary and critical texts, as agents in the process of institutional birth and death. That undertaking will make us rely more acutely on our ability to imagine history, to recreate its forces and its limitations. That is a narrative as well as a discursively analytic enterprise. But it also demands increased attention to the present and to the imaginable future, to the actual settings in which we inscribe readings of texts and ask students to carry on, for their own purposes, the kinds of descriptions and interpretations we initiate. This is a matter of radicalizing the liberal tradition so that the deconstructively bracketed though still uncontested notion of critical freedom and interpretive autonomy can be replaced by the far more difficult but necessary realization of the reader's and writer's immersion in a network of social forces that both grant and limit the possibility of intellectual authority. Specifically this means that criticism and teaching must de-idealize as far as possible the act of reading in order to show how interpretive authority is derived from institutional practices that at present encourage personal innovation while denying interest in or identification with popular social struggles.

One way to achieve a more actively social and political consciousness as a reader is to resist the temptation to closure which is at work in theoretical writing. We can regard this as an old Kantian ambition to describe the boundaries of knowledge, most of all to define the limits of thinking, though I do not see any need to identify oneself in this effort as a "Kantian" or a "Marxist" or any other kind of writer, since each tradition has built-in blinders to be resisted. The greatest closure now threatening literary criticism is the tendency toward monolithic theory, abstract rationalistic inventiveness (structuralism, semiotics, reader response theory, deconstruction, and so on) that overlooks the evaluative function of critical judgment. Certainly Kant does not provide a framework or vocabulary to avoid this difficulty, since his writing was devoted, both knowingly and unknowingly, to a transcendental perspective that insufficiently positions itself within its actual intellectual and social fields. Marx, as Mark Poster has shown, succumbs to dangers inherent in his own historical moment. "By excluding mental operations from the domain of historical materialism, Marx remains within the traditional, Enlightenment metaphysic," a perspective that inflates the "universal" capacity of reason to be free of all forms of dominating interest and that "gives the intellectual power over the liberation movement."[10] The result is that theory dominates practical critical activity by abstracting it from the world. No matter how politically acute any particular theory may take itself to be, the only way it can avoid an idealistic retreat from the actual conditions of social life is by naming as accurately as it can the relation between intellectual work and the organized forms of power that appropriate or thwart that work.[11]

As a step in that direction, Raymond Williams's investigation of culture provides a way of pursuing Gramsci's concept of hegemony into the native textuality of our own tradition. To say this is immediately to be called upon to remember the institutional nature of "textuality". and "traditions." Anything we say about our heritage and everything we find in texts is a product of the assumptions and disciplined expectations we bring to them. We not only read *from* texts that situate us in different historical eras and in earlier social configurations; we read *toward* (and, yes, *into*) texts with generalized concepts of what we are to find and how we are to decode whatever we find there.[12] That, I take it, is what graduate training is mostly about: situating relatively eager young readers in the prevailing understanding of their cultural past so they may continue, as they mature professionally, to place their reading and the understanding of their students and readers more fully within the textual and social conditions of our heritage. Williams gives us, with canny good humor, a view of culture as a concept and a historical area constantly under revision. Whatever we attribute to the ethos and the artifacts that ground our living moment, we cannot fail to take account of the turbulence of those values and objects. Culture is a rolling event. It gathers us to it even as we try to detach ourselves to see where we are, where it comes from, what "it" is in the first place. Therefore the image of culture as a battleground, the site of disturbance and ideological warfare for very definite political stakes, should not come as a shock to anyone trained to read texts and history:

> We live in a transitional society, and the idea of culture, too often, has been identified with one or other of the forces which the transition contains. Culture is the product of the old leisured classes who seek now to defend it against new and destructive forces. Culture is the inheritance of the new rising class, which contains the humanity of the future; this class seeks, now, to free it from its restrictions. We say things like this to each other, and glower. The one good thing, it seems, is that all the contending parties are keen enough on culture to want to be identified with it. But then, we are none of us referees in this; we are all in the game, and playing in one or other direction.[13]

Williams, unlike many critics, locates us in our genuine circumstance.[14] First of all, he reckons the confusion of the term: "culture" is both the series of objects, events, and monuments gathered into academic canons composing an official memorialized past and a "way of life" or a constellation of dispositions collected around a language and a national terrain. One image of culture is elevated and mostly in the hands of scholars; the other is dispersed throughout a society, high and low and everywhere in between, and forms the linguistic and ethical diversity that makes possible many kinds of behavioral and artistic styles, including that excluded and demoted "idea of 'working-class culture.'" Second, he comprehends the long history of our current transition—that this particular moment of social upheaval evolves from very specific institutional forces that can be plotted through literature, forces that separate us from earlier historical eras in distinct ways that can be named and finally understood for the purpose of evaluating cultural changes. The three great shifts Williams traces through the period 1780–1950 are the evolution of *industry*, the rise and transformation of *democracy* as a political reality and as a revolutionary idea, and the development of *art* (both the concept and the practice) as a compensatory or alternative area in opposition to commercial markets. The use of these elaborations in Williams's survey shows up in his discussion of *community*.

For Williams, and here we are in an ineradicably English setting, the evolution "of the idea of culture has, throughout, been a criticism of what has been called the bourgeois idea of society." The disputes this criticism has fostered lead to another idea,

> the idea of community, on which all in general agree, [but which] has been differently felt and defined. In our own day we have two major interpretations, alike opposed to bourgeois liberalism, but equally, in practice, opposed to each other. These are the idea of service, and the idea of solidarity. These have in the main been developed by the middle class and the working class respectively.[15]

Now the resistance to bourgeois values cited here comes from the long history of a society, stratified in distinct cultural and economic classes for centuries, with a tradition of deep ideological disagreement. The notion of culture in that setting, as Williams shows, has been a reconciling notion, a way to overcome ideological and economic differences in the imagery of communal cooperation. If England today suffers from the failure to integrate these two images of cooperation—of community based on service that essentially protects the status quo and of community based on solidarity between people who take an "active mutual responsibility" for one another—it is because the class system these ideological differences reflect has not been leveled as it seems to be, or as many think it has been, in the United States. Nonetheless, the "transitional" pressures facing England and North America may very well be similar: a shift of institutional affiliations due to "the growing distance between political democracy and socio-economic democracy," as Nicos Poulantzas characterizes the crisis in contemporary state capitalism.[16] But the failure of community in the United States, and of the idea of community also, emerges as the shock of history against the communal myth on which this country was founded: its sense of a redemptive mission. As Sacvan Bercovitch makes clear, the United States from its outset defined its destiny in terms of capitalist progress. The individual's success both ensured and verified the success of the nation. In distinction to British and European cultures, "America" has been based on promise, boundless hope in a future richer than its present, endlessly expanding and sweeping every citizen with it. This faith produces "a tyranny not of the majority but of middle-class thought," "a culture bound by an extraordinary ideological hegemony" that affirms and constantly reaffirms America's obligation to be the redeemer nation for individual and world alike.[17]

That this myth undermines the making of communities by an increasingly obscene justification of power which squanders local energies by "unifying" both national and personal identities within a single standard of success (crassly materialistic, essentially authoritarian) can be seen in the newly reconstituted North American "consensus." Once again commandeering general cultural space, this is an ideological consensus—that is, one that is *imposed* rather than democratically evolved—a carefully constructed practice of excluding or defaming political dissent that too sharply challenges dominant cultural attitudes. The "textuality" of our tradition, as I called it awhile back, is very much at stake in all this in precisely the way Bercovitch makes apparent:

> None of our classic writers conceived of imaginative perspectives other than those implicit in the vision of America. Their works are characterized by an *unmediated* relation between the facts of American life and the ideals of American free enterprise. Confronted with the inadequacies of their society, they turned for solace and inspiration to its social ideals. It was not that they lacked radical energies, but that they had invested these in a vision which reinforced (because it emanated from) the values of their culture. Their quarrels with America took the form of intracultural dialogues—as in Thoreau's *Walden,* where "the only true America" beckons to us as a timeless image of the country's time-bound ideals (minimal government, extra-vagant economics, endless mobility, unlimited self-aggrandizement); or in Whitman's *Leaves of Grass,* which offers the highest Romantic tribute, the process of poetic self-creation, as text-proof of America's errand into the future. In these and other key instances, the autonomous act that might have posed fundamental alternatives, imaginative or actual, became instead a mimesis of cultural

norms. The works of our classic writers show more clearly than any others I know how American radicalism could be turned into a force against radical change.[18]

This is the cultural situation everyone in the United States who now writes critically is forced to take account of, only to find in doing so that the critical act is also hegemonic. To the extent that a critic seeks authority as well as inspiration or solace in such texts (in the native literary tradition), the temptation will be to find in them all that is deviant and capable of maintaining self-reliant skepticism. Bercovitch notes that he "may offend just about everybody" who cares about these writers. His aim, however, is not to reduce "their achievement to ideology" but to clarify "the ideology that links high literature and popular culture in the United States."[19] That ideological linkage is as much a record of interpretive communities and of material or political communities as it is of the literary culture we inherit. These realms in fact overlap to create the actual circumstances of reading and writing. They activate the terms of our choices as citizens and as professional interpreters. Here Williams's reflections on the topic of community become problematic. Since *community* is a term that deserves some privilege in a critical vocabulary because it marks the place where culture starts, the place where knowledge breeds human health, how can we use it now constructively rather than nostalgically?

That is an extremely difficult task. Today we live in the worldwide community of an impending nuclear winter. Cultural and professional as well as national communities give way to the sullen integration of a technological holocaust, the prospect of the final human community. Or rather, the community of human mortality is now nearer and larger and more sublime, more instantaneous and impersonal, so that the improbability of cross-cultural, transnational solidarity (a community of global citizenship) is confirmed in the strategies of art and journalism by the swift, sure image of common peril. It seems to me that the general recognition of this apocalyptic unity does not offer much hope of reconciliation between rival factions at the academic, state, or international level. Intellectual culture (literary and philosophical culture), far from inhibiting the great nuclear superpowers, seems almost powerless to name—much less to challenge—the organized violence that allows the rest of technological reality to grow as if nuclear weapons and their paranoid logic were imagined, not active, threats. What Williams or anyone else means by *community*, therefore, can be reckoned only against the actual military hardware now in place and against the emerging information structure that is linking the globe, continent to continent, with a computerized data and surveillance network. The two, military superiority and communications technology, support each other.

For anyone who wants to pursue this subject, Herbert Schiller's *Who Knows: Information in the Age of the Fortune 500* documents the interlocking operations joining the giant multinational corporations to North American state power.[20] At the heart of the emerging computerized world we find a contradiction. The development of computer technology and the enormous push throughout the school system for computer literacy both rest on boldly advertised promises of enhanced educational opportunities, greater human efficiency, and increased knowledge and leisure for everyone.[21] And yet the development and research costs to create an evermore elaborate, constantly expanding worldwide communications system have been directly subsidized by the United States government to the benefit of private corporate wealth and American military strength. Several features of this activity are worth noting. A new information environment is in fact being developed around the world. Its center is the United States, primarily within the big computer and data-control industries such as IBM, Digital, Texas Industries, and RCA, and it relies on extensive cooperation from a select group of major universities to train future employees, to produce specialists in various scientific and technological areas, and to further research.

Behind the ostensible aim of producing information to be made available to more and more people, a struggle for increased secrecy is being waged by government and private industries alike. The battle concerns not only strictly military information but control of all technological knowledge that might give competitors and rivals an immediate advantage.[22] Perhaps the most interesting aspect of this struggle is that the alliance between the state and private sectors has produced a transnational corporate system that supersedes all state boundaries and national sovereignties. This system of international business is being forged by greater and quicker information capacities—by the enhanced control of data between far-flung points—but it extends through a variety of industries (banks, insurance and real estate management, and heavy technologies, as well as military and information-intensive activities). The result is a privately owned global empire of wealth and knowledge with allegiance to the international position of the United States but largely outside its territorial borders. Such an interdependent world of high finance, continuously expanding markets, and instant communication is more capable than ever before of extending capitalist, Western-oriented control over "underdeveloped" and largely exploited countries whose entrepreneurial class seeks American culture, Western consumer items, and transnational capital. The cost of that development, however, is not only loss of the indigenous culture and old communal patterns but a diminished capacity to control the communications and surveillance equipment that "upgrades" urban life for a small part of the population while giving military and economic assistance to North American interests.

The same process goes on, at a lower level of assistance and technological sophistication, on the Soviet side of the world. Indeed, the USSR's activity provides the justification for Western expansion. What is lost and subject to even greater devastation is regional autonomy, national state sovereignty, and nonaligned political interests. When huge state powers play the world as a gigantic militarized chess game, the weak and disadvantaged become pawns. Viable communities, entire countries such as Cambodia and Afghanistan, succumb to massive coercion from distant political pressures. And *community*, for the critic, becomes a word that washes out. It suggests everything that supports people and social solidarity. Against the new information order it becomes a mere concept, a dim hope. In the meantime, the unregulated expansion of capital and private control continues. Whatever intervention criticism and teaching may attempt, therefore, must be framed in precise terms, in terms of the actual (not sentimental or vaguely utopic) possibilities of resistance to cultural, economic, and military aggression.

That the political uncertainty and social irresolution of criticism contributes to the maintenance of the current global structure is a thesis worth discussing. The moral perplexity of academic "neutrality" stifles needed dissent within the university, dissent in particular against the misappropriation of knowledge and intellectual skills by the university-corporate-military arrangement building an integrated transnational business community.[23] This "community" of the powerful is not communal in any sense of the word as Williams uses it. It is a community of interlocking political interests, finances, and directorates free from public accountability—a community devoted to ensuring the unopposed barbarism of the profit motive. Its main features, aside from extraordinary wealth and the privilege wealth buys, are these: (1) institutionalized support by a number of government agencies—for example, the National Security Agency, the Department of Defense, and the National Aviation and Space Administration (NASA)—as well as by covert and explicit affiliations with the various branches of government; (2) virtual freedom from interference or inspection by national and international regulatory authorities; (3) development of a "stateless" international marketplace beyond the control of national laws (and for that matter national needs); (4) most intriguing of all, perhaps, a literally daily enhancement of the privately owned worldwide information system that collects and transfers data quickly and secretly in order to monitor markets on a global scale. These developments are advanced by a growing communications network beyond the reach of public oversight but in contact with the university laboratory and the deliberations of university trustees.

I bring all this up because the absence of a fully articulated concept of community that could be sought or worked toward as the twentieth century heads to a close leaves the humanities in the dreary position of preserving a fairly narrow range of texts, traditions, and values without any real sense of the social—that is, the human—consequences of critical effort. That this position replicates the short-sighted and undialectical perspective generally attributed to bureaucracies and to businesses is, at minimum, ironic and potentially tragic for the future of criticism. Humanist intellectuals efface all possibility of developing a workable concept of community—of local or regional communities of politically affiliated (though necessarily contentious) people, of interpretive communities as well—by carefully discriminating textual concerns from the contextual pressures, limits, changes, and nuances that vivify texts. Which alone bring texts into existence to begin with, I might add, because texts are records not only of verbal or conceptual possibilities but no less of communal and interpersonal possibilities. Most of all, critics need to comprehend the context of reading as innate to the situation (to the situating) of texts. Good readers are trained to pay close attention to texts and to the formal and sometimes the ideological condition of texts. Such close attention usually involves looking at the historical setting of a given piece of writing as the site of its context, as something *there* in the documentary record of past events to be recovered or taken into account. The conditions of knowing in which we are placed, the *here* and *now* of our potential understanding, are equally a part of every text's way of being in the world and participating in what I will call its territoriality. My point here is that interpretation is not merely or even essentially an archival activity, an affair of text-on-text or of texts activated mainly in an academic "intertextual" dialogue. Rather, interpretation seizes texts as available (and more or less suitable) occasions for asserting meaning, for ideologizing or de-ideologizing as the case may be. The question is: Whose meaning, whose ideology, whose politics are in play?

My position, following Gramsci, Williams, Chomsky, Said, Ohmann, and Weber, is that intellectual authority derives from the state
to begin with, from its organization of people and functions and
institutions in some form of working order propelled by economic,
cultural, and bureaucratic energies. This is certainly not the image we
like to pose for ourselves of a freely chosen profession, itself autonomous in its supervision of texts and values evolved through a rich and
untotalizable history. But I think we come to admit the unavoidable
fact of state power and even of state intervention in intellectual affairs
by analyzing the territoriality of intellectual work.[24] The relatively
new feature of state power, its dispersion across national boundaries,
its integration in a system of economic and cultural formations outside traditional political identities and responsibilities, anomalously
reinforces the finite and too often dismissed placement of the critic
and the critic's work within the aggressive impersonality of capitalist
marketing.

First, most intellectual activity today occurs within the fairly strict
division of labor that defines modern society everywhere from the
factory to the boardroom, a division in which specific functions are
delegated to people trained or authorized to occupy particular roles.
No one need be surprised that humanistic labor, which pretends to a
kind of wide-ranging generality searching through the whole of
human history, conforms to this practice; the division of university
catalogues into different schools and departments, each subdivided
into areas of specialization, verifies that conformity. And these sub-
divisions do not reveal the whole tendency toward greater specificity
and narrowing in intellectual labor. One of the primary conditions of
the territoriality of intellectual work is its self-imposed but altogether
institutionally mandated position in advance or to the side of the
central blocks of knowledge that hold the means to radicalize public
consciousness. Obliquely but nonetheless provocatively (as Jürgen
Habermas's critique of cultural modernity suggests), Jean-François
Lyotard's *Postmodern Condition*[25] calls attention to this "paralogical"
self-legitimizing circumstance.[26]

Second, in addition to professional specialization we must add the
encompassing realm of the school or university where knowledge is at
once generated and disseminated. This is a subject for much more
investigation, some of which has begun already in the writing of
Michael W. Apple, who locates "the school as part of a system of
mechanisms for cultural and economic reproduction."[27] Apple's Althusserian research joins that of a group of writers, mostly in England, concerned with the role of schooling in maintaining a society's

cultural hegemony. A central interest there is the "hidden curricula" that reinforce existing power relations by legitimating the norms and categories at work throughout institutional reality.[28] The point of this research is.very much in line with Ohmann's analysis of the politics of knowledge distribution which permeates normal school operations first and then the culture as a whole. In this regard we must remember how important schools are to the effective functioning of the entire social structure. No aspect of a society's economic and professional activity, from banking and legal training to the training of doctors and engineers, escapes the crucial influence of educational regimes.

The third territory of intellectual work follows from the second: the specific workplace or institution in which an individual conducts research and teaching appropriate to his or her area of special interest. As we all know, universities vary in their styles of bureaucratic management as well as in their styles of scholarly and pedagogical performance. The recent controversy over the designation of a "Yale school" of criticism suggests the depth of these differences and the passions they can arouse. In particular, though, I have in mind here the way a group ethos, subtler but no less important than the kind advertised by the fame of the Yale critics, permeates every laboratory, every department, every college and research institute. Groups have patterns of rivalry, support, expectation, and achievement in some genuine sense unique to themselves, or at any rate capable of varying the standard routines of assumption and performance that count for quite a bit in the way individuals feel useful as members of their small social units. One of the areas of potential investigation for anyone wishing to understand the way knowledge is transmitted from teacher to pupil, from colleague to colleague, is the academic department as a central node in the national and international network of information exchange. Some departments foster students and faculty in ways that deserve emulation, while others retard or dampen the kinds of excitement and support that stimulate the most creative flow of knowledge. These tendencies may not be so strictly correlated with the mythical ranking of departments as national surveys, those in the *Chronicle of Higher Education* for instance, suggest. The deviations we find from school to school, from department to department, are subject to change as their faculties change, as shifts in national and professional attitudes occur. No doubt they evolve as economic forces necessitate changes in school budgets and resources. But the usefulness of thinking about the differences to be found between departments or between specific intellectual work sites (between national regions, for that matter) lies in its ability to help us avoid homogenizing the influence of state power—of all those systemic pressures generated by the state—upon intellectual effort. Very real differences can be seen in the ways intellectuals fulfill their roles, and those differences are not merely personal or temperamental but institutional also, products of the cohesion of the minicommunities in which intellectual work takes place.

The fourth territory I want to specify is the general context of national and international power, an area so large and so troubled that anyone who points to it as a sphere of influence on intellectual and cultural life risks elimination from the competitive affinities of theoretical debate. Though I cannot briefly construct an analysis of domestic or interinstitutional power that would properly explicate the international context in which state influence on intellectual effort is situated, I can note here the disciplinary hermeticism that isolates intellectual activity in pockets of small managerial competence over well-circumscribed bibliographical terrains. In such a decontextualized world "the university ceases to provide a usable cultural context for any of its subjects," as Gerald Graff points out. Not only the self-disabled technical agility found everywhere that reductive forms of argumentation rout invitations to build collective intellectual arrangements (to enhance both the cognitive and the political grounds of critical work) but the "inability to *disagree*" about the central topics and problems impinging upon scholarly production prolongs the perpetually deferred university-wide debate concerning the social consequences, the human impact, of knowledge.[29] For knowledge now and after is a product of institutions, of institutionalized activities; knowledge is an institutional event (or set of events) that succumbs to the massed strategies of local and global institutional operations. The failure of university complexes to direct a significant portion of sustained scholarly production toward institutional self-scrutiny—and not as professional publication alone but as ongoing curricular and procedural self-scrutiny with a mandate to restructure disciplinary segregation—protects established interests within the university's fiefdoms and beyond, where information counts as "news." The unexamined consensus by which the professionalization and rarefication of knowledge are reproduced by (in terms of) predictable habits of authority, in which the generation of authority is the essential "natural" result of institutional constancy, can be looked at as the primary ideological component of a culture devoted to transforming information while obscuring the institutional ground, the material and economic interests, shared by universities and the state and corporate network that defines a major part of the general context of national and international power.

At this point an examination of material and institutional realities such as the postponement (amounting to a repression) of debate about what role critical learning plays in the university's production of knowledge becomes an examination of the reigning ideological and cultural structure that drives (one might say enables) the development of both state and institutional power in their current embodiments. I mean that, without an ever-reaffirmed concept of *authority* in its various professional roles and guises, without a continually manufactured, persistently mystifying reenactment of expertise throughout the world of commerce, government, learning, and the professions as a whole, the *state* as we find it everywhere that taxes are collected and military arsenals grow in size and sophistication would need to rely on a distinctly different institutional order. It would need either more coercive means or more persuasive means, or some yet-unseen amalgam of the two revising the seductive constraints on which professional behavior thrives. To bring the material and institutional realms so closely into contact with cultural and ideological "rationality" is to encounter continuously demoted forms of class struggle. It allows us to recognize that professional authority obscures the cooperation between professionalization and institutions that gain their relative autonomy from intellectual habits that isolate mental work into small units of expert knowledge. This relationship, prevalent throughout the Western and much of the non-Western world, breeds attitudes that erode responsibility to general human well-being over parochial self-interests.

In this sense the problematic and all but undesignatable territory comprising state and international power is far closer to intellectual action than it seems, and more explicable too. When terrorism becomes a spectacle of confrontation between an ever-menacing horde of unseen maniacs and a well-coordinated counterattack by a highly visible state, rehearsed endlessly on national television for worried citizens aroused after years of post-Vietnam suspicion to renewed patriotic zeal, a critic's responsibility to professional intellectual authority cannot be distinguished from responsibility to marking out (publicly, professionally) the narratives and rhetorical strategies that divide the world into convenient roles. Thus "the terrorist," like the Arab or the Jew, becomes a metonym for hate, eliminating the complex causes of the individual's or the state's terroristic logic. And "the critic," also, can become a metonym—this one indicating goodness or marginalized nobility.

Everything that can be meant by an *interpretive community*, a community of readers and writers which now substitutes for the fuller, more generous, and more passionately immediate communities passing from existence, is situated firmly within the reach and logic of state power. That power develops within the cultural, economic, and political combat of international relations. This set of overlapping territories, made visible, calls attention to the critic's involvement with the facts of authority, bureaucracy, hierarchy, technocratic rationality, and "official" (managed, commercially compliant, sometimes state-controlled) information as much as with academic learning and professional knowledge. No critical writer works independently, regardless of the still unembarrassed myth of intellectual autonomy that surrenders unknowingly to the normalizing logic of global imperialism by keeping viable the ideology of imperialism in the figure of personal triumph. And so now critics must name the logistic as well as the rhetorical and epistemological patterns that inhabit intellectual dependencies. When criticism, traditionally but paradoxically, aims to create an audience of open-minded people "free" to choose the form if not the result of their work as intellectuals, it erodes yet also draws upon the institutional closures that both create and demand authority in its corporate and in its personal, "expert" forms. This simultaneous tearing down and rebuilding of its own enterprise is part of what Samuel Weber points to as the logic of *institutionalization*, "the process by which institutions *take place*, by taking the place *of others*, to which, in varying and complex ways, they remain constitutively indebted."[30] This is a logic of assimilation. Institutions, like individuals, exclude or shun what they cannot incorporate. More wily, North American critical work, as a collective body of individualizing scholarly or critical projects, as a collection of personal careers, has assimilated greater textual scope in essentially decontextualized modes of knowing that effectively take the place of those without authority to read professionally, legitimately, while also taking the place of those cultural and material territories knowledge depends on in the first and last moments of cognition.

If the most influential intellectuals do not account for the way interpretive work is situated, how certain interpreters gain power (culturally significant if nonetheless slight), and how criticism as an institution develops concrete reading practices that enable and potentially disable complacent professional behaviors, the future of critical learning may be secure as a famous esoteric field. My sense here is that critics must remember what intellectual effort can accomplish in the world of human action. One of the tasks involved is a clear and accurate assessment of the intellectual's role in relation to state power. That role is mediated and even filtered by the complex overlapping of numerous territories that obscure the impact of information and of practices as specific as literary criticism and critical theory. But given the place of capitalism and of North American institutions internationally, critics at work in the United States must make maximum sense of the relation between intellectual territories and their international context. Critics might ask what they mean by an "interpretive community" and how such a community fits into a world that is now evolving new forms of domination and cultural control.

5

Theory and the
Interpretive Community

No term in current critical practice is more beguiling than *interpretive community*. The phrase proposes a body of closely affiliated writers joined to maintain group identity and mutual interests, people on the same side of reality who, even in disagreement, face common tasks and privileges. Concern for such communities has passed into contemporary criticism thanks largely to Stanley Fish, who, along with Thomas Kuhn, has drawn attention to the institutional nature of textual practices. For Fish, "interpretive communities are made up of those who share interpretive strategies not for reading (in the conventional sense) but for writing texts." That agreement, as he sees it, accounts for the "stability in the makeup of interpretive communities and therefore in the opposing positions they make possible," a stability that "is always temporary (unlike the longed for and timeless stability of the text)."[1]

I call this now crucial critical term "beguiling" because it promises to justify the current organization of professional criticism. To talk of "communities" of interpreters and interpretations accentuates the dialogical, the positive and productive (the institutionally regenerative), side of academic practices. It delays the moment when the distance between professional interpretation and the surrounding human world must be reckoned. It also makes less likely the critic's responsibility beyond the guild of professional readers and writers—outside the circle of literary "fellowship," as Fish calls it, where "the nod of recognition from someone in the same community" constitutes the "only 'proof' of membership."[2] It is appropriate, then, that in the title essay of his provocative collection of essays *Is There a Text in This Class?*

Fish looks at the *situated* nature of understanding in general and of interpretive work in particular. These activities take place *"from within a set of interests and concerns,"* Fish writes, "because a way of thinking, a form of life, shares us, and implicates us in a world of already-in-place objects, purposes, goals, procedures, values, and so on." Even more particularly, "it is only in situations—with their interested specifications as to what counts as a fact, what it is possible to say, what will be heard as an argument—that one is called on to understand" in the first place.[3] Remarkably, Fish's stern reply here to M. H. Abrams's worry that interpretive experimentation is eroding professional critical authority remains vaguely existentialist, refusing to clarify the sorts of values and interests that are actually carried forward by an institutional understanding of texts. In fact, Fish's reassurance that solipsism and relativism cannot terrorize professional criticism leaves writers even more enclosed within "the institution of academic America," since, he tells us, "as actors within an institution they automatically fall heir to the institution's way of making sense, its systems of intelligibility."[4]

If this reassurance is supposed to dissolve fear about the disunity of contemporary criticism by stressing the shared assumptions that link interpreters to one another, more than anything else it has the effect of pointing out the strict if sometimes unnoticed professional limits that define the field of inquiry we call "criticism" and "textual interpretation." Fish accepts this fact, as he acknowledges in a short piece for the *Times Literary Supplement,* "Professional Anti-professionalism," when he writes that "arguments, reasons and evidence, rather than standing to the side of interpretive disputes, where they can serve as independent points of reference, are more often than not what is *at stake* in interpretive disputes."[5] His point is well taken; it describes the perpetual contest for authority between critics and critical positions. But Fish's service to current interpretive debates is just that, a description of existing professional combats which reaffirms the status quo by accepting as unalterable in principle or practice the literary "community's assumed purposes and goals" that make agreement possible. One of the benefits of this position is its clear delineation of what truly occurs in the critical establishment. But Fish leaves little room, and finds no particular motivation of his own, for institutional change—for an enlargement of critical territory and responsibility. Instead he champions "the context of evidentiary procedures," which constitutes "the click and snap of having arrived at a conclusion, that is, of having been convinced."[6] Critics persuade one another not by standing in conformity with the institutional circumstances of their professional authority, Fish proposes, but by reassessing textual evidence and inserting new viewpoints within the community of discourse, by debating, confounding, deviating, adding, violating, in sum, by exercising all those rhetorical operations writing is capable of when it wrestles with new or well-worn issues and with long-established conventions.

Fish may not mean to eulogize the academic status quo; in fact he gives us reason to think he means to celebrate its changes, the way adjustments and fresh perceptions enter the field of combat. But the narrow and self-confirming critical authority Fish clarifies, which he lauds as the proper (indeed *necessary*) vantage point for literary intellectuals, clings to the formalities of privileged critical debate now prevalent and, if anything, growing stronger. What I mean is this. Once you move the source of professional critical authority from a determinate core of central textual meanings to an evolving realm of central interpretive dialogue (from text-specific meanings to institutionally generated meanings)—and this is Fish's primary theoretical goal—in what way have you broken the essentially priestly function of the authoritative interpreter? By emphasizing the communal or professional nature of critical work, one secularizes the way knowledge is viewed as a creative and highly mediated, never fully stable, body of interpretations that collide and undo or dislocate one another. Thus one desacralizes the text by keeping it from becoming (or relapsing into) a transcendent body of purifiable significance; and that is useful because it diminishes the opportunities for critics to mystify the act of reading by reducing the text to authorial meaning. At the same time, however, the notion of established "communities" of interpreters succumbing to the "context of evidentiary procedures" isolates the critical act by emphasizing the specialized, the rarefied and potentially clubby world of professional textual knowledge. I do not disagree with Fish's understanding of this fact as we face it in academic life. It suffuses every facet of professional literary criticism. I am arguing that the model of professional competence that Fish upholds reinforces the insular clerical function of well-trained literary savants, each of whom demystifies texts only to remystify the role of literary interpretation in a society uncongenial to the political self-consciousness of literary strategies.[7]

No doubt Fish's emphasis in his concern for "interpretive communities" is somewhat distinct from mine. He means, if I read him correctly, to make sense of the fragmentary and agonistic conditions of modern literary understanding. He admits, in other words, the provisional nature of the ceaselessly re-forming "communities" of academic interpreters—an admission, however, without any will to situate the academy or its critical and humanistic activities in the larger human world. Fish's discourse alludes to a world of concrete social events that might somehow invade or inform what texts produce, what readers find relevant, but it stops far short of its own implied awareness. Here, for example, is the strong conclusion of a recent essay, "Interpretation and the Pluralist Vision":

> Pluralism and liberalism are the same thing, identical in what they oppose—the sectarian, the merely political, the exclusionary, the normative—and in what they valorize—the free marketplace of ideas, the suspension of judgment, the imaginative and sympathetic consideration of points of view other than one's own. To put it another way, liberalism is the political form of the ideology of the academy, of the disinterested inquiry into unsituated and timeless truths; and it is no wonder that for many academics the truth of liberalism (which is the truth of pluralism) is self-evident and beyond dispute. It is because he speaks (or thinks he speaks) from so secure and admirable a position (the position, paradoxically, of having no position) that the pluralist is so often complacent and even self-righteous. He believes himself to be a person of exemplary generosity, distinguished from other men and women by a capacity to entertain any number of perspectives and to refrain from insisting too strongly on his own. Whatever else a pluralist is telling you, he is also telling you that his heart is in the right place . . . the right place is every place and therefore nowhere at all.[8]

Certainly Fish has created a position for himself, but the irony is that his apparent dissent underwrites the very pluralism he scorns. Who has provided a better theory to account for divergent beliefs and critical viewpoints that individually spar with one another but collectively establish the institutional habit of tolerant skepticism—the position of "persuasive" intellectuals, removed from political engagement, in "sympathetic consideration of points of view other than one's own"?[9] In fact the academy is not at all generous to views that truly call into question its communally validated forms of doubt. We can see right here, for example, that the object of Fish's position is not so much an "accurate" recording of the factual basis of literary criticism as it is an effort to deflect theoretical interest from the traditional text-centered universe of literary study in order to place it in the midst of interpretive combat, the taking of positions and the making of arguments among critics vying for authority. This effort not only depends upon, it also embellishes and even resuscitates, an already viable set of practices: the pluralistic, self-contained (self-neutralizing) operation called Criticism.

In all of this Fish performs a fairly astonishing repression of the institutional context of interpretive activity. He does so, rather audaciously, *in the name* of institutional contextualization. The essential prerequisite for critical argument in Fish's scheme is an active forgetting of everything that does not immediately relate to professional intellectual behavior. His is a neatly ordered if also contentious world, the world of literature professors and critical theorists who debate with one another about what texts and argumentative moves should be admitted into the circle that constitutes the "business of criticism," as he calls this work—business that is negotiated, Fish insists, by persuasion rather than demonstration, since "critical activity is constitutive of its object."[10] Interpreters and theorists, by this formulation, need not assume a docile relation to their work. They do not need to seek certainty or obtain agreement from others about the true nature of their intellectual reality (or about the world's or, for that matter, any particular text's reality) because the stability of the interpretive community resides in its permission to create and challenge its own conventions. That permission, in fact, generates the "business" of criticism (the writing of books and articles), which in turn is monitored by the critical institution. We have, therefore, a beautifully closed world: "interpretation is constitutive of the center [of the interpretive community]—of what will count as a fact, as a text, as a piece of evidence, as a reasonable argument—and thus defines its own limits and boundaries."[11]

The result, Fish assures us, is "a greatly enhanced sense of the importance of our activities."[12] But in what realm can a persuasion model of critical expression enhance self-esteem and institutional status unless it is a depressed and potentially irrelevant realm to begin with, a realm suffering from a diminished self-image? No doubt the erosion of humanistic prestige lends a certain poignance to the embattled critical theorist's sense of self. But as Gramsci shows in his monumental work on cultural hegemony, mostly scribbled in fragmentary notes "in prison, under atrocious conditions, with a fascist censor scrutinizing everything that he produced," the critical theorist in fact contributes to the efficiency of social formations.[13] No state or nation, no government organization or party program can succeed without mediating intellectuals who pave the way for its citizens to accept or at least tolerate the inequities it produces. Since the fundamental pacifier in advanced democratic capitalism is consumerism itself, the system of material rewards and comforts, the role of the critical intellectual turns out to supervise (and to enhance or diminish, to approve or erode) the professional norms and the system of authority and prestige which support the complex structure of consumer society. Everything Gramsci meant by "civil society" (as distinct from "the state," although Perry Anderson has shown that Gramsci wavers by assimilating these terms to one another) is supervised and in the final analysis sanctioned by its reigning intellectuals and intellectual institutions. That is why a shift of perspective such as the one recently inaugurated by radical faculty members in the Critical Legal Studies program at Harvard Law School—a shift from a body of theory based on the assumption of innately rational legal grounds to a context-specific examination of values, traditions, roles, and practices—poses a threat to vested interests there and to the perpetuation of institutional capitalism.[14] As soon as the law professor represents the legal system as an assemblage of morally contestable rules and assumptions, the traditional stability of long-protected practices and values begins to crumble. Hierarchy and its conventional self-evidence are then open to judgment and reversal. Such a threat was precisely what we saw being countered in the model of intellectual work put forward by the research strategy group (a "community" of interpretation itself) connected to the Pentagon's National School of War when they found that the ongoing humanistic tradition provided "a way of contemplating literature and art appropriate to our civilization," a way of dealing with texts that maintains "our judicial systems and concepts, our political philosophy, our mode of communication, our ideas of mobility"[15]—maintaining, in brief, the stability of the Western way of life.

Hardly a wonder, then, that such ferocity lurks among things as elegant as interpretations of literary and cultural artifacts. What is at stake there is intellectual authority, and that authority is both professional and moral. Professional authority derives from the interpreter's status in the academic world, moral authority from the kind of ideological clarity a writer asserts. Intellectual authority thus derives from the authority of texts. But the authority of texts—or their authorizing power—derives from the institutional control of interpretation. Intellectual authority, as Fish's theory of interpretive communities makes apparent, is exercised in what people who are empowered professionally to read and write texts actually *do* with those texts: how they link them, separate them, open them, and reject or circulate deviant models of textual appropriation. We can see here why Fish's work might be genuinely useful in reorienting both legal and literary interpretation. Unlike many theorists, Fish is not so much concerned about arguing the nature of linguistic referentiality and its semiotic properties as in debating what an interpreter does as an active reader of texts, as a writer. "That is to say, the act of reading is at once the asking and answering of the question, 'What is it that is meant by these words?,' a question asked not in a vacuum, but in the context of an already in place understanding of the various things someone writing a novel or a [legal] decision (or anything else) might mean (i.e., intend)."[16]

This emphasis is meant to open the interpretive field to the whole spectrum of strategies and positions, since "an intention"

> is not private, but a form of conventional behavior made possible by the general structure of the enterprise. This of course does not mean that intention anchors interpretation in the sense that it stands outside and guides the process; intention like anything else is an interpretive fact; that is, it must be construed; it is just that it is impossible *not* to construe it and therefore impossible to oppose it either to the production or the determination of meaning.[17]

So then we are left in the swirl of interpretive disagreement and adjustment, the maelstrom from which the most persuasive readings (and readers) emerge to command, and ensure, the authority of professional interpretation. Yet in putting this view forward Fish assumes that interpretation is professionally responsible primarily to canonical literary texts and occupies a self-sufficient space unattached in any necessary or demonstrably contingent way to the rest of cultural life. Nor does the territory that professional interpretation occupies seem linked to the adjacent professional enclaves (law, medicine, business, government, and so on) which share the cultural contradictions that simultaneously stimulate and confound interpretive practices in every field—this despite Fish's participation in the now-growing debate about the relation between law and literature, since his notion of institutional territory is relegated to purely ideological grounds. "Interpreters are constrained," he tells us,

> by their tacit awareness of what is possible and not possible to do, what is and is not a reasonable thing to say, what will and will not be heard as evidence, in a given enterprise; and it is within those same constraints that they see and bring others to see the shape of the documents to whose interpretation they are committed. . . . interpretation is a *structure* of constraints, a structure which, because it is always and already in place, renders unavailable the independent and freely interpreting reader.[18]

The point is not whether interpreters can be wholly independent (they cannot) but what framework of practices actually constrains their work. In contrast to this unsituated structure, the professional critic's understanding of what is "reasonable," of things that are "possible to do," is directly dependent upon his or her affiliation (employment, professional compliance, material connection) with the university, with a particular department as a specific work site, and with the entire institutional context of professional reality which is "constrained" by forces more strenuous than interpretive rationality. How reasonable is it, therefore, within these enveloping terrains, to pursue an oppositional context-oriented interpretive practice when that practice, too, will become at best one more critical position within the quarreling that passes for work in the academy? Once we see how thoroughly the critical institution is constituted by these internal skirmishes, is there any use in challenging the noncommunal (it may in fact be the anticommunal) nature of professional competence where "the central question is, 'What is the source of interpretive authority?'" and that source turns out to be the privileged circumstances of the interpretive community?

At present that is a "community" in name only, and calling attention to this fact merely stimulates more debate. Indeed, as Gayatri Spivak sees it, no other result is possible: "for the bourgeois intellectual to look to join other politico-economic struggles is to toe the line between hubris and bathos."[19] If so, Fish is free of such error. Instead of locating the authoritative interpreter within a national and global order that literally depends upon stable interpretive practices and a secure network of interpretive authority (a stability and security that critical opposition ironically reaffirms), Fish's altogether orthodox assertion of social and literary distance dematerializes, depoliticizes, and finally justifies the self-defined autonomy of separate professional communities (of law, criticism, journalism, and such), each an interpretive fiefdom in its own right, each divided into minikingdoms of strong textual performers.

Not only that. Interpretive communities, as Fish defines them, persuade their members of the relative isolation appropriate to their professional well-being.[20] Apparently the notion of "community" to begin with is defined by the bureaucratic divisions of knowledge that are maintained by departmental and disciplinary specializations. Like the rubrics in *Time* and *Newsweek*, reality is permanently housed in categories called "religion," "law," "art," "education"; the difference is that, in Fish's world, professional interpretive communities imitate the university catalogue. These assumptions depreciate the intellectual impact of texts and interpretations on students and on readers generally. Fish's emphasis on competitive persuasiveness leads us to imagine authoritative readers as technicians of language games, people mainly seeking professional recognition.

It is a small move from the interpretive game of so many scrambling academicians to the big game of capitalist empire building. The *Wall Street Journal* can be thought of as defining an interpretive community with subcommunities that perpetually reposition themselves, each seeking a larger piece of real estate and greater recognition among peers and rivals. How do we discriminate between hermeneutic strategies (which "are, in effect, community property," Fish says) and financial strategies or strategies of corporate merger when, after all, the humanist interpretive community "is not objective because as a bundle of interests, of particular purposes and goals, its perspective is interested rather than neutral"?[21] The term *community property* does not designate general social property open to all citizens any more than *private property,* applied to the sort of things negotiated in business dealings, designates land or capital available to everyone. In other words, those vested interests that make up the "authorizing agency" for criticism—for the "business of criticism," as Fish dubs it— comprise "the literary institution: texts, authors, periods, genres, canons, standards, agreements, disputes, values, changes, and so on."

This institution in itself contains territory and manipulates real estate. First of all, it seeks "to establish by political and persuasive means (they are the same thing) the set of interpretive assumptions from the vantage of which the evidence (and the facts and the intentions and everything else) will hereafter be specifiable."[22] This is material as well as formal space that is at stake, since the kind of "evidence" that will be admitted into curricula and thus into the educational domain as a whole, the particular readings and attitudes that will be recognized as legitimate, and the scholars who will be permitted to remain within the circle of interpreters are all under judgment here. Second, although the power of such capital and the scope of such real estate may not be great, the literary institution does in truth command chairs of many kinds; it occupies space in university buildings and in various research institutes. Without question, that control is conditioned by the larger administrative apparatus of those institutions. But the oversight and the power of judgment and influence involved there are nonetheless considerable, especially if one thinks of the way the literary institution—unlike perhaps any other academic institution or subset—touches every educated person in one way or another along the entire journey through school, from the earliest years in grammar school with the first reading lessons all the way to the training of graduate students for teaching careers at various levels of the educational system. The ways in which texts are taught to high-school students and to college students in freshman humanities or general survey courses, for example, influence patterns of comprehension that guide the student's lifelong professional and private reading habits. The "importance" Fish wants to grant literary work is accorded right there for the most part, in the way texts are taught, in the way students are trained to imagine the relations between words and values, between values and practices in the world.

If the "bundle of interests" that defines the territory of criticism is directed to a significant degree toward retaining material space within universities (and by that means is able to perpetuate influence in society generally), we can hardly imagine interpretive authority to be distinct in any important sense from the authority of capitalist business practices that dominate our intellectual and cultural lives as well as our material and political existence. Anyone tenacious enough still to be committed to the humanities should be able to see that the structural position of literary study has not changed even though society has. This is not something within the control of humanists. For the most part, scholars and theorists occupy the niches they are given. In this respect nothing has changed substantially since the expansion of the university system and the development of the modern multi-faceted research and teaching institution in the late nineteenth century. While interpretive ideologies have come and gone or shifted focus, the social function of literary education has remained constant: to project the core of Western "democratic" values—belief in the value of possessive individualism, respect for legal processes that largely favor property and extraordinary capital interests, and tolerance for the institutionalization of technocratic rationality.[23]

And yet something else lurks in the background of the critic's work. Education has always extended a promise of community of some imaginable sort. At least *literary* education, education in the conscious uses of texts, has seemed to promise an invitation into the diversity of outlook and expression that encompasses human differences, distinctions formed by nationality, language, religion, culture, and politics as well as by artistic style. The notion of community for that reason necessarily remains larger and more hopeful than its incarnate neighborhoods or settings ever justify. But that idea also refers to cultural and political energies that sustain the promise of cooperation against factionalism and discord. A "community" is not just a myth, one more enviable fiction. The notion of community is grounded on facts of human exchange. It suggests negotiation rather than force or exploitation as the basis of human reality. Most of all, it asserts respect for the unknown and sometimes unwanted "other" (neighbor, foreigner, as yet unassimilated intruder) and posits the usefulness of creating habits that establish solidarity between people who do not really know one another but who, in the absence of familiarity, agree to trust that the other is more rather than less like themselves. Community, in sum, is part image, part fact. It subverts commercial and military systems. Too often (almost the rule, as we know), communities define themselves negatively—by reference to a common enemy. But an interpretive community, or the interpretive community of professional literary critics, at any rate, need not be a negatively defined group or territorial enclosure. Whatever else it is, such interpretive work may be thought of as affirmative in its opposition to authoritarian policies, inclusive intellectually, and generous by inclination and intention if not always by deed and professional execution. Regardless of the failures of national or local communities strained by the conflicts of domestic and international competition, the interpretive community that scholars and teachers of literature identify with as the region of their professional well-being could articulate a common and socially productive purpose. Such a purpose need not be, as it stands today, a narrow professionalizing and ultimately technical self-definition: a concept of community based on superior linguistic dexterity with critical terms, canonical texts, and publishing formats. It might be a purpose gained by clarifying for one another, and for students of texts at every level, the affiliation between interpretation and the world in which interpretations live and die, the way they are accepted and inhabit existing political realities or, left alone (ignored, rejected, patronized), become dissenting—sometimes successful—antagonists of the dominant system.

I have in mind Kenneth Burke, kept too long on the periphery of the academic critical mainstream. Frank Lentricchia's *Criticism and Social Change* may help to correct this neglect.[24] But the drama of the overlooked or disfavored oppositional writer is repeated elsewhere. Theodore Adorno, despite the respectful attention he has received, is an example of a critic whose dialectical strength still has not been fully assessed.[25] Others, less theoretical, more corrosive, could be cited. Frantz Fanon, Martin Luther King, Jr., the Merleau-Ponty of *Signes* and the occasional political essays. Hardly less anomalous but equally stimulating is the writing of I. F. Stone and Paul Goodman. One can think also of a familiar but nonetheless underutilized figure such as E. P. Thompson, whose *Making of the English Working Class* is possibly the most evaded historical or critical "classic" in the whole of literary study. The institutionally specific awareness of journals like *Telos* and

Social Text and the important contributions to an antihierarchical theory and practice in the writing of Catharine MacKinnon, Nancy Hartsock, Teresa de Lauretis, Adrienne Rich, Gayatri Spivak, and other feminist writers open contemporary criticism to previously unheeded or dismissed political facts embedded in the act of reading texts. I could keep adding writers who contribute to the intellectual solidarity of the left in particular and to the formation of a socially conscious criticism generally. The important task, however, is not to create a new canon of outcast, undervalued, or emergent oppositional writers but to find common ground in the actual circumstances of human reality to exert critical force. The important work for critics today is to extend the range and insubordinate urgency of critical intelligence in a world that seems predicated on disabling all forms of communal well-being. This means seeking, by diverse means, to create intellectual solidarity beyond the territorial struggles of the academy.[26]

The line that most sharply divides interpreters today falls between those who actively seek a social role for interpretive work and those who seek purely textual knowledge. The terrain of literary criticism is fractured by that difference. But how, exactly, does this disjuncture affect the possibility of a critical "community" of intellectual solidarity among interpreters? This difficulty may not be so easy to resolve as it may seem at first, because "consequences" of reading and of interpretation always turn out to be writing practices, rhetoric, and rhetoric inevitably (as Paul de Man has courageously tried to show) contains both resolvable and irresolvable complexities for the reader's subtlest art. De Man suggested, shortly before his death, that "once a reader has become aware of the rhetorical dimensions of a text, he will not be amiss in finding textual instances that are irreducible to grammar or to historically determined meaning, provided only he is willing to acknowledge what he is bound to notice."[27] Substantively, de Man chastens everyone, himself included, by insisting on the "undecidable enigma" curled blissfully within texts—critical and polemic texts no more or less than others. He does not say that texts are utterly undecodable, only that the assurance anyone wants to gain from determinate readings will always dissolve, demanding one more look, another rereading, with interpretive ambition demanding further readings, and so on and on. The history of this process is literature itself, for de Man, and it constitutes the whole of critical reality, a cycle or spiral or any other appropriate figure of bedeviling and bedeviled interpretive attempts. This literary and critical corpus creates the giant palimpsest on which we write as teachers, scholars, and critics.

One might stretch this metaphor to say that the canonical and sub-canonical master list, perpetually revised without too much change of shape across time (and with no startling change in the range of attitudes and strategies available for deployment in any event), is the "territory" of criticism's interpretive community. Not the institutional context or social structure but the irreplaceable ground of rhetoric and its established landmarks provides the determining frame of interpretation.

But this revelation, if that is what it is, produces a dilemma even more troubling than the one Paul Bové ascribes to de Man's position. While Bové sees "de Man's commitment to the absolute self-aware fictionality of all literature" as "an unexamined presupposition" or moment of blindness in the great demystifier of critical self-consciousness (the demystifier himself mystified),[28] I see it as a problem curiously akin to the one posed by Stanley Fish's ideologically loaded optimism. A kind of faith in deconstructive progress underlies de Man's work, an unstated belief in the gathering strength of literary and critical theory despite the pervasive confusion about theory which de Man goes to considerable lengths to make clear. De Man's difficult work in *Allegories of Reading* and his essay "The Resistance to Theory" disarm Bové's criticism of the "earlier claim [in *Blindness and Insight*] for fiction's total separation from the world."[29] Not only has de Man always shown that a positivist search for "truths" and stable institutional values is deluded by its inevitable failure to say what it intends to say unequivocally, he shows also that the "relationship between trope and performance is actually much closer but more disruptive" than a speech-act-oriented reading, for example, could reveal, since such a reading empties "rhetoric of its epistemological impact" and thereby relegates linguistic force to the "purely affective and intentional realm." For de Man this orientation "opens up dreary prospects of pragmatic banality," equating rhetoric with psychology rather than with epistemology, where the "performative power of language can be called positional."[30] While this formulation seems sympathetic to the reader-response emphasis Fish puts forward—indeed de Man, like Fish, finds "referential authority" to be an agreement that "is merely contractual, never constitutive" of meaning[31]—it actually undermines the experiential basis of understanding so crucial to Fish's perspective. At the same time it carries even further a preference for the radically contested nature of statements, meanings, interpretations, and rhetorical positions which anchors Fish's model of reading. The difference achieved by this extension or development can be seen in de Man's belief that a deconstructive reading "does not occur between statements, as in a logical refutation or in a dialectic, but happens instead between, on the one hand, metalinguistic statements [in a particular text] about the rhetorical nature of language and, on the other hand, a rhetorical praxis that puts these statements into question."[32]

In essence de Man, like Fish, is vitally aware of the worldliness of rhetoric (in a highly restricted sense), but his understanding of that world is dazzlingly skewed by the complexity of agreements, by the difficulty of comprehending the grounds or methods or outcomes favorable to an accurate understanding of texts. The ironic conclusion to his way of reading—and everything in de Man is ironic— comes to this: Even "a 'truly' rhetorical reading that would stay clear of any undue phenomenalization or of any undue grammatical or performative codification of the text," while "irrefutable" in the consistency of its interpretive logic, would nonetheless produce "an unreliable process of knowledge production that prevents all entities, including linguistic entities, from coming into discourse as such."[33] In other words, the most accurate theoretical inspection of texts and of the production of texts will itself be positioned self-consciously yet impractically (i.e., hypothetically) at the extreme boundary of language as we use it—and where it makes sense—in the collective interactions of tropes and narratives. This means that the enabling condition of reading is theory, but that theory is itself an interpretation and a fictional project that is disabled by its own ambition for scrupulous clarity. Thus theory universalizes its performance even as it erodes and renders futile the very accuracy it desires. The disturbing consequence of the assertion that criticism is at once necessarily theoretical and necessarily resistant to the conditions of its own theoretical effort is its depoliticized optimism.

The reason I find de Man's formulation hopeful, a sort of evolutionist bad faith despite its self-destructive (self-excusing) irony, is that it predicts an inevitable growth of the critical institution, not just in numbers but in professional strength. Look at his entangled insight: "Nothing can overcome the resistance to theory since theory *is* itself this resistance."

> The loftier the aims and the better the methods of literary theory the less possible it becomes. [Note the irony once more: "less possible" to accomplish affirmatively, "less possible" to resist productively.] Yet literary theory is not in danger of going under; it cannot help but flourish, and the more it is resisted, the more it flourishes, since the language it speaks is the language of self-resistance. What remains impossible to decide is whether this flourishing is a triumph or a fall.[34]

Well, maybe. Somehow, nevertheless, one knows that de Man's clos-ing puckishness is not ambivalent. To enter such deliberate self-con-sciousness and its uncontrollable displacement by language is to "tri-umph" by a "fall" into uncertain knowledge, ever startled, ever pleased, which is the only way one can "flourish" here. This languid turbulence provides the mode and the mood of our interpretive com-munity itself. Readers are condemned to disagree, and readings exert themselves only to arrive at the possibility of beginning once again. And yet, when resistance to and acceptance of the same activity con-stitute an identity, the pragmatic considerations (pedagogical, ideo-logical, social) of that enterprise are aborted for the sake of enhancing institutional harmony. Far from being the evil godfather who gives "the impression of having a grip on truth,"[35] de Man assures us that truth of any kind is elusive and that the best interpreters can do is to execute their tasks without worrying about the overt discontinuity between cultural life and theoretical clarity, which, we can see now, conceals the covert continuity between interpretive self-containment and political pessimism.

The institutional authority of criticism as it stands will not create the community of readers and writers needed to challenge our world's cultural smugness, the systematic exercise of power obscured and made possible there. It may be that rehearsing capitalism's contradic-tions cannot, in the end, change much, but the humanist's avoidance of "the permanent intervention of the state to organize the markets and ensure the process of accumulation"[36] for transnational develop-ment enhances neither the intellectual solidarity nor the technical skill of professional interpreters. Critics thus seem destined to work "be-tween the *Numen* and the *Moha*," as R. P. Blackmur once called the predicament of people susceptible to ideals but equally vulnerable to self-deception and moral or political complacency. The *Numen* is fa-miliar enough, that power of inspiration which "resembles the force of the sublime described by Longinus—the blow that transports us." But *Moha* is vaster, less elusive, more brutal:

I suppose some people would call the *Moha* the devil; but it is much more human and ornery than that; nor is it the mere *miseria* of the spirit. *Moha* is a Sanskrit word I got from a physicist (one time a poet), who in turn got it while studying that language for relief at Los Alamos during the war. I suppose the atomic bomb was a labor of the *Moha*. At the juncture when I got the term it was given as an attribute of the faculties of high institutions of learning—bodies of men and women by nature subject to incalculable, capricious explosions of behavior. The attribution was cor-rect. *Moha*, then, is a term for the basic, irremediable, irreplaceable, characteristic, and contemptuous stupidity of man confronted with choice or purpose: the stupidity because of which he goes wrong, without which he could not survive.[37]

Blackmur's physicist-poet is Robert Oppenheimer, and the systematic harassment that plagued the final years of his career, a malicious inquisitorial debasement of government review boards that judged him "disloyal" and suspect, a potential security risk, makes the word *Moha* squalid with accuracy.[38] *Moha*, Blackmur continues, "refers to what is sottish, oafish, and drunken, to what is slothful but active in man's nature. . . . *Moha* has something to do with the basic lies we tell." Whatever truth there is in the belief that humanist criticism has kept itself contained by its own political sloth or theoretical complacency, the *Moha* it enacts would be its refusal to risk the hubris and the bathos Spivak points to.

Several of Blackmur's late essays are helpful here. They illuminate the material and cultural imbalance between advanced capitalism and what is now, thirty years or so after they were written, called the "Third World." Contemporary critics, especially younger ones, will find a sobering dedication to the social usefulness of interpretation in those texts, a body of writing that separates Blackmur from the New Critical mainstream, where he is often misplaced and ignored—a dedication, I might add, particularly alert to the concrete institutional milieux of writing.[39] We could call what Blackmur accomplishes in those late essays "cultural criticism," but I think it is more accurate to call his work there "political criticism," since it seeks to show how the world of intellect is immersed in a stricter, less forgiving world. For anyone interested, his essay on the "new illiteracy" taking hold in the mid-fifties throughout the Middle East ("Toward a Modus Vivendi") provides a place to rethink the idea of an interpretive community. Such a community would have, for one thing, an active oppositional purpose: to expose and contest the invasion of beleaguered countries by consumer culture (then mostly "comic books and picture magazines, along with grade B and C" films). It would work against the devalued status of *generally* educated people, that part of the intellectual work force that forms an academic proletariat, "a class of persons who have no fixed and vital position in society" and who are regularly deposited "further and further outside the economy which they express in its human consequences." Such is our reality once again. Most of all, a politically conscious interpretive community would see that the relationship between critical writing and everything worth attacking and defending is lost when theory and scholarship become too specialized. Thus Blackmur held out, in his characteristic way, for those discriminating "means of getting along without loss of vital purpose in a concert of conflicts with which we necessarily find out our problematic relations with others, nations, jobs, or friends."[40] For Blackmur it followed that "professionalism is a form of illiteracy."

Many would dismiss Oppenheimer's Sanskrit term and Blackmur's meditation as too eccentric. Blackmur, however, believed that the world's best hope resides with those who promote cultural diversity and political clarity. In such work scholarship and criticism find their justification. When we think of the lack of political will and institutional energy to foster self-determining communities, when we contemplate "the end of the subordination of individuals to the 'division of labor'" which Marx thought could be accomplished by rational force, the role of the critic can be seen for what it is: a mostly undefined and still uncertain accomplice of revolutionary ambitions that, in the United States at the close of the twentieth century, seem unthinkable, illegitimate, or hopeless.

6

Intellectual Identity

Anyone who writes criticism today cannot avoid the awkward, obscure, and even incapacitated movement tetween texts and the institutions and social struggles that define our era. The shrewd literary theorist reminds us that we cannot plunge from texts into history. Writing (including critical writing) is now a visible empire of signs and warring parties. Writing is where history is made—or where it is comprehended as it is made by material and political events, and by cultural events also, among which the critic's efforts count. How, then, in intellectual space so aware of its boundaries, could any identity or critical consciousness break free of the professional mediations that keep scholarly and evaluative writing distant from the educated working citizen? What would it mean—and is it possible—to intervene critically into the ruling cultural habits of a media society too contradictory to be summarized but too powerful and too historically ignorant to leave unopposed?

To this point I have argued that the main effort of oppositional criticism right now can be directed only at the critical institution itself. Before intervention into the world of public consciousness can take place in any significant way, it will have to gain strength in the university as a debate about intellectual identities. Such a debate has just begun, initiated by a few writers on the left who are by no means in systematic agreement. Criticism may now, at any rate, begin to see that it is already "intervening" in a culture that ironically appropriates the model of the nonintervening, pluralist, and apolitical intellectual vanguard as a strong institutional ratification of its innate justice. The comic element in this situation is that the radical right, in the absence of a genuine critical left, attacks liberal intellectuals (lumping a few notable professors with more prominent, apparently more dangerous journalists and media executives) as dire threats to civilized morality. The common ground between the liberal critic and the Hollywood film maker or New York television baron probably comes down to a shared appreciation for cultural diversity and free speech—acceptance also, no doubt, of the material benefits the resurgent political and religious right wing seeks to protect by cultural terrorism.

The growing controversy about intellectual identity may well reveal what many would otherwise not see: that criticism in the United States has created a community of writers who, as a group, do not forcefully or in any concentrated way challenge the North Atlantic state system and its power. Literary culture remains incidental to institutional or political critique. Critical theory, as Jonathan Culler confessed to the English Institute in 1983, is unaware of the state; the state is something Culler, for one, admits he knows very little about and does not want to know about.

So it is that part of capitalism's "democratic" state power derives from the self-disabled status of extremely articulate, powerfully educated writers who unknowingly (or unthinkingly, at least) cooperate with the public and private organization of Euro-American military and financial policies by keeping to their cadres of expertise. The state's power is preserved, guiltless and efficient, in part by the lack of harassment experienced by those in power throughout the professional and corporate order. I am aware, in saying this, of what everyone at work teaching and writing about texts knows quite well. The literary critic, the teacher, and the theorist have no real audience beyond themselves and a few curious readers here and there. Yet the activities of each of them is in contact with a wide public after all. Each extends intellectual force beyond the small circle of professional readers and writers every time the classroom exercise begins. The issue here is not *if* literary intellectuals have a possible and potentially important influence in North American culture. They do. The issue is what *kind* of force is involved in critical activity and what role a politically conscious critic should play.

Although many, perhaps most, university literature teachers focus on training the future literary scholar or critic, a commitment to the departmental major which may to some extent undercut the importance of literary and critical training for students outside purely literary areas, the classroom with its exchange of ideas and writing practices nonetheless forms a subprofessional, not yet completely homogenized world of intellectual give-and-take where criticism has an impact beyond strictly disciplinary and orthodox lines. Questions can be raised there about the *purpose* of reading texts. Why read these texts (the literary and philosophical classics)? Why read in this or that particular way? What are the alternatives? Most of all, what theoretical and practical consequences emerge in the world of daily business—the business of law or publishing or teaching or whatever else—as a result of thinking of texts and textual practices in one way and not another? In this way as opposed to that one?

These are the necessary questions, or some of the elemental ones, that the critical institution (the teacher or critical theorist) represses at the peril of keeping students somewhat mystified about the practical value of a literary education. Traditionally, the intellectual left has admitted the political basis of interpretive work more readily than its opponents have.[1] But even here, the question of what to make of that fact, what intellectual identity to uphold, becomes a source of confusion and real disagreement. We can see, for instance, how troublesome Antonio Gramsci has proved to be among those few critics who have taken his work seriously. We find Paul Bové chastising Edward Said for using Gramsci to shore up an "image of critical consciousness [that] is essentially a legitimation of the *status quo* of intellectual life" (an opinion that seems designed to capture ground further to the left) while Frank Lentricchia, who aligns himself with "the university humanist, because [the humanist's] position as a social and political actor has been cynically underrated by the right, left and center," rejects Gramsci as a writer who takes intellectual work too far outside the academy to revive the specific political function of literary critics.[2] The issue is far more complicated, so I will return to it in the next chapter, but the fact that a figure so distant from the traditional concerns of criticism in the United States can provoke such interest and such different assessments among professional readers in itself suggests the unsettled quality of the contemporary critic's identity.

Gramsci has helped recalculate the intellectual's political purpose. His distinction between the "traditional" intellectual, who preserves cultural traditions and helps maintain social cohesion by reinforcing dominant social values, and the "organic" intellectual, who seeks to create cultural and political solidarity among demoted or disempowered people, provides a point of departure for Michel Foucault's concept of the "specific" intellectual. By that term Foucault means someone whose identity as a critic is not based on global or large-scale class interests as defined by a vanguard political party (or by a personal conceptual generality) but who, instead, considers his or her particular workplace a site for political opposition. That opposition is directed against the cooperation between intellectual practices that claim privileged access to truth (to "true discourses") and a society that depends upon those practices to construct and organize its power. For Foucault, social control and institutional power are not outside the realm of intellectual activity. They coincide so that those forms of thinking and writing that are considered "true" extend and disseminate existing power. The "specific" intellectual's job, therefore, is to disrupt the stable functioning of "truth." That is a matter not of exposing the ideological contents and false consciousness of statements or texts but of showing how intellectuals themselves inhabit positions of power that are related to the entire structure of social and political power—showing how much even critical activity that thinks of itself as "oppositional" can in fact verify and help maintain an unjust social order by failing to demonstrate how power circulates through language that cannot be used neutrally. The "specific" intellectual's job is to examine the relation between truth and power within particular discursive practices and within the institutions they support (law, medicine, the penal system, etc.), a procedure that Foucault believes puts the specific intellectual in a distinctly subversive relation to "normal" professional activity.

Against these three intellectual identities we can pose a fourth and somewhat strangely unrepresented one. It is the "provisional" or "intermediate" and unformed intellectual identity of the college student. I have in mind here undergraduates for the most part, since graduate students, even in their first semester of work, have already made a conscious choice of an intellectual or professional identity and are quickly made aware of the rules of the game by which they will succeed or fail. Most undergraduates, in a large part of their activity in colleges and universities, are very much in personal and professional transition. Their intellectual identities, such as they are, can be thought of as in flux, often confused by the attempt to sort through requirements, choices of majors, and the means of writing essays that will satisfy various professorial tastes and assignments. In the normal run of college activity, undergraduates are seldom if ever invited to think of themselves explicitly as "intellectuals" but rather are put through numerous, frequently bewildering exercises. I offer this fourth category of intellectual identity, first, because at any one time most people who are actively engaged in studying texts, writing essays, attending (in some form of consciousness) to ideas, are students, not professors or professional writers. This is a fact to be reckoned not as a by-product or incidental feature of the professional critic's work. Students are not merely the necessary audience (or clientele) for the propagation of knowledge and the continuation of intellectual traditions. They provide immediate access to the future. The purpose of intellectual work is not just to advance theoretical understanding and to enrich intellectual practices but to widen and deepen the social relevance of knowledge—to put ideas into more useful contact with democratic principles, to make all institutions within the Western sphere of influence more democratic, to make democracy as a national political force (as a cultural ideal) more prominent, less prone to the massive assault of commercially induced apathy. I open the notion of the unformed or "provisional" intellectual because students are genuinely intellectuals-in-process whether they recognize it or not, even though they are not granted such status in the organization of knowledge itself. Within the dreary reality of global illiteracy (including much illiteracy among students themselves), people who undergo education of the fairly rigorous kind to be found in most good four-year colleges and universities certainly can be counted as intellectually trained and intellectually oriented, even if, at the rudimentary stage of development achieved with the college degree, they cannot be thought of very easily as practicing or as self-consciously critical intellectuals.

Something that Gramsci and Foucault both point to, despite their different orientations, emerges from this recognition of a "provisional" or "intermediate" intellectual. The teacher's purpose, especially the oppositional teacher's purpose, is to promote an intellectual identity in students who in large measure are vulnerable to the pacifications of the common culture that organizes capitalist reality: advertising, commercial television, and the onslaught of rock and Hollywood pop culture.[3] The teacher's job is to breed the kind of critical capacities that allow students to resist such disabling forces. This task can be seen as opposed to the preparation of students for the professional hierarchies that wait for the most competent. It can also be thought of in the way Gramsci postulated the "organic" intellectual's activity: as the preparation of students to confront the relation between ideas and social power—to confront, specifically, the way the reading of texts (including the master texts of the humanities curriculum) raises both intellectual and political issues that need first to be defined and debated, then developed in writing and in critical strategies that question the actual shape of institutional reality.[4]

The structure of North American schooling stands against that aim, and the teacher or critical theorist who takes it seriously seeks to spark an anomalous individuality in students, a freely constituted, self-directed desire that leads them, in the process of questioning received assumptions and conventional practices, to challenge authority not by temporary (and mostly futile) rebellion but by working wherever they work in the long-drawn-out effort to create resistance to domination and cultural indoctrination. What such teaching needs to look at within the reading and teaching practices that make up the contemporary student's intellectual life is, in essence, the question of capitalism itself. What is the morality of the marketplace and how does it influence and even determine public life and the structure of institutional behavior?[5] The first obstacle to such an inquiry is the relative ignorance of most students about anything that could be considered an alternative vision to capitalist reality. The second is the student's identification with commercial culture. In other words, the oppositional teacher actually seeks to intervene first and most forcefully in the student's already well-ingrained sense of urgency and self-worth within the hierarchical order, where success means accepting what authorities of various kinds demand, where "playing the game" without much dissent or antagonism seems necessary.

The oppositional teacher's introduction of a provisional and formative intellectual identity (an introduction, I should add, to the exhilaration as well as the challenge of making interpretive choices) is much like Gramsci's notion of creating class consciousness among the working classes. This may seem a strange idea, even wrong or foolish, since many of the most receptive students are preoccupied with upward mobility toward well-paid, well-protected positions of power and authority within the capitalist order. But students can be taught to read so that they see their own relation to social power and intellectual authority. They can be educated to confront their identities as intellectually privileged, if also frequently confused or mystified, people who, as Foucault suggests, can make a difference in the world by knowing how to examine specific work regimes in the effort to advance human solidarity over capitalist hierarchies and professional cynicism.

To make a persuasive case for this notion of the teacher as a critical or oppositional intellectual allied with intellectuals in formation—an alliance promoted to resist popular cultural indoctrination and the democratic indifference of professional routines—I would have to demonstrate how, for example, this kind of teaching contests its own assumptions (overtly, graphically) in order not only to appear fair to an often skeptical and somewhat resistant audience but to exercise the kind of analytic agility that opens up alternative readings and does not close texts and problems within the seamless web of a monolithic interpretation. Each assumption and each interpretation offered young readers must (to the best of one's ability) be made available to opposed readings, different assumptions—especially those that students bring to bear, often naively. If not, the student is given little choice and hardly encouraged to develop critical—that is, imaginatively analytic—moral skills among discrete possibilities that always narrow as well as intensify what anyone can finally posit as alert social and textual intelligence. In sum, to make my case I would have to say more about the way critical skills can be.developed in the short time of a twelve- or fourteen-week semester.

For the moment I will make one further comment on the political function of the oppositional teacher. I think my experience as a teacher is not dissimilar to what most literary teachers at work in colleges or universities in the United States encounter. The central influences upon a teacher's identity as a professional humanist deny the historical, the material, and the institutionally specific nature of that identity. For one thing, the literary establishment seldom looks at the kind of work critics perform as an activity (as an *action*) within a field of cultural and economic forces. It is generally not interested in the social effect of literary understanding. Therefore most critics and teachers of literature think what they do is of use somehow, even important in a way difficult for them to make clear, but essentially distinct from the concrete placement of such effort as a professional and an academic (an institutional) event. The literary teacher's job, after all, is to educate in both general and particular ways that engage the reading of texts. I am now inclined to think of that work as *training,* since the influence that passes between teachers and students, limited as it is, forms the potentially most rigorous clarification of the student's choices and institutional options. Critical training, in this assessment, attempts to visualize the concrete conditions as well as the intellectual and moral behaviors that organize public reality. It projects the student toward the actual world in which interpretations and literary understanding take place. It also asks the student to imagine becoming a thinking, willing person who may resist institutional pressures, a person who can oppose abuses of power and privilege.

This idealistic projection of the individual as an intervening force is at odds with what we normally, with good reason, think of as the appropriate condition for institutional change. We know not only from Marx's writing and from the history of Marxist struggles, but from resistances and oppositions without affiliation to Marx or Marxism, that institutions are moved to alter policies and material conditions for the most part because of the large-scale pressure of individuals gathered into a collective force. The single person righting "wrongs" stands little chance in most circumstances and is usually defeated in advance by a hundred signals that resistance is not merely deviant but stupid, economically or politically suicidal. A lifetime's training in common sense dissuades most people from thinking of alternatives to "the system" in the first place. But in a nation where social vision is permitted minimum cultural expression even as it is denied in professions and in executive behavior, where does the will to change rituals, expectations, habits, and policies that constrain such imagination come from if not from individuals trained to exercise intellectual courage, people encouraged by critical training to exert their intellectual and moral force?[6]

That preparation and the knowledge it carries with it, knowledge that teachers and critical intellectuals are uniquely positioned to distribute, constitutes the political function of critical work. When Frank Lentricchia reminds us that "theories of reading or interpretation (theories are interpretations of interpretation) help us do intellectual work, but even to say it that way, to speak of *intellectual* work, courts an idealism, a split between theory and practice that is the secret ground of despair for most academic intellectuals," he accurately summarizes the institutional confusion I am concerned with here. Nevertheless, he overlooks a not so subtle distinction still to be affirmed. Theory and practice are interrelated and inextricable, and not just "in theory." A critically engaged intellectual teaches from the basis of his or her writing, and that writing evolves from an immediate relation to teaching—for both teaching and writing are practices, both "theoretical" because they are continually reformulated and revised, both "practical" because they are consistently shared in the interaction of intellectual and personal commitment (conversation, instruction, dialogue, interrogation, the rethinking of fundamental ideas and positions *with others*). I agree with Lentricchia here: "Whether or not one calls oneself a Marxist, one could, I'd say one should, always check one's effectivity as a teacher of the literary classics by asking oneself the following questions: Does one's approach to the text enable or disenable— encourage or disencourage—oneself and one's students and readers to spot, confront, and work against the political horrors of one's time?"[7] I think the individual teacher and critic does just that by making affiliations between knowledge and power an explicit topic, a demonstrable institutional context for interpretation.

I am suggesting that critical intellectuals share as much as possible of their own reality as writers and teachers with one another and with their students while avoiding any temptation to dramatize or inflate that activity. The oppositional teacher is not a hero or a marvelously combative derelict. No opposition or intellectual resistance takes place outside the system of power relations; the most radical critic is in some degree supported by the profession and the culture whose values and practices he or she challenges. The critic, in other words, is close to things to be opposed because they are intimately connected to the work and the identity of the critic. They are entangled with the critic's authority. Opposition, therefore, is as much directed to the false and compromising choices any intellectual may make (may have made many times, in fact, because those choices suffuse professional life) as it is directed "out there" against countless foes who represent tyranny. Criticism at root is a clarification of intellectual positions that a writer is disposed—by temper, choice, and training—to take in company with others. It is first a self-clarification that prepares for an unending reclarification in league with anyone who will join the work of understanding the costs and consequences of choices. Therefore criticism is not work *on* texts. It is work *with* texts, an effort to demonstrate through them the lines of institutional force which connect texts and intellectual practices to one another. One way to put this is to say that criticism moves *from* the world toward texts and *through* texts back again into the world. Another way, more accurate, is to say that criticism and texts never leave the world; they are always situated, and the task of criticism is to make that situation explicit. The fundamental purpose of criticism is to create the intellectual means for intelligent human action. Its specific task is to prepare educated people who complicate interpretive suspicion by transforming knowledge from text-bound information to constructive public debate.

Thus it is disconcerting to find Fredric Jameson, who is unquestionably one of the most astute critics at work today, proposing that interpretation of a Marxist or socially committed variety is, like all other forms of critical effort, like every other theoretical enterprise, "an essentially allegorical act which consists in rewriting a given text in terms of a particular master code."[8] Is that what critics do? Is such work—whether it proclaims itself to be Marxist or not—necessarily a "rewriting" of texts, and does such rewriting operate from the basis of "a particular interpretive master code"? While Jameson poses "new forms of collective thinking and collective culture which lie beyond the boundaries of our own world" as his primary hermeneutic and political goal, he remains indebted to (perhaps also imprisoned within) the overall academic master code, which entices even a writer of his range and ambition to outtheorize other theorists and, by outflanking their less "dialectical" positions, to entrench himself more deeply in the game of academic rank. Of course, as that game is played, everyone who cares to write critically is condemned to engage (if not to embrace so thoroughly) the positioning and repositioning that literally define the self-contesting, self-neutralizing consciousness of the critical establishment. The problem in Jameson's contribution to the game is not that he plays it so well and so seriously; nor is it that he finds himself, like others, caught within the limits of the enterprise; it is that he poses his genuinely socially alert effort so unselfconsciously (I think incompletely) *within* "the boundaries of our own world," which in this specific instance is the world of theoretical exercise. The game of professional criticism may generate acute analysis, as it does in Jameson, but unless one finds a more concrete political strategy, that analysis is imposed upon texts and circulates whimsically, if entertainingly, within the commoditization of academic production.

Jameson, in other words, is a stern contestant in the struggle for critical authority. But what is troubling and somewhat surprising, given his Marxist inclinations, is his failure to confront this most self-mystifying feature of academic criticism. Even when he approaches this issue, as in his essay "Marxism and Teaching,"[9] we find no strategy for allying criticism with teaching in the effort to create a critical community with political force outside the profession. Instead, we find an appropriate concern not "to defend the privileged position of cultural criticism in a self-serving way," a mild discomfort about the identity and role of the critic in a badly fractured, wholly stratified society. Jameson asserts quickly, however, that "it is a historical fact that the 'structuralist' or textual revolution . . . takes as its model a kind of decipherment of which literary and textual criticism is in many ways the strong form." This "revolution," he continues, "liberates us from the empirical object—whether institution, event, or individual work—by displacing our attention to its *constitution* as an object and its *relationship* to the other objects thus constituted."[10]

The group so liberated, as it turns out, is that body of practicing critics whose authority hardly needs further embellishment to execute the task of textual decipherment. But the greater irony involved here is the way this self-affirmation on apparently "new" intellectual ground (structuralist, textual) avoids recognizing just how much its own celebration of hermeneutic power actively propagates the very stratifications Jameson's Marxism is designed to level. We are still in the world of intellectual expertise, a world divided between those who know and who have access to knowledge and its instrumentalities and those who are disempowered, exploited, marginalized, or underrepresented—all those, in sum, whom Jameson seems to want to champion. Jameson seems unaware (at least to this point he has not fully faced the fact) that the critic's authority exists to a considerable extent—and that extent, of course, deserves debate—at the expense of those unauthorized people who have neither political nor cultural representation in the dominant hierarchy of power, privilege, authority, and values. Writing from the self-assured vantage of cultural analysis, of Marxist "rewriting" of texts and hermeneutic codes, thus seems to defer the task of grappling with the apparent social impossibility of bridging the gap between knowledge and its victims. The problem in Jameson's politically committed form of criticism is its political uncertainty.

To get a sense of the dilemma facing politically oriented critics we ought to ask ourselves, as literary and critical professionals, how theory and the interpretation of texts will stimulate social changes. How will the critic's activity intersect with institutional practices other than the academy's? How can theory and criticism become socially productive, intellectually disruptive in ways that generate compassion, democratic decision making, a willingness to negotiate cultural and political differences? The first requirement is that the critic who means to contribute to building an intellectual community beyond the stable confines of the academy must think of interpretive power and hermeneutic authority as events or enablements that do not reside only with specialized professional territories. The theorist who means to promote human power—the "community" of citizenship opposed to military and cultural hegemony, opposed also to legal and institutional exclusions that invent, replicate, and ensure the domination of profit and bureaucracy—must be willing to work *against* the current model of critical authority. This effort cannot fail to be paradoxical, since it means placing authority in its present forms in the service of people and cultural values that lack authority. It means encouraging other professionals and professionals-to-be (students) to think of critical activity as moral effort rather than careerist self-validation, as the work of creating an intellectual authority based not on texts and on the professional appropriation of history and traditions, but on a commitment to apply knowledge (including the knowledge of reading texts) to specific social and institutional situations. Such authority would be defined by intervention in relationships of power and knowledge that work against the general human interest.

Needless to say, just what that common body of interests may be is not at all obvious, and to speak of creating an active and oppositional intellectual authority that does not lapse into easy accommodation with existing power and privilege is to raise the issue of the general human or social good. Anyone who does so risks political naiveté, crass and uninstructable idealism, or mere intellectual banality. Critical authority today is bound to be based on specialized skills, on discrete bodies of knowledge—on the division of labor and on segregated professional areas also, since authority emanates from actual institutional conditions. Intellectual authority reflects and truly embodies social organization. Yet despite these realities, my objection to Jameson's position is motivated in part by its practical (and political) incompleteness, its conscious or unconscious reinforcement of intellectual order as we have it. Jameson writes about the political "horizon" of all interpretation while explicitly postponing "that exploratory projection of what a vital and emergent political culture should be and do."[11] Yet he jeopardizes those interests when he frames critical teaching as an act of specular theorizing in which the Marxist teacher introduces the social and historical problems with which Marxism is concerned. The result is a pedagogical focus "less on the work [the text] itself 'as it really was' in the past, than on the ideological categories through which contemporary readers receive, rewrite, deform, those works of the past."[12]

Jameson offers a shift from isolated texts and static historical contexts to interpretive frameworks that make reading the generative component of knowledge in order to assert the "uncomfortable presence" of Marxism "in the present-day supermarket of American pluralism." But that presence emerges alongside the superior reality of academic work in its competitive commoditized marketplace circumstances. Marxism as Jameson offers it is a curiously unresisting, inactive, even stable partner within the overall interpretive tumult. While Jameson takes aim at ideological categories that are frequently the unnoticed elements of knowledge, he fails to wrestle with the fact that his position is wholly compatible with that most indigenous of all ideologies, academic professionalism. He demonstrates his avoidance of that uncomfortable fact in three ways: first, by leaving the critical or academic "inside" segregated from an unspecified political "outside" where theory encourages action and clarifies values; second, by formalistically emphasizing criticism as an application of interpretive codes instead of as a form of work specifically placed (with particular rituals, privileges, and limits) within a social system that absorbs and thereby resists the "subversive" intention of the authoritative critic; and third, by imagining the teacher's and critic's work as an exercise of hermeneutic expertise. These choices embrace the tendency of academic criticism to ignore the social basis of its authority.

I want to make some sense of this set of choices because it has important consequences for the political impact of criticism. Though Jameson may seem a surprising instance of critical isolation, his promotion of a derealizing, apolitical hermeneutic appears at every point in his attempt at "working through contemporary interpretations" of literary masterpieces in order to reveal the "insufficiencies" of viewpoints less dialectical than his own.[13] The startling thing here is that Jameson, even as he emphasizes the need for "historicizing the present and making the student aware that this present is of a piece with the past," poses the student as a spectator to the instructor's clarity. Two problems emerge here. Experience is overwhelmed by necessity (that is, the student's sense of self is shown to be a code within a larger, uncoded form, History, which breaks down into a series of events that cannot be decoded but nonetheless are ceaselessly interpreted); the drama of Marxist criticism and teaching therefore is trapped within a history where "the cultural monuments of the past" are both "Utopian *and* ideological simultaneously." In other words, to be a reader in Jameson's sense is to suffer an unending seduction by the promise of interpretive clarity, which dissolves perpetually because texts at once invent and exceed their own grounds. Jameson leaves us with a historical vision inexplicably defeated by abstraction and by the subordination of interpretive choice and personal experience to a hermetically textualized world:

> History is therefore the experience of Necessity, and it is this alone which can forestall its thematization or reification as a mere object of representation or as one master code among many others. Necessity is not in that sense a type of content, but rather the inexorable *form* of events; it is therefore a narrative category in the enlarged sense of some properly narrative political unconscious . . . , a retextualization of History which does not propose the latter as some new representation or "vision," some new content, but as the formal effects of what Althusser, following Spinoza, calls an "absent cause." Conceived in this sense, History is what hurts, it is what refuses desire and sets inexorable limits to individual as well as collective praxis, which its "ruses" turn into grisly and ironic reversals of their overt intention. But this History can be apprehended only through its effects, and never directly as some reified force. This is indeed the ultimate sense in which History as ground and untranscendable horizon needs no particular theoretical justification: we may be sure that its alienating necessities will not forget us, however much we might prefer to ignore them.[14]

This is the final paragraph of the eighty-five-page opening chapter, "On Interpretation: Literature as a Socially Symbolic Act," in *The*

Political Unconscious. Several things are immediately apparent. The writing is immensely abstract. But that density, which appears at crucial moments in Jameson's arguments, is a symptom of a deeper problem. Since Jameson reads the world as closed by a historical "necessity" whose "inexorable form" cannot be seen directly but needs to be explicated, critical readers who pursue Jameson will find themselves inscribed within the logic of history's macrotext. History, from this viewpoint, is less a series of events or social tendencies than the unavailable result of forces that cannot be named or grappled with but can only be alluded to vaguely as "Necessity." History turns out to be a text, or rather "a narrative category in the enlarged sense of some properly narrative political unconscious," and not really a "ground and untranscendable horizon" of any discernible human or institutional variety. It is truly an "absent cause," a blank abstraction that can be filled in however anyone wishes. Reading Jameson's view of history, one arrives at no comprehension of the empirical form of history or politics or interpretation itself. The entire scene is played out among categorical stereotypes, so that anything we say within the orbit of their logic is impossible to challenge or to verify and of no real importance anyway, since history and necessity have already won.

But that is not the end of the difficulty Jameson creates for those who follow him. In his attempt to avoid a heroically independent critical voluntarism (the autonomous bourgeois writer or Sartre's engaged but free existential Marxist), Jameson dissolves experience. Like Althusser, Jameson believes that experience is inhabited utterly by "the imaginary relationship of individuals to their real conditions of existence"—by ideology, in sum.[15] The only way out of that trap is to deny experience any value and to replace it with "the concept of the text," which substitutes structures that can be decoded for empirical objects that are mute. In a passage from his essay on Marxist teaching in which he depicts the subordination of experience and of texts to the historical forces with which Jameson is concerned, we find the "opening" in history that dictates a possible interpretive strategy:

> There has never been a work of art in human history which was purely progressive or revolutionary, without entertaining some kind of ideological complicity with domination. Let the motto for this assertion be Walter Benjamin's great observation, "There is no document of culture which is not at the same time a document of barbarism." By the same token, there has never been an unqualifiedly reactionary work of art of any value either: the most elitist masterpieces also contain Utopian and progressive impulses, the most hermetically formalist works are also ultimately and inevitably social in their resonance. To teach works this

way is to recreate the living and ambivalent, concrete situation of social struggle from which they emerge; it is to respect them as human praxis and symbolic action far more adequately than is done when we content ourselves simply with awarding them the prize of a progressive qualification or the stigma of reactionary content.[16]

Note that Jameson draws the conclusion of intellectual culpability and of the interpreter's resistance in terms of texts, not of practices, including the teacher's and the student's act of bearing responsibility for the use of knowledge. Human "praxis"—that is, choice, interpretation, commitment—is equivalent to "symbolic action" in this passage. They are not distinct here despite the "and" that seems to join them and keep them separate. Jameson never shows how history motivates or takes hold of the maimed individual in a way that could cut through ideological knots. Instead, everyone succumbs to ideological closure, and the best possible outcome seems to be a reading of that closure. One must be an interpreter to resist history.

Jameson has replaced experience with interpretation, but he has reduced interpretation to a rather formalistic interplay of texts which now becomes the vital realm of human action. This vitality eventually closes in upon itself. At the end of *The Political Unconscious,* when he deals with Benjamin's loaded passage at a more leisurely pace in order to show how the "concept of class" motivates "a Marxian version of the hermeneutics of meaning," we are placed in a strange conceptual landscape "in which the ideological would be grasped as somehow at one with the Utopian, and the Utopian at one with the ideological." Such identification, Jameson adds, leads anyone who follows this logic "to formulate a question to which a collective dialectic is the only conceivable answer."[17] My particular resistance to this model of Marxist hermeneutics evolves from two related and problematic elements in his perspective. First, his stress upon the literary text and the "text" of culture as sites where "the production of false consciousness" is entangled with Utopian and critically dissonant elements creates a textualized world so dense that even the fairly competent student or critical reader may feel overwhelmed by the inextricable meshing of texts and consciousness, texts and cultural substance. This is hegemony writ large. The problem here is that when the world becomes utterly a matter of decoding texts—and when the world seems merely an extension of texts—then the reader and the writer are actually and inescapably within an interpretive regress, texts leading to more texts, interpretation counteracting interpretation. I do not want to say that this is not in some sense an accurate depiction of the bibliomanic energy of academic reality. I want to note instead how much it lacks a clear sense of the structure, of the social hierarchy, within which texts are used to advance choices and policies. It needs that frame of reference if it is not to wash out into infinite textualization and potential interpretive vertigo. The question that may be formulated alongside Jameson's interest in "a collective dialectic" is this: How are texts and interpretations used within the interactions of institutions? How do they generate and participate in the relations of power and social ordering?

Jameson does try to show how texts are situated. For him, literary and critical clarifications of existing social relations are subsumed by "the ideological function of mass culture"—"a process whereby otherwise dangerous and protopolitical impulses are 'managed' and defused, rechanneled and offered spurious objectives."[18] Such a massive cultural closure as Jameson finds in our society is essentially impervious to rational change and critical opposition, however. The specific reason that critic and critical text alike are immobilized is the "complex strategy of rhetorical persuasion [at work in society] in which substantial incentives are offered for ideological adherence" to the norms of consumer culture. In other words, capitalism pervades society through advertising and popular culture. That seduction implicates even those who renounce the materialistic rewards the system hands out; it corrupts the rest.

Jameson's view of this seduction creates the second problem I alluded to a moment back. "We will say that such incentives, as well as the impulses to be managed by the mass cultural text, are necessarily Utopian in nature," he asserts. But this is puzzling. If *Utopian,* as Jameson uses it, means what he says it does—that "even hegemonic or ruling-class culture and ideology are Utopian, not in spite of their instrumental function to secure and perpetuate class privilege and power, but rather precisely because that function is also in and of itself the affirmation of collective solidarity"[19]—then no teacher will easily (if ever) find the means to encourage in students what Daniel O'Hara has called, modestly but accurately, "a style of intellectual production that they can admire and find morally satisfying."[20] In fact, the means to a form of intellectual production that can be politically useful, and not only morally satisfying, is undermined by Jameson's conflation of the Utopian and the ideological functions of culture. He arrives at that formulation by three interwoven routes: through Ernst Bloch's readings of advertising slogans, through Adorno's and Horkheimer's analysis of fascism, and through the "Hegelian formula, that the *truth* of ruling-class consciousness (that is, of hegemonic ideology and cultural production) is to be found in working-class consciousness."[21] All of this, including Jameson's use of Benjamin, relies upon an extremely mobile concept of repression which Jameson's Marxist form of hermeneutics intends to unlock so that submerged energies in our culture may express their truly "Utopian" purpose. Only an enormously vague and relentlessly affirmative notion of totality, of a liberating but hidden "unity" in the social whole (the lost or suppressed human community), could support this enterprise, however, For Jameson, redemption lies somewhere within or just behind the false consciousness and brutal instrumentation of late capitalism. His aim as a Marxist theoretician and teacher is to reveal that hidden promise, to stimulate political and intellectual movement to recover the "Utopian" and constructive form of desire within the degraded, merely ideological desire we all live with.

That is an ambition that anyone who cares about improving rather than maintaining society may find difficult to reject. It is an appealing project, one of the most seriously committed and critically useful statements of the political function of the critical intellectual which North American writing has produced to date. But here is my central worry about Jameson's effort: Although he finds that "ideological commitment is not first and foremost a matter of moral choice but of the taking of sides in a struggle between embattled groups,"[22] he depicts the university setting in which critical consciousness is developed as neither moral nor political nor, for that matter, affiliated with work in the social world. I find this assumption in his representation of his teaching practice as delivering Marxist concepts and intellectual practices *to* his students in the relatively stabilized, unproblematic demonstration of so many texts and concepts "out there" (or "over here") to be learned and put into motion. Jameson establishes a model of his Marxist teaching as one more academic enterprise within the bourgeois university. His topic is Marxism; his intellectual wares are interpretation and theory. His students, he tells us, are fairly sure that they

> don't need [Marxism] now; but if we're right about history, there will come a time when suddenly this presently merely abstract doctrine will come back into their minds as a solution to urgent problems. At that point, retrospectively, the things we all taught them, in apparently imperceptible accretions that left no trace, will come back and be activated for the first time. That is it seems to me no negligible function for us to play, even if it offers very little immediate personal satisfaction.[23]

This is either intellectual modesty or pedagogical embarrassment, because the task of teaching is not to plant in students small pieces of doctrine or information that will be retrieved later at some moment of consternation or duress. The task of teaching—a very difficult and often failed project—is to get students to transform their thinking and their writing immediately, however tentative and subject to regression or erasure those efforts may be. The task of the teacher, Marxist or otherwise, is to get students to see their world differently, *distinctly*, from the first day intellectual discourse begins. The job of teaching is to put students into intellectual crisis so they must *digest* texts, *transform* information, *question* intellectual positions, *read* the institutional world, and begin to work out a way to *name* reality with a conceptual clarity that is open to improvement and maturation of the sort Jameson may have in mind but that does not have to be deferred until the course or the college experience is over. One indication of how little Jameson imagines his teaching practice as truly situated within an institutional context that demands immediate and repeated subversion is the uncertain location of the pedagogical (and the critical) transaction. He assumes, quite rightly I think, that the "power of purely intellectual persuasion which is available to us in the classroom" is limited and should not be overestimated. But is "our major problem in teaching Marxism . . . to keep the students from turning their hearing aids off," as he believes?[24]

I think not. No doubt teaching has to respect the vast ability of students—who want to be entertained before all else (who experience themselves for the most part as "captured" prey)—to resist activation, to mimic thinking and imagining. Undoubtedly most students even at the conclusion of their college years still do not have much idea of, and almost no practice with, *critical* and historically alert writing. But the question that should trouble critics and teachers is not how to avoid losing their students, a negative objective, but how to engage the dormant curiosity and sleeping critical instincts that really do come alive (however imperfectly) when people are shown their own stakes and inherent interests. This is the context in which intellectual identities can be formed and set in motion.

The negative aim, the fear of losing the unattentive or resistant student, guides Jameson's pedagogical theory and leads him to two useful strategies that fall short of putting students fully to the adventure of working among demonstrable intellectual and ideological alternatives: "When you have to work through the framework of teaching a specific literary text, it seems to me that there are two options or strategies open to Marxist pedagogy: I will call them the strategy of historical reconstruction and the dialectical or reflexive strategy of the critique of contemporary interpretations."[25] The first option, historical reconstruction, calls for a demonstration of "the living and ambivalent, concrete situation of social struggle from which [texts] emerge." This option, as we saw earlier, leads Jameson to invoke Benjamin as an ally. The second option, the critique of contemporary interpretations, requires one to sharpen one's own interpretive practice by demonstrating the "insufficiencies" of others. This combined effort of bringing the past alive and historicizing the present seems to me the necessary prerequisite for critical intelligence, its ground but not its stimulus. The stimulus is an intellectual situation that demands of students both choice and persuasive clarity. The critical teacher cannot succeed in radicalizing or transforming a resistant student (or an overworked and confused or intellectually immature student) by demonstration alone. No Marxist analysis, no historical density or entertaining intellectual complexity is going to rouse the slumbering intellectual identity of the newly bedazzled mind. The teacher capable of showing how texts and cultures exist with a historical strangeness that can be approached and named, who is able also to situate students among the interpretive standpoints that actually define intellectual options in the contemporary world, needs to plunge the young writer into an exercise that cannot easily be faked. The student who begins to see how alive texts and interpretive positions really are is a writer who finds a way to argue *for* something that seems worth defending. Such an argument is necessarily generated against opponents and potential detractors. Its chances of being persuasive are enhanced to the extent that the writer imagines an audience beyond the classroom and addresses the institutions, values, and practices at work there. It is quite possible, therefore, that a certain amount of autobiographical self-concern may be necessary as a way "into" texts and problems, not just into historical ground and interpretive perspectives but into the self-confidence that allows a writer both intellectual space and motivation. No fledgling critical intellect will go very far without some sense of self-worth, and this sense is not always encouraged (or cultivated) by classroom ethics. Even the radical and sympathetic teacher may overlook the oedipal dynamics that hamper the development of young critics.

I have no reason to think that such blockage can be charged to Jameson. I am concerned, however, about his underrepresentation of the scene of instruction, about the vague and rather conventional notion expressed in the essay "Marxism and Teaching" that "by inviting the student's initial complicity with these standard interpretations [comprising academic reality], you make the study of the text into a process of self-knowledge and self-critique."[26] That is a desirable aim. But my point all along, perhaps the central point in this book, has been that the critical intellectual and the oppositional teacher must go a great deal further in examining the institutional particularities of cultural order. They must look at the social framework of intellectual roles and, in doing so, encourage students to grapple with the forces, values, and practices that will steal their best energies unless they define themselves in active and articulate resistance.

We can think here of Freud, an interpreter who found himself instructed by his patients. So the radical teacher means to place his students before texts and contexts that will instruct them; but that teacher must know how much in the reading and in the pedagogical interchange will be lost or mistaken. Thus the need for a kind of humility or deliberate suggestiveness that does not *inform* or *instruct* directly so much as it places young writers before tasks, creating for the student an obstacle to be encountered, which is the student's desire, confusion, and misplaced or unused curiosity. How good teachers do this is mysterious to some degree. Each effective teacher has several ways of goading, disarming, misleading, cajoling, seducing, clarifying, entangling, and finally enabling emergent intellects. My sense is that useful teachers are, as Freud learned, themselves instructed by people who are on their way toward clarity. Strong teachers learn from struggling speakers and writers.[27] The teacher's role as a critic is to initiate and whenever possible to intensify that struggle.

Without question such struggles have an agenda that a teacher such as Jameson can put into play. For one thing, the immediate context of learning, the school or university, can be seen for what it is: a site of ideological as well as institutional conflict, a field of contention and dispute about the use of knowledge, about what constitutes "knowledge" to begin with (what deserves to be thought of as "true," as Foucault frequently reminds us). In fact, that struggle can be defined for students in the United States and elsewhere in much the same way Paulo Freire has defined it for dispossessed and uneducated Third World peoples, as a struggle to own one's own labor, including one's intellectual labor. The aim of the effort so conceived is for young writers to see how much of their own unfound, as yet unmade, identities as thinkers and "workers" (of any sort) is within reach only of those who name and thereby grasp their own critical relationships. My objection to Jameson's outline of his Marxist pedagogy derives from his overcommitment to, or at least his overstatement of, a latent and recoverable social "totality" in which Marxist concepts and their usefulness will "suddenly" burst forth for the student at the appropriate moment of cultural crisis or economic breakdown. If the hege-

mony of a homogenized cultural closure is as great as Jameson says it
is, so great that it holds the "Utopian" opposition of cultural and
intellectual difference (of political opposition too, no doubt) within it,
then what chance is there really that students trained to entertain
Marxism and capitalist commercialism simultaneously will turn one
against the other? If Marxist opposition and the concept of insurgency are dissolved or suspended within liberal mass culture, what social
or political formation will emerge, if and when capitalism falters, to
activate their use?

I think that Jameson's concept of creating intellectual identity—of
producing among the middle-class students he teaches "a revolutionary intelligentsia"—is far too abstract to initiate the sort of struggle
such students need. It is too bogged down in Marxist urgencies,
Marxist aims and exclusions, to excite much opposition to capitalist
"authoritarianism" or socialist "totalitarianism." Opposition to domination, hierarchy, militarism, and every other form of coercion and
oppression need not wear Marxist colors; but it does require increased political awareness, a task that begins with the *form* of intellectual instruction. The lesson here is to historicize the student's present
not in terms of a past animated by "social struggle" which can be
decoded, but in terms of choices that confront the student as unwrit-
ten possibilities that no teacher can make fully visible or supply an
adequate interpretive code to construe. In other words, the classroom
itself and the teacher's work are as vulnerable to the forces of cultural
domination and interpretive blindness as any text from the past ever
was. To demonstrate "the living and ambivalent, concrete situation"
from which texts emerge, then, is to prepare the student to ask questions of every subsequent environment in which reading is a necessary
act of self-definition and social interaction—which is to say, in brief,
everywhere, since critical understanding is the art of knowing how to
name social forces and their ideological manifestations within "texts"
of every kind, including the teacher's and the student's work.

I am quarreling with Jameson's depiction of ideological combat and
social struggle all around but somehow never fully in the classroom
itself. The scene he sets up to demonstrate interpretive "insufficiencies" cedes a certain unnamed but nonetheless inappropriate power
to the teacher making interpretive sense for students. The Utopian
and ideological possibilities he points to are not *there* in texts to be
decoded but are elsewhere, in the act of writing: in the forging of
vocabulary, of perspective, and of real human problems to be confronted or evaded. Certainly Jameson knows all this, yet he prefers to
look at the critical act as an essentially textual event. It is, as he shows

us, a historical and social event also. But for the critic, for the interpreting intellect, it becomes an essentially academic practice. Jameson, to be blunt, never quite situates his students. He seems to assume that he is himself already situated by displaying various interpretive methodologies, by deconstructing literary texts with a particularly forceful Marxist awareness. But as a writer of texts, including that prefatory text which the oppositional teacher means to provoke in his students so they may find their own identity and motivation as critics, Jameson leaves himself short.

I am not saying that Jameson has sold out or that criticism in the United States, even on the left, is bankrupt. I am saying that the recasting of preestablished institutional molds that keep criticism safe for a rather stagnant form of democracy presents more serious difficulties than most critics know how to pursue. The underrepresentation of this circumstance in Jameson's writing is not its final problem. He is both praised and blamed for accommodating himself to the critical mainstream. I would point out that this assimilation by the critical institution not only is a nearly inevitable occurrence that Jameson helps clarify—a fact of "the present-day supermarket of American pluralism"—but is actually part of his strategy for advancing Marxist theory. I want to point out how congenial Jameson makes his position to academic containment. Perhaps the ambition that most galvanizes the promise of *The Political Unconscious* is its concern for "the priority of the political interpretation of literary texts," in which, as Jameson insists, "the political perspective . . . [is] the absolute horizon of all reading and all interpretation."[28] This concern translates into an awareness of the perennial suppression of political interpretations—that is, of openly Marxist or radically left-wing interpretations—in which all political information is "recontained" by "an idealistic conception of the history of ideas." He is right about this, and every teacher of literature stands to gain an enormous leverage over old, unwitting habits of ahistorical interpretive closure by following his explorations of specific narratives (Balzac's, Conrad's, Frye's, Lévi-Strauss's) as well as from his investigation of "that uninterrupted narrative" which comprises class struggle, alienation, and history itself.

There is much to recommend Jameson's project, not the least being his concern to clarify the theoretical context of contemporary reading and writing. And yet, despite a heroic interpretive totalizing that seeks a hermeneutic self-consciousness of almost monstrous proportions, a brave if nearly maniacal urgency for *Aufhebung*—or truly, I think, because of it—Jameson never provides any real sense of the

institutional and ultimately political context that could help the critic
and the teacher to escape that "ideological double bind, between anti-
quarianism and modernizing 'relevance' or projection," which snarls
most contemporary critics who are aware of Marxist theory. I take it
that Jameson wants to fend off both old-style Marxists who flirt with
empirical certainties and their "autonomous" opponents. "When
properly used, the concept of the 'text' does not, as in garden-variety
semiotic practices today, 'reduce' these realities [i.e., 'political power,
social class, institutions, and events themselves'] to small and manageable written documents of one kind or another," Jameson believes,
because the idea of textuality places us amid the structural realities of
force and history.[29] The result, however, is that Jameson fails to show
how such interpretive work joins the class struggle, advances political
and intellectual solidarity, or undermines repression. The question
here is not merely how Jameson's theory will move the student or
professional reader to political action. It probably will not, and it is
not really designed to do so. The question is what actual constraints,
what real and namable blockages, prevent criticism as powerfully motivated and as intellectually acute, as politically concerned, as Jameson's from gaining adherents.

I do not mean to convey the impression that Jameson is unique in
understating impediments to his project, in failing to name specific
obstacles, resistances, and targets of opposition. The fact is that Jameson's writing makes these topics worth pursuing. Its sheer ambition
lifts his criticism to maximum academic value. Yet precisely what does
Jameson mean when he talks about "the hidden logic of historical
dynamics" or the "determination of consciousness by social being" or
"the mode of production, a concept which ought to end by raising the
most urgent issues of the difference between capitalism and pre-
capitalistic societies,"[30] unless it is that the cultural sphere (and everything within it that constitutes intellectual or ideological hegemony)
elaborates but also works in concert with the power relationships that
define the capitalist state? And if that is what he means, how does
Jameson's form of self-consciousness, his hermeneutic decoding,
open up the world of power that limits criticism by encouraging it to
be aloof or otherwise disengaged? The question for Jameson and for
every critic who cares about the use of criticism as a form of political
opposition—or as a means to that opposition—is this: How are readers to move from the academic world of texts and interpretations to
the vaster world of surveillance, technology, and material forces
(from the academy's practices to those of less restrained forms of
corporate capitalism) if the connections that join them or if the politi-

cal possibilities they commonly encounter are left vague and even doubtful? The result must continue to be that most people who work as critics will find themselves unable to move from one realm to the other. They will continue to assume that some insuperable hidden logic prevents them from knowing how to represent the affiliations and contradictions between theory and reality. The tacit sanity of this arrangement is that critics are not supposed to look at politics and the mechanisms of power, of cultural and social control, of institutional collaboration with the state's cumulative force.

We have two fundamental ways to identify power and its relationships as well as to identify intellectual resistance. We can, along with Gramsci, think of power as molecular—as the struggle of institutions, classes, powerful interests, and even powerfully situated groups (and, at moments, of uniquely situated individuals). This view leads, as I think we have seen, to critical interest in the forms and uses of authority, the way authority in some real sense makes power possible, or at any rate makes it effective in molding a civil state, a culture that stabilizes and helps to reproduce the state. Power, then, is an extremely contested operation. It is the result of choices, attitudes, decisions, and most of all of struggles that carry out those preferences and values. Power is up for grabs, and the authority of the intellectuals who verify one form of social coherence (of civil and political behavior) against another exerts a powerful effect in consolidating power's legitimacy and force. The intellectual, therefore, knowingly or unknowingly works for large-scale interests beyond the small institutional rivalries of the academy. Practicing critics and scholars may imagine that their efforts remain isolated within purely professional boundaries, but the effect of intellectual debate is to ensure the overall maintenance and efficiency of a certain structure of values, policies, and practices.

Thus "organic" and potentially revolutionary intellectual energy exists in competition with "traditional" humanistic authority. These two forms of critical identity are really variations of what Foucault calls the *universal* intellectual, who "derives from the jurist/notable and finds his fullest expression in the writer, the bearer of values and significations in which all can recognize themselves."[31] Against that general intellectual identity, Foucault offers the "specific" intellectual as a more accurately conceived contemporary figure, someone who carries particular expertise that cannot, without real risks and compromises, be aligned with universal or global interests. The difference between Gramsci's and Foucault's readings of the intellectual's political function evolves from divergent understandings of the power that defines the state. That difference leads to considerably distinct views of the structural position of intellectual work in society. Since for Foucault intellectual influence is no longer based on its general discursive force (its ability to persuade and set cultural and political agendas), since it is relegated to the particular knowledge or body of expertise that has an immediate point of application within the system of economic and cultural functions, the *specific* intellectual has a local political influence. Such influence amounts to the ability of anyone whose work derives from specific knowledge and training to direct or to interfere with the conventional ordering of professional roles, beliefs, policies, and purposes. Underlying this difference between Gramsci's general intellectual and Foucault's specific expert is the difference between post–World War I Italy (and prewar Sardinia) and post–World War II Europe and North America. In other words, in the course of this century the mode of capitalist production—including, of course, intellectual and cultural production—has carved out more complicated economic and professional territories based on greater diversification of roles, products, and international relations. Foucault's definition of a narrowed intellectual identity and a shrunken critical influence reflects that complexity.

Foucault's definition of power and its system of relationships also reflects a reading of the increased cooperation of capitalist interests internationally and of the knowledge and professional roles they rely on nationally, which for him prohibit opposition as a molecular struggle of subordinate against large capitalist interests. Power is beneath and beyond global political resistance, as he sees it: "power relations are rooted deep in the social nexus, not reconstituted 'above' society as a supplementary structure whose radical effacement one could perhaps dream of."[32] Gramsci's notion of the struggle of classes and of powerfully opposed groups vying to control civil space and its cultural and political apparatus is displaced here by the concept of subversion and the erosion of techniques of social control which define human identity and knowledge in its particular uses. Foucault imagines the struggle against domination, exploitation, and subjection occurring in the political sphere not as a contest of programs and policies, nor as an "outside" application of force and rational clarity against the state's order, but as an internal attack on the images and practices of expert knowledge which (in a tightly knit institutional and professionalized society) control "the simultaneous individualization and totalization of modern power structures."[33]

To look at these models of power and intellectual identity—to see the situated and contestable forms of power and the confrontational immediacy Gramsci constructs versus the dispersed and unmanifest system of power along with the strategic intervention Foucault announces—is to be given a choice of political combat. One may take Gramsci's focus on the state as an invitation to think of criticism, for example, as one among several forms of intellectual resistance in which "the taking of sides in a struggle between embattled groups" becomes an explicit political task, a personal and professional commitment more than a clarified interpretive horizon. One may equally take Foucault's emphasis on techniques of power and strategies of resistance, which intersect at "points of insubordination" in the social system, as a way of encouraging discrete interventions in the otherwise smooth functioning of power and its logic. The problem with a Gramscian or "revolutionary" critical identity is that, in the absence of a politically active intellectual community, without an established or emerging political base, "taking sides" becomes an individual effort of the maverick writer. The problem with a Foucauldian or "subversive" critical identity is that it risks keeping professional expertise in place with the hope that intellectual skepticism—which cannot, as Foucault admits, change the nature and organization of power—may somehow create sufficient antagonism to the system of subordination to sustain "a permanent provocation" that could at least frustrate technological coherence.

In the context of Gramsci's overt political ambition, Foucault's concern with discourse and with dispersed local practices turns out to be as politically vague and socially amorphous as Jameson's interpretive totalizations. The "specific" intellectual, like the "traditional" academic Marxist, provides little help to the student who needs to situate intellectual practices in the framework of institutional force and political struggle. The common blindness (perhaps it is a common disavowal) that links Foucault and Jameson, despite significant differences, is their depreciation of the problematic status of intellectual authority. Both Jameson and Foucault accept the authoritative role of the professional intellectual without finding any need to specify how, precisely, that authority supports or can be brought into relation with the victims of power each wants to champion. Such abstract projections of solidarity leave power—whether it is seen as in control of culture and commodity exchanges or as a structurally incontestable series of continually reformed, remobilized actions—unchanged unless the institutional authority and the political consensus linking institutions can be confronted and finally altered. In the face of the authoritative intellectual's interpretive agility and skeptical irony, the question such writers as Jameson and Foucault must answer is this:

How can interpretation, theory, and intellectual practice improve the world's material and political conditions?

Foucault is doubtful that they can, and Jameson, while promising an interest in just such issues, leaves us politically and even intellectually unsituated. Instead he offers a solely academic urgency "to go about the principal critical business of our time, which is to forge a kind of methodological synthesis from the multiplicity of critical codes."[34] Such "critical business" (an interesting phrase in itself) amounts to promoting and demoting interpretive authority, finding the intellectual means of reading texts with greater skill within the relatively stable critical community. The threat to Jameson's avowed Marxist ambition is his own substitution of verbal dexterity for the thankless job of building class consciousness: of arousing among students an awareness of the dominance of capital formation and its ability to direct or merely to pervert intellectual clarity and political reality.

Marxism, in brief, is easily reduced to an interpretive method. But if "methodological synthesis" is now the main task of criticism, how does it inspire or link up with readers whose persuasion and effort must pass out of the academy if they are to achieve strong results? In what way will methodological synthesis retrieve criticism from its commoditizing mentality, its ceaseless writing, its constant production of interpretations for their own sakes—or, truthfully, to advance careers but not to build an organization of people who might work together to train politically mature students? I think the answer is obvious. No one who writes criticism today can fail to encounter what Jameson calls "the ideology of the text," a phrase that points to the noncommunal and subjectivizing fragmentation of most critical energy in this society. Indeed, I think it is only fair to turn on Jameson his own commitment to undo idealistic "transformations in our modes of *thinking*" which overlook "those of more concrete structures or situations."[35] Jameson, too, succumbs to the priority of texts over situated energies. Almost every tendency in criticism—from its inflation of texts and authors to its reliance on an ethnocentric body of critical objectives to its focus on the individual reader and its adherence to the value of the critical luminary—forestalls the possibility that intellectual community and critical solidarity might be generated not by interpretive synthesis or methodological agreement but by challenges to the institutional forces that exclude most people from power, forces that subject specific groups to cultural manipulation and both legal and economic control.

The forces that thwart the exploited and underprivileged also thwart the possibility of intellectual and critical solidarity across fields. They thwart, too, the common interests of all kinds of labor that do not define themselves by reference to democratically negotiable public space. These forces are not alien to criticism. They are ideological forces, institutional forces, the force of knowledge (its habits and orthodox assumptions) used in specific and specifically powerful ways. Criticism as it is practiced in capitalist democracies is an institutionalized activity, and as such its knowledge, which is the production of theory and its applications, bears a relation to power throughout the institutional network. Knowledge carries the effects of power within itself. What does it mean, for example, to practice criticism in the United States today, after Vietnam, after Watergate, after the victory of the "new right"? Are these obviously dramatic political events merely passing disturbances on the surface of cultural reality, events that rise and fade from national consciousness, leaving the professional critic and teacher no better informed about the scope and purpose of dealing with texts analytically and perhaps even lovingly? Or are they, as I think they are, rather crude designations of a genuinely "political unconscious" within criticism itself: signs of the failure of literary education to create, in the "best and brightest" graduates of the finest North American colleges, the social responsibility and the critical compassion that moves from texts into the world and from the world into texts with a well-developed understanding of the human costs of intellectual blindness?

Regardless of the way such questions are answered, criticism needs a far greater understanding of the institutional context within which students and teachers do their work—from which they can see their work as interpreters to be situated with concrete social and political consequences. This is Edward Said's ambition. It is also lately Frank Lentricchia's. I agree with Lentricchia that "our potentially most powerful political work as university humanists must be carried out in what we do, what we are trained for. We might do it very well because we have the technical knowledge of the insider. We have at our disposal an intimate understanding of the expressive mechanisms of culture. We know how culture works; we know, or should know, that culture does *do* work."[36] I agree even more with Said when he pushes us to see how the political impact of humanists derives from their social and professional authority as people who occupy positions of real if also somewhat contradictory influence in the production and dissemination of knowledge. This relationship between critical work and its social authority is most often idealized rather than examined analytically as a relationship existing within the overall network of

institutional power, since "very little of the *circumstances* making interpretive activity possible is allowed to seep into the interpretive
circle itself."[37] The result of that idealization is a literary and critical
imagination, the young humanist who moves through the profession
unable to discern where critical intelligence and literary knowledge
stand in the world. The inference, as always, is that they stand nowhere in relation to real work and arguable social goals. The critic's
identity remains the unnoticed surplus of capitalist business.

7

On the Political Use
of Critical Consciousness

It's all against all. There aren't immediately given subjects of
the struggle, one the proletariat, the other the bourgeoisie.
Who fights against whom? We all fight each other. And there
is always within each of us something that fights something
else.

—Michel Foucault, July 1977

The sudden death of Michel Foucault in the summer of 1984 was
an occasion to mourn the passing of a writer whose work will continue
to shape critical debate for a long time to come. It brought with it a
need to reassess the political commitments of radical left criticism.
Anyone who read Foucault's work as it appeared will feel the absence
of his voice, his ability to disturb critical thought, moving it toward
unexpected turns and unconventional hypotheses. What will be
missed most is the seriousness of his enterprise. Foucault changed the
intellectual map. One can no longer view the world or history or texts
of any kind as one did before reading his books and interviews.
Foucault was the uncompromising theorist of intellectual subjection,
of the incapacity of theory in its present forms and circumstances. His
aim was to propel readers, by whatever means, toward a truly insurrectionary knowledge. It follows that he became the focus of much
effort to generate politically aroused critical energy. One of the questions now facing critics of a radical persuasion is the nature of Foucault's legacy. What projects will his work make possible, which will it
impede?

Radical critics in the United States, the few one can find, have a
distinctly indecisive impact on literary studies, perhaps in large part
because they are so openly political, defining themselves against the
main line of critical respectability, opting for a brave if somewhat

friendless search for secular moorings. The "threat" from the critical left is its desire for change, an intemperate wish to move intellectual work beyond the academy, to reshape society toward saner, more just conditions. And yet from the left in North American criticism one hears very little about justice as a social problem that intersects the critic's authority. One hears almost nothing at all about assaulting capitalist inequities with the political resistance that theory might arouse.

Foucault's role here is difficult to assess, since his writing sought a genuinely *strategic* scholarship, a kind of learning that stakes out the actual political and cultural terrain against which it means to operate. Simultaneously it offered itself (unintentionally for the most part) as another system—an antisystematic system of genealogical interpretation—to be decoded, debated, and canonized as the intellectual's perpetual bad conscience. Foucault is *the* theorist of intellectual hegemony. More than any other writer in our era, he plotted the complicity between intellectual practices and the maintenance, distribution, and almost impervious enforcement of power throughout society. Power acts, in Foucault's estimation, with a liquid continuity. Power is everywhere. It is seamless and efficient.[1] The complicity of intellectuals and of intellectual efforts, from his point of view, is mostly unconscious or unknowing, because power is insidious even when it is not monolithic and wholly unopposable. This is a significant feature of Foucault's position. The determining aspect of intellectual production appears to be outside human agency, beyond the controlling or resisting eccentricity of the individual writer. Thus Foucault's challenge to critical intellectuals indicts the arrogance and, for him, the fatuous self-deception of traditional accounts of the "knowing self," of self-correcting self-consciousness. Knowledge is essentially systematic and regulatory. It is dispersed among the relationships of social reproduction and actively directs human energies. Such things as choice and decision, the prerogatives of the single situated individual, are subordinate to the institutional context of knowledge. This is Foucault's posture.

The critical act is therefore threatened by absorption into the "power-knowledge" complex that defines late capitalism's institutional coherence. Radical criticism is particularly vulnerable to the superior strength of the "liberal" disciplinary state, an order that ensures its stability not by censorship or by ideological indoctrination (although the social field is saturated by ideological consensus) but by the structural omnipotence of relationships of force which are masked by the appearance of the creative and freely choosing subject. In other words, domination and control take place in the exercise of ostensibly uncoerced scholarship no less than in the more overt forms of subjugation that regulate society—law, police work, punishment, taxation, and so on. Power soaks into the tiniest, least imaginable areas of normal life and, for Foucault, creates a constant "agonism" (as he calls this unbreakable internal social struggle) between individuals and groups and the organization of force and intellect.

The important aspect of this situation for the critic is that critical work cannot be thought of as distant from the central assumptions that orient all other institutions. Everything in the social field is permeated by power's strategies. The irony here for "normal" freely creative critics who mean to exercise interpretive skill, as for "radical" critics who intend to influence the institutional force of the schools or fields in which they work, is the unconscious cooperation everyone lends to the stability of the reigning order.

The difficulty of assessing Foucault's contribution to critical acquiescence in such impacted territory is that his writing means to create ruptures in the institutional grid that keeps power secretly circulating out of reach of normal investigation. It does so both by institutional analyses (of the prison, of the clinic, of the humanities, of the family, for example) and by a more overtly political or strategic discourse, undertaken largely in interviews and occasional lectures and essays, meant to arouse political involvement among intellectuals. What makes that apparently useful effort difficult to judge pragmatically can be found within Foucault's central insight. In a world so closed and given to normalization, who is to say what concrete effect anyone's analyses of power and of institutional regimes will have? Since the hegemony of existing institutional relationships is so strong as first to mask its affiliated linkages and then to absorb or contain efforts to restructure social order, writers who make this their prevalent theme may well fall prey to pessimism or construct an essentially academic resistance. That is precisely what we have in Foucault's position as it stands, an ambivalent attitude of resistance and impossibility. Reading Foucault, one has the impression that capitalism, big bureaucracy, official science, the state, and consumer culture together constitute a Western Gulag. This ramifying carceral network subordinates intellect even when it erupts strategically, cunningly. As one reads Foucault, there seems to be no way to reverse the system of subtle (and not so subtle) dominations that keep things in line.

Edward Said's essay "Criticism between Culture and System" describes this overtotalized outlook better than I have done here, but Said takes a position against "Foucault's flawed attitude to power" which opens him to attack by Paul Bové. In Said's judgment, Foucault does not take seriously resistances to power and dominating authority which are at work in the world; he seems more devoted to pursuing, defining, and theorizing the closures throughout the social field which defeat revolutionary change. Bové charges that Said misses the real point of Foucault's work, which is to delegitimate the intellectual's claim to an effortless or unproblematic authority, an authority without ties to the hegemonic power of the state and its leading institutions. Foucault's contribution to the debate about intellectual roles and identities, Bové asserts, is his exposure of the link that connects intellectuals and intellectual practices to the "regime of truth" that all knowledge operates within (and in fact constructs) under the pressure of reigning institutional assumptions about what is "normal," desirable, and, finally, necessary. Said, in his estimation, has posed a serious challenge to Foucault's increasingly popular standing among left-leaning critics, but at the same time he "has chosen to ignore Foucault's figure of a 'regime of truth,'"[2] which, if one accepts it, complicates the possibility of projecting general principles for political conduct.

This disagreement about Foucault, to which I will return, is significant for a number of reasons. One of them is that criticism currently and traditionally is an almost solely elitist academic effort without social or political commitment to people who stand outside the circle of institutional authority and political power. The way critics of a radical inclination assert themselves professionally, as morally and politically adept people, will thus determine what kind of involvement literary scholarship and critical theory can have, directly or indirectly, with oppressed and unrepresented people. This is not a small issue because humanist knowledge and oppositional critical practices will find some way to join their persuasive public energies with the plight of systematically outcast individuals and groups or will leave themselves thankfully unburdened by our militarized, wholly stratified world. The choice here is graphic and not at all imaginary. The debate about Foucault's work, then, will have a lasting bearing on the way many people choose to define their efforts—on the way the critical establishment, as a collection of diverse academic interests and political inclinations, throws its weight.

Said's essays on Foucault help us to judge these issues. For him, critics still have partial autonomy; Foucault doubts that they do. "Between the power of the dominant culture, on the one hand, and the impersonal system of disciplines and methods (savoir), on the other, stands the critic," Said writes.[3] Foucault's reading of the power-knowledge complex that constructs the cultural coherence of contemporary society does not allow the critic room to stand as an independent agent or theorist of opposition. The critic (in this instance, the genealogist of power) is inscribed within the dominant culture and within the operations of power which he wants to contest. He is, in some undismissible sense, an agent of that power.[4] In other words, Foucault's understanding of the critic's position places the work of critical opposition *within* "the impersonal system of disciplines and methods" where the critic is an expert of a certain sort. Even in opposition, the critic's effort is a structural component of the cultural complex; it carries out the possibilities it has (including dissent and subversion) within the hegemonic whole. In sum, the critical intellectual is relegated to a specific cultural and institutional locale (the university, the laboratory, the clinic, the law office, and so on)—the chosen site of political resistance in Foucault's theory—because that is where the critic's small counterpower resides: in the opportunity to challenge a particular embodiment of knowledge by revealing its systematic affiliation with the entire ensemble of social forces.

It still remains for anyone in such a position to be persuasive, to influence others, and to convert them to an opposing understanding of what is at stake in normal intellectual and institutional practices. Without the power of persuasion, the "specific" intellectual is isolated, without use. The question of authority, therefore, remains to haunt Foucault's attempt to deauthorize intellectual work. Intellectual, critical, and oppositional authority of some sort will be necessary or nothing changes. Merely to assert suspicion about one's institutional affiliations with a prevailing set of conceptual and methodological habits does not alter those habits or cause others similarly placed to find oppositional ways of entering into transactions with the social world. Intellectual subversion of what Foucault calls the " 'general politics' of truth" will not in itself revise or reverse the status of demoted people; it will not initiate in any predictable way a greater access to authority and power among those shut out.

Nevertheless, the critic in Foucault's model is a point of interruption in the otherwise smooth continuity between intellectual practices and overall power. Said is right, however, to object to Foucault's too limited vision of critical opposition, holding out instead for "criticism, as activity and knowledge," which is "openly contentious."[5] Following Foucault, one can think of such contentiousness only in very restricted terms. The critic is dissuaded from attempting a general oppositional stance not so much because the base of critical practices in our professionalized, highly differentiated society is itself quite narrow, but because such generality inevitably replicates the profound categorical logic that underlies existing rationality and social order. Critics, as generalists or as open combatants against social ills, betray the disruptive power of their own intellectual obstinacy: "deprived of drugs," Foucault tells us in a book review on Gilles Deleuze in 1970, "thought possesses two horns: one is perversity (to baffle categories) and the other ill humor (to point to stupidity and transfix it)."[6]

One finds in Foucault a continual rejection of the bourgeois forms of thought and feeling that link people variously within divergent communal groupings. The perversity and ill humor he advertises are directed not against people but against the roles they play, the stable structures of approved social normality. Thus the function of critical opposition is essentially antagonistic. It becomes more like insubordination than dissent. Not at all concerned with social vision or with the mapping of conceptual alternatives for common political purposes, such opposition is meant to incapacitate the system of information and knowledge that organizes and provides content for a media-rich society. Foucault is as detached from (if not in fact hostile to) the notion of creating a generalizable principle of justice as he is from the idea of working to achieve a popular, self-generating democracy. His thought is insurrectionary. But despite its obvious militance, it may be ineffective as an intellectual position because it is incapable of fomenting sustained resistance from the very class it addresses, the professionals who own the disruptive potential on which his strategy depends. Foucault may well be right in one sense. Perhaps the best hope of creating a less tyrannical society would be to rebuild the educational system, to release political prisoners, most of all to seize newspapers and television networks so that such fundamental questions as the exercise of power—who has been and who will be in charge of property and labor—might become immediately important and not just philosophically interesting. But until that revolutionary moment comes, Foucault's position is self-aborting. It is desperate and a bit theatrical, too, I think. Instead of attempting to arouse consciousness and enhance critical choice within the framework of present opportunities, Foucault wants to rattle the foundations of major institutions directly. But "the question to ask," Magali Sarfatti Larson writes,

is whether the possession of scientific and technical knowledge can now confer political power upon its possessors. Implicit or explicit in the asking of this question is the notion that expertise, because of profound transformations in the structure of society, may be in the process of superseding formerly dominant factors of power: in capitalistic societies, the power claims inherent in the ownership of capital and, in state-managed socialism, the claims inherent in party position or in doctrinal purity. Expertise, it can be argued, increasingly provides a base for attaining and exercising power by the people who can claim special knowledge in matters that their society considers important.[7]

In other words, those who might join Foucault in the revolutionary destabilizing of existing institutions enjoy a certain real power that can by jeopardized by the kind of insubordination and resistant obstinacy Foucault champions. In effect the centerless power he opposes resides precisely here, among those he calls on to disrupt a system they uphold by expertise that circulates outside political inspection and political accountability. Aside from the considerable cultural and economic strength of both the capitalist and socialist state systems, aside from the booming worldwide population explosion, which seems all too likely to reinforce existing global divisions even as it strains political arrangements, competition for positions of expert power and privilege diminishes the likelihood that many people will risk personal loss for the sake of challenging such an anonymous force. In the first place, most professionals will not agree with Foucault's reading of the world. The experience most people who are comfortable cannot help embracing, somewhat self-deceivingly, is that their daily identity is grounded *personally* and not constituted systematically outside their own influence, as Foucault says. Second, the subversive energy Foucault favors is atomized, left without collective force or interaction. It is another version of the politically neutralized, hierarchically constrained expertise that has allowed capitalism and bureaucratic socialism to amass power. Foucault's "opposition" is hermeneutic or theoretical and not political in any actively public (and achievably revolutionary) sense of that term.

To some extent, of course, any critical activity, especially any theoretical activity, may be accused of lacking adequate political force. Theoretical debate seldom filters out of the academy. But is that isolation inevitable, and is it desirable? What kind of effort would it take to move criticism and theoretical activity into the world in some effectively cross-disciplinary, interinstitutional dialogue—to move it toward a general and sustained disruption of the stable continuities that keep political discussions of national priorities and state policies free from the harassing inspection of critically trained, textually proficient people? What kind of intellectual solidarity in what form of political affiliation could penetrate the tightly held control of the concepts and political analyses that dominate televised news and most public discussions of major issues?

Whatever form it might take, it would have to be more overt in analyzing power's centers and margins, in describing and contesting the specific habits of authoritative groups and individuals who control (who actively choose and form) public images, institutional practices, and most of all the setting of agendas about what issues are to be debated or inspected and, by extension, what issues are to be overlooked. I regard Foucault's form of opposition as hermeneutic rather than fully political because, despite his plea that his work does not unearth meaning but only maps the intellectual ground that transforms material reality into social and institutional regularities, the view of power he proposes is extraordinarily abstract and even somewhat shrouded in mystery. The work of genealogy and of the opposition it creates turns out to be, if not the revelation of a secret (power's hidden unity or strength), then something very close to it.

Foucault's work is dedicated to showing the determining constraints that produce individual and collective behavior. It employs a variety of methods to examine the limiting apparatus and normative regimes that restrict, modify, and condition everything that may be thought of as humanly spontaneous or eruptive. Increasingly his last work turned toward the "productive" aspects of power, the way desire is constituted and controlled by moral techniques. The constant throughout his writing, nevertheless, is the question of power. Foucault's position is consistently and more or less openly that power is ubiquitous, essentially unopposable except at specific points in the system where knowledge carries a definite circumstantial relation to culture and its entangling network of microfiliations. What makes this clearly strategic intention predominantly hermeneutic in its thrust is the repeated emphasis on power as an elusive interrelational phenomenon, something that escapes detection but is prevalent and formative, not subject to seizure or blockage and yet available as a theme or an operation at work in the whole social fabric which the critical scholar can account for—must beware of and, finally, warn others about. Foucault, in other words, is an expert at tracking an almost invisible quarry. Power's enigma shows up in his hermeneutic lessons as "regional but productive constraints upon the writing and subsequently the interpretation of texts," Said notes. More, "Foucault's most interesting and problematic historical and philosophical thesis" (his explicit hermeneutic goal, in fact) "is that discourse, as well as the text, became invisible, that discourse began to dissemble and appear merely to be writing or texts, that discourse hid the systematic rules of its formation and its concrete affiliations with power, not at some point in time but as an event in the history of culture generally and of knowledge particularly."[8]

Said allows us to see that Foucault's project is a complexly unfolding story of the disappearance of intellectual *practice*, an analytic narrative about the way power hides in routine functions that permeate society without any apparent source or leverage. Power, like discourse, hides within the naturalized, altogether acceptable and normal operations of authority which define social order. The genealogist's task therefore is to break through the appearance of legitimacy which obscures authority's rule—which validates the official discourse of prevailing intellectual practices by making them not at all a set of choices or interpretive acts, but forms of expertise with self-confirming insight.

Said accurately sees Foucault's project as "making discourses visible not as a historical task but as a political one." But if the political task of an interpretive practice is developed in the strategy it propounds for meeting, joining, and eventually inserting itself into the world of authority and power, Foucault's project may not be quite so political as it seems. Not only does Foucault constantly hold himself distant from any interest in the relationship between personal experience and the process of intellectual discovery, he explicitly disavows the role of individual and group consciousness in political events. This stance relegates him to a strangely unmotivated sphere of relationships, a world in which political resistance appears as a play of opposing forces in which the determining influence of choice, personality, and human creativity has been effaced by the superior technologies of social control:

> Every power relationship implies, at least *in potentia*, a strategy of struggle, in which the two forces are not superimposed, do not lose their specific nature, or do not finally become confused. Each constitutes for the other a kind of permanent limit, a point of possible reversal. A relationship of confrontation reaches its term, its final moment (and the victory of one of the two adversaries) when stable mechanisms replace the free play of antagonistic reactions. Through such mechanisms one can direct, in a fairly constant manner and with reasonable certainty, the conduct of others. For a relationship of confrontation, from the moment it is not a struggle to the death, the fixing of a power relationship becomes a target—at one and the same time its fulfillment and its suspension. And in return the strategy of struggle also constitutes a frontier for the relationship of power, the line which, instead of manipulating and inducing actions in a calculated manner, one must be content with reacting to them after the event. It would not be possible for power relations to exist without points of insubordination which, by definition, are means of escape. Accordingly, every intensification, every extension of power relations to make the insubordinate submit can only result in the limits of power.[9]

This is, I think, a sobering strategic model. It warns the naive or nostalgic radical that the road to social change is littered with the remains of men and women who have been "willing to risk their lives" to reach its goal.[10] It is all the more provocative when one thinks of the normal operations of reading and teaching texts in North American schools. How many teachers and students think of critical work as involved in social struggle, as an active element in advancing political interests? Despite the occasional Marxist or Foucauldian critic, the fact that interpretation and the analysis of texts are exercises in political combat has been denied if not carefully hidden. It is against just such obscuring of situated interests that Foucault's work becomes most useful. Here, too, his somewhat abstract estimate of structural antagonism between the vested power of dominant strategies, classes, institutions, and the state itself, on one side, and attempts to depose or at least relax power, on the other, becomes problematic. It does so because the critical act, once it understands its own relation to institutional circumstances, is capable of supporting social change. Criticism can encourage insubordination, resistance, and political alertness. It can help prepare for the destabilizing of points of control and of institutional regulation which make power not a "thing" or a "fact" but a system of loosely coordinated relationships that preserve social hierarchies. This ability makes critical opposition a form of general political opposition.

But notice how predictable and orderly all this seems in Foucault's depiction. Power and resistance are posed as dependent upon one another, just as crooks and cops are said to define themselves in relation to each other. There seems to be a kind of dynamic balance in the flow of resistance and response which links opposition (or subversion) with domination. Foucault gives us a static model. A relationship of power, he tells us, "is a mode of action which does not act directly and immediately on others. Instead it acts upon their actions."[11] That is an accurate, if also highly schematic, way to characterize cultural and political reality. It accounts, nonetheless, for the obscurity of power despite its openness, its invisible effect across the surfaces of daily life. Once power is so thoroughly desubstantiated, made into a capillary network of branched microshocks that cascade endlessly throughout the interinstitutional system, in what way can resistance to tyranny or to any of the concrete forms of oppression all too prevalent in our world be thought of as potentially successful? Indeed, Foucault is aware of the reversal of power's programmatic intention when, in *Discipline and Punish*, he shows us how the prison as a technology of coercion both hides the penal consequences of the legal order and creates an organized delinquent population that can be assessed only as a "surplus" result of the normalization of disciplinary logic. Science, law, social theory, architecture, the police force, "correctional" training, and any number of state agencies join forces to create "the carceral city" now overflowing with prisoners. Foucault's point is that such a massed ensemble of power relations works through the prison as an integrated technology for the creation of "coerced individuality." But "ultimately what presides over all these mechanisms is not the unitary functioning of an apparatus or an institution, but the necessity of combat and the rules of strategy."[12]

But of what do such "rules" consist? Foucault does not say. He shows us repeatedly, however, that the hidden hand in this display of integrating, ultimately cooperative power is a tacit agreement never publicly negotiated but rigorously enforced: the normalization of behavior throughout the major institutions of society. The disappearance of public cruelty, of torture as a legitimate practice and regular social spectacle, he tells us, severed the law and the court from punishment, thus relieving them of responsibility for their violence. Bureaucracy, the penal system itself, and specialized knowledge (criminology) therefore not only hide punishment but integrate it into the normal operations of a society based on ever more subtle means of control. "Prison continues, on those who are entrusted to it, a work begun elsewhere, which the whole of society pursues on each individual through innumerable mechanisms of discipline."[13]

There you have in miniature Foucault's major thesis. It is a view designed to infuriate anyone who believes that Western "democracies" are dedicated to preserving human rights, but it also has the effect of overstating the continuity of power and thereby closing off the very counterdiscipline of political resistances that Foucault's own position might elicit. "The carceral 'naturalizes' the legal power to punish, as it 'legalizes' the technical power to discipline," Foucault writes. But his understanding of a pervasive disciplinary power that frequently exacts punishments silently and efficiently within many institutional locations (the school, the office, the family, the military, the economy as a whole considered as a system of debt and credit) never seems to invest interest in the latent anger and profoundly self-conscious dissatisfaction smoldering just below the threshold of eruption among millions of unemployed or victimized laborers, a powerful force needing strategic political awareness and solidarity forged by common interests. Foucault is alert to these possibilities, of course, but he denies the role of political instruction to the intellectual as a public or semipublic figure who might indoctrinate the masses "from the top down." This is the pivotal point in the argument between Said and Foucault, since Said imagines the critic moving "skeptically in the broader political world where such things as the humanities or the great classics ought to be seen as small provinces of the human venture" which might "preserve some modest (perhaps shrinking) belief in noncoercive human community."[14] Foucault, in contrast, sees the humanities and the work they perform as preserving the image of sovereign individuality—the "normal" well-regulated and idealized self—against the false "liberations" of consumer society. The critic sold on Said's vision becomes, in Foucault's judgment, "the rhapsodist of the eternal," someone fooled by the appearance of opposition in work attached to institutions that enforce beliefs that maintain power.

Foucault's enormous skepticism makes the critical intellectual of no use to oppressed people. Or if a use can be discerned, it is ironic and inadvertent. The radical critic, like the mainstream or traditional critic, serves as an opponent, a potentially disempowering seducer of those without power, privilege, and access to intellectual authority. The political effect of Foucault's critique of intellectuals is to sever the classes, leaving no possible liaison between them, no point of conspiratorial affiliation between disenchanted radicals and the truly victimized. Foucault's position is essentially this: Intellectuals can at best rearrange their own realm. The outcast and undone must organize themselves. The lessons of the classics, and Foucault's own writing, cannot help those who have already been defeated by that culture.

Foucault's understanding of power as systematic—divided between material and discursive (or cultural) technologies, on one hand, and strategies of domination, on the other—depreciates the notion of human agency. Can we say in all this working out and working together of power and its mechanisms that the people involved in social combat are of little or no interest to theorists and to strategists of power, to political and critical practices? Just to choose a struggle close to the critic's home, imagine the difference between a university administered by John Silber (the current president of Boston University) and that same school run by, say, Jesse Jackson or, to pick a less preposterous example, by Foucault himself. The difference would be genuinely significant for nearly everyone who worked or studied there, even if not everything at stake in the institution would be immediately affected.

I do not want to propose a view that reidealizes the great leader or the revolutionary intellectual. I believe, however, that Foucault adds weight to the general political pessimism of our time. If one were to write and teach entirely from his perspective, something very much like the present sense of academic unworth, of humanist gloom and irrelevance, would come to seem necessary and even inevitable. In the last analysis, Foucault underplays and, I think, truly undermines the value of intellectual commitment to nonspecialized, global human interests. When one imagines Foucault's audience, it can only be those well-read citizens of the empire Foucault's work challenges at an extraordinarily high level of expertise and engagement, a level so removed from concern for the troublesome questions about political means and about the objective struggles one should aid that nothing in the state's counterrevolutionary vigilance needs to be looked at very closely. Theory such as the complicated, self-disrupting theory Foucault has produced can continue uninterrupted because, distant from such work as Nelson and Winnie Mandela's, unlike Gramsci's prison writing in Mussolini's Italy, it threatens no one in power. Nothing will really be changed by the logic of Foucault's writing. A few intellectuals will be instructed. Some will be enlivened by a historical and critical effort sympathetic to the oppressed. But Foucault's work shows the teasing incompleteness of a theory defined by its rejection of class consciousness. It is aware of its audience. It recognizes the necessity of political combat. But it is content with an academic authority that it questions systematically.

What other conclusion can one draw when the theme of normalization and its "productive" containments lead to a judgment that intellectuals "are themselves agents of this system of power" (which they often are), thus turning radical intellectuals against "the idea of their responsibility for 'consciousness' and discourse"?[15] If intellectuals are not to be responsible for their work, responsible particularly to the concept of a general public good and therefore responsible to some kind of support for and commitment to public political consciousness as well as the specific consciousness of demoted groups, then what can we really say Foucault's writing leads to or works for? Can it be for the greater clarity of a small number of academic critics and not much else? I can understand the inappropriateness of projecting the public function of critical activity in a country such as France, where the more obvious politicization of universities and the greater involvement of radical intellectuals in public debate has to some extent affected public attitudes but not the distribution of wealth and power and certainly not the institutional control of populations. This "biopolitics," as Foucault calls it, is still organized by the incorporated power of knowledge to count, chart, summarize, and finally define social space. But in a country such as the United States, where compelling political ideas of any kind, especially ideas from the nonliberal left, are seldom heard publicly (and then frequently distorted), where everyone who speaks or writes to the left of a fairly narrow political center is potentially a "communist" or a "godless traitor," the intellectual has a responsibility to instruct public consciousness in order to promote unpopular views otherwise shut out of political debate altogether. This is, of course, an ideal that can degenerate to self-deceived revolutionism or avant-garde theatrics. Yet the intellectual's responsibility to a concrete position within the public sphere must be fought for against a commercially controlled consciousness industry that will only grow more fatuous and successful if its intellectual enemies are weak.

Is it really the case, as Foucault says, that Truth itself—the organized knowledge that fosters the capitalist and totalitarian state systems more or less pervasively—must now be the object of struggle? Is it not political power and the control of state policies, agencies, and budgetary decisions that need to be contested? It matters immensely who runs America's bureaucratic juggernaut. But the issue of political power, and of the intellectual's small but real responsibility in the overall effort to shape a safe and just world, cannot be replaced (and in effect given up) by a total reliance on the salutary consequences of theoretical endeavor. The specialist (even the cross-disciplinary and historically grounded theorist) would then be affirming the distance between one form of expertise and another, most of all between those who know and those who govern.

This division between intellectual authority and political or administrative authority is the outcome of slighting the importance of decisionmaking, the fundamental place of moral values, and the capacity of individuals and groups to challenge oppressive policies and sites of power in a tightly organized but still not sealed state system. Despite closures and ill-conceived priorities within the industrialized sectors, the only way of producing sufficient change to redirect the scope and purpose of government practices is by political action.

I find in Foucault's work the will to imagine revolution but a scholar's sure awareness of futility—of the individual's immersion in structures of convention, regulation, and institutional control which withstand any attempt to alter them. For Foucault, individuals and individual activities are (politically) effects of knowledge and (behaviorally) the result of cultural demands and limits. This is Foucault's central certainty. Anyone who is familiar with the repeated celebration of originality and creative freedom in Western literary criticism, perhaps the major ideological fixture in the humanities, should appreciate Foucault's effort to correct or at least modify its habit of putting the single self ahead of historical and social forces. But even as I admire Foucault's stubborn attempt to make humanist scholars and critics consider the *effects* of intellectual work, to see the subject of knowledge and writing as itself a product of the entire cultural and institutional ensemble, I suspect his emphasis on containment causes his form of strategic scholarship to impede the political action it is designed to facilitate. Left out, or left unclear at any rate, is the way similarly inclined critical people might work together politically: how to go from the individual's impacted situation to the socially productive condition of group agency and collective action. Also blurred in his studies of the penal system and the family, of epistemic structures and the birth of the clinic (lost, too, in the abstraction and generality of his comments on sovereignty and the state), are the specific targets and forms of resistance that make freedom possible as opposition and struggle—something created by social interactions that elude containment and, as Said points out, cannot be reduced to texts or discursive systems.

The difficulty I see in assessing Foucault's intellectual legacy evolves from the fact that his writing authorizes a disarmingly cool appreciation of domination and institutional control. There is no question in my mind that Foucault is on the side of radical involvement. But his constant emphasis on the regimented and normalized institutional domain and his inadequate emphasis on the ordinary creativity of the ordinary citizen leave the political ramifications of his frequently recast theoretical undertaking up for grabs.

Foucault's depreciation of the individual's potentially powerful creativity shows up vividly in the debate with Noam Chomsky to which Said has called attention. In 1971 on Dutch television, Foucault and Chomsky discussed the question of human nature and its implications for political action. Their initial concern with Chomsky's view of human creativity—that innate knowledge of a universal kind is aligned with a "creative principle" in humans which allows the development of speech and thought—generated a disagreement not only about what human nature is but, more important, about how to approach the relation between knowledge and choice or action. Reading the transcript of that debate, we find a significant difference that largely accounts for their divergence. Whereas Foucault focuses on "the productive capacity of knowledge as a collective practice," looking at the creativity involved in great epistemological leaps across historical development, Chomsky stresses "the normal creativity of everyday life" which prompts the emergence of language, culture, and both individual and social practices that cannot be thought of as regulatory or repressive in any systematic way, but rather as life-giving and constructive, genuinely experimental.[16] Chomsky, in sum, grounds human action on self-sufficient and "fundamental properties of our intelligence" which lead to, among other things, resistance, obstinacy, and a will to rebel against intolerable social conditions.

Foucault, of course, is always suspicious of anthropological concepts, but one finds that his exclusive concern with "official" knowledge and with thought of essentially epochal proportions gives way to its own sort of anthropological identity. "Man" appears in his writing in the role of the expert. Foucault would deny that there is anything "natural" or elemental and a priori about the specialist. Yet the central place Foucault assigns the specific intellectual in a society based on the production of knowledge and on the worldwide distribution of information makes that function the prototype for human "liberation" as it now might be conceived. "Man" is no longer an integrating concept but a rumor replaced by a role, the subversive specialist. "Man" is the absence or categorical opening filled up by so many specialist functions defined by capitalist divisions of labor. The global identity of Man as thinker, Man as worker, is reduced to an instrumental position within the system as a whole. The generic type, however, is the expert, someone who knows precisely what can and cannot be done at a specific place in the system. This is not an essentializing abstraction but a functional identity.

Foucault's final position, consistent with what he wrote for fifteen years or so, insists that "the political, ethical, social, philosophical problem of our days is not to try to liberate the individual from the state, and from the state's institutions, but to liberate [all of] us both from the state and from the type of individualization which is linked to the state. We have to promote new forms of subjectivity through the refusal of this kind of individuality."[17] This is not so much a positive program of constructive political and social vision as a decreation of all those ways of speaking and thinking that posit a stable "subject" or identity upheld by, and in turn upholding, social hierarchy, scientific and legal rationality, and the sovereignty of the state. The role of the specific intellectual here "is not to discover what we are, but to refuse what we are" in our present circumstances. In other words, the Nietzschean hermeneutics that Foucault employs ascribes agency (true human creativity in its negational force, the opportunity to reverse the dominating consequence of social order) to his own position—to the Nietzschean intellectual whose authority in large part derives from a favorable relationship with power. That the function of such interpretive work is to reveal the secret between power and truth, to some extent undermining its own status in the culture, cannot obliterate the fact that the one form of opposition with some hope of undoing or obstructing power appears to reside with those who enjoy intellectual authority in the culture. The bad news is that the force of such agency, as Foucault conceives it, at once lacks concepts that could galvanize mass action and is blunted by the arrangements of institutional reality.

Thus the intellectual's task at present, as Foucault reads it—to throw sand in the gears of technoscientific rationality—is essentially disruptive rather than constructive, since there is no standing point or cause or ideal that could join intellectuals to citizens generally. The disability created by this hyperpessimistic analysis is not unique to Foucault. His is, I think, merely the subtlest and the most vigorously ambivalent embodiment of the political uncertainty of knowledge. As politically alert as it is, as politically committed as it seems to be, Foucault's theoretical work nonetheless legitimates power by making it appear to be incontestable except by those who "know," and who can contest it only by a form of delegitimating activity. But (we should ask) what if such things as science and law and government, areas of interest such as philosophy and criticism and literature, were all in one way or another delegitimated by consumer culture and by the inability of intellectuals to imagine an active, positive, and politically productive role in society? What if, as Jean-François Lyotard has suggested, learning is cut off from its traditional idealistic accounts of knowledge, history, and human purpose, leaving us with so many language games and the sheer might of information production ("research" in all its forms) within the context of a university that produces skills to compete within a global economic system but no ideals for restructuring it?[18] In that delegitimated realm, in which knowledge is purely instrumental and seems incapable of aiding the victimized or excluded (incapable of an emancipation function), what purpose does further disruption or skepticism about the efficacy of intellectual work serve unless it is to reinforce the dominant attitude—a distinctly nontheoretical attitude—embracing capitalist values and the logic of the market?

My point here is that Foucault's writing is severed so totally from the communally revitalizing concept of *justice* that it leaves us with a material regime undisturbed by the quakings of theorists. Only as theory moves into the neighborhood and televised newscast, only as the inequities of power and wealth become items of debate and passionate reflection among the population as a whole, can the force of ideas finally count in some way capable of changing, not merely reaffirming, the present distribution of authority, opportunity, and privilege. In this regard Chomsky's response to Foucault seems useful.

In the face of Foucault's power-driven universe, Chomsky proposes two intellectual tasks. The first is "to create the vision of a future just society" that will depend upon some "humane concept of the human essence or human nature." The second is "to understand very clearly the nature of power and oppression and terror and destruction in our own society." But while this analytic task is fragmented in Foucault's hermeneutic strategy, relegated to endless forays against particular sites of subordination and command, with Chomsky the hard work of political opposition is made possible by the seizing of theory as an act in the struggle against the autocratic rule of enormous financial institutions and the general coercion of marketplace values. In other words, Foucault succumbs to the postmodernist reading of a world so wholly bureaucratized, so closed by the hegemony of its ruling institutions, that opposition can take place only outside or beneath the political process. Since abstract and anonymous power circulates everywhere, since power is its own end and motive, the only way to "justify" political struggle is in terms of power—the infinite, scattered power of intellectuals and revolutionaries, without any integrating force or focus, against the infinitely dispersed but nonetheless localized and integrated power of economic exploitation, class oppression, state oversight, and disciplinary regulation in schools, laboratories, homes, and elsewhere. Yet this model of opposition carries the danger of refusing to name a goal other than the obstruction of power (or its seizure). It imagines the ordinary person as more or less co-opted, even trapped by the system, while subversion of a sort that might change society rests with intellectuals and anyone else who is situated at a privileged place. Not only does this model fail to imagine the role of justice as a political goal that, almost alone as a credible ideal, can arouse popular interest; it also defeats the one reliable source of authority critics might develop further—moral argument in the service of intellectual and political solidarity.

Foucault's genealogical method is founded on breaking the link between intellectual practices and moral accounts because, like Nietzsche, he distrusts the malleability of ideals and the coercive consequence of interpretation. In Nietzsche's terms, "the cause of the origin of a thing and its eventual utility, its actual employment and place in a system of purposes, lie worlds apart."[19] In Foucault's formulation, "the idea of justice in itself is an idea which in effect has been invented and put to work in different types of societies as an instrument of a certain political and economic power or as a weapon against that power." In brief, the notion of justice, he believes, "functions within a society of classes as a claim made by the oppressed class and as justification for it."[20] Chomsky's appropriate response is that, first, one must make "an argument that the social revolution that you're trying to achieve *is* in the ends of justice, *is* in the ends of realizing fundamental human needs, not merely in the ends of putting some group into power" which may or may not create a more equitable reality. Second, such a revolution can be pursued only "in the *name* of all human beings." And third, it ought to work toward "the value of decentralization and participation" by the greatest number of citizens in democratic processes at every level of social life.

In a society devoted to what John Schaar has called "bureaucratic epistemology," it is hard to imagine getting to Chomsky's world from our current situation. Public discourse goes on, day after day, as if value-free decisions were actually possible, especially where large, impersonal institutions concoct policy based on technological, scientific, and quasi-rational estimates of what is possible at any particular moment in the capitalist market. What is almost always repressed, of course, is the situated nature of interests: how everyone who owns power and policymaking privilege is invested within the system of values and exchanges called capitalism. The radical intellectual is no less invested there, even though the critical act, as Emerson said of Shakespeare's work, may seem to "take no stronger hold of real nature than the shadow of a passing traveller on the rock." Nonetheless, we can pose the situated context of intellectual authority as the first, most intimately contestable object of critical inspection. Thus one might expect Foucault's view of "all against all" in a ceaseless competition for capital and prestige to drive the radical intellectual, if unwilling to argue for attainable justice by whatever means (violent change, parliamentary process, or peaceful civil disobedience), to explain how theory and critical opposition to normative ideals prepare a better, more humane society.

Foucault did not give us that explanation, in part because his position is bleak. He points to the historically failed effort of socialism, which adopted the bourgeois model it might have been expected to overturn or correct, as evidence that it is difficult "to say exactly what human nature is" and what form of society we might hope for in a postcapitalist world. The truth of the matter is that Foucault is not at all optimistic about people's ability or willingness to communize and cooperate: "the proletariat doesn't wage war against the ruling class because it considers such a war to be just . . . [but] because, for the first time in history, it wants to take power. And because it will over-throw the power of the ruling class it considers such a war to be just."[21] This statement projects revolution in purely violent terms, minimizing whatever chance of social change there might be in a deeply conservative, tightly policed society such as the United States. It is also cynical: "One makes war to win, not because it is just," Foucault asserts. The banality of this logic replicates capitalist and totalitarian aggression, the "victory" of amoral power.

What becomes evident in this debate is the absence of any positive sense of communal bonding—of a politically achievable concept of justice—among contemporary critical theorists. Certainly Foucault's position speaks only for itself as one among many strategic postures. But is has become prominent in the United States in large part because it offers access to the appearance of radical action (or its theory) while actually diminishing the more complicated task of envisioning concrete social goals. Foucault's understanding of epistemic structures and the massive flow of interinstitutional power leaves very little room for the individual critic. Nor does he posit a way to understand collective action and political effort (intellectual solidarity as well as intellectual contention). "All against all" may describe our current circumstances as academic professionals and as individuals in the capitalist grinder. It does nothing to formulate critical work as political agency, a power to enable people to work *with* as much as against one another: with others outside professional enclosures who are not at all beyond the effects of such work. Chomsky's eccentric emphasis on an "instinctive" or inherent basis of human community, the common inclination to know and to speak and to share with others, seems far more able to get us (as a body of heterogeneous peoples) from where we live today, skewed for the most part by institutions and policies that serve no one very well (including, I would argue, the rich and powerful), to somewhere more intelligent and politically mature.[22]

"We have no political or moral teaching that tells men they must remain bound to each other even one step beyond the point where those bonds are a drag and a burden on one's personal desires," Schaar writes.[23] That observation may do a good deal of disservice to the Bill of Rights, which holds a singular vision of individual liberties that can be maintained only by just social interaction. Nonetheless, as critics, we have no secular philosophy of cooperative individuality to ground a statement of political and intellectual responsibilities as well as rights. Contemporary criticism in its "delegitimated" confusion about social and epistemological frameworks leaves writers without vision, will, or commitment to intersect the world as citizen-activists.

That aim, I think, has been the particular goal of Edward Said's work. Like Foucault, Said has been concerned with the containment of critical thinking in our culture. But real differences about what sort of repression or disablement the critical writer faces divide them.

We could, as Said has done, look at such a difference as an instance of the limitation of theory, an occasion to examine the way "theory becomes an ideological trap," since the tendency of theories and theorists, he tells us, is to wrench ideas out of context for strained, inappropriate, and overtotalized applications. The danger of theory for criticism has usually been seen to lie in its reductive rigidity, its tendency to assimilate nuances and subtleties to doctrinal regulations that overwhelm the specific life and contradictory openness of texts and problems. Now Said has given us a variation on that expectation. The danger of theory is not merely the futility of programmatic interpretive formats; nor is it the habit of orthodoxy, codification, and institutional self-enclosing. It is the possibility that "if theory can move down, so to speak, become a dogmatic reduction of its original version, it can also move up into a sort of bad infinity . . . a theoretical parody of the situation it was formulated originally to remedy or overcome."[24]

This warning comes in response to the way Lukács's powerful analysis of reification as the central tendency of capitalism, undermining people's ability to see how they are situated within a social whole, migrates from *History and Class Consciousness*, written amid the revolutionary struggle of the Hungarian Soviet Republic in 1919, to Lucien Goldmann's more limited and scholarly entertainment of that analysis in *Le Dieu caché*, written some thirty-five years later in post–World War II Paris. Goldmann's treatment, in turn, travels to Cambridge, England, where in 1970 it informs Raymond Williams's theoretical hunger to escape his own reified intellectual landscape. The "scholarly imperative" in Goldmann's borrowing of a previously "insurrectionary" theory tames the militant and politically insurgent force of Lukács's position. By the time Goldmann's use of Lukács reaches Williams's pages in *Problems in Materialism and Culture*, an idea (reification) that was originally meant as a tool for the development of revolutionary class consciousness has passed through a scholarly translation that turns the notion of class solidarity (and for that matter the notion of intellectual or critical solidarity) into "the expression of a tragically limited social situation."[25] Williams finds here a motive for reflecting on his own position as a critic distant from the kind of revolutionary struggle Lukács had in view.

A similar theoretical displacement shows up, in Said's estimation, when Foucault's exploration of discursive systems and regions is transferred from the essentially French history it deals with to critical writing altogether unconcerned to test what Said has called the "central reality of power and authority in Western history, at least since the period from the end of feudalism on, [which] is the presence of the State." Such disregard for the social environment of criticism provides concrete examples of the reification process, one of which is "oppositional debate without real opposition." For Said, in our present culture "the whole concern with oppositional knowledge (that is, a knowledge that exists essentially to challenge and to change received ideas, entrenched institutions, questionable values) has succumbed to the passivity of ahistorical refinement upon what is already given, acceptable, and above all already defined."[26] Foucault's unwillingness to embrace justice as a concept that gives criticism an immediate object of human as well as theoretical purpose lends itself to such emptiness. "It matters how we teach and talk about justice," Schaar reminds us, because the fragile link between customs, hopes, and constitutional guarantees of liberty and due legal process, on one side, and the establishment of general interests and public welfare, on the other, resides with current intellectual practices.[27] Justice is always incomplete, jeopardized, and subject to negotiation. Thus the appeal to power over justice vacates any source of moral authority a critic or a revolutionary movement might achieve. We need to ask, not only of Foucault's work but of the humanities and of theory generally, in what way they increase human agency, critical strength, and the possibility of justice within our economic and political system. These are questions about how people talk to one another, how they address professional institutions and professional audiences with an awareness of capitalist behavior and state power—an awareness also of the habit of professional abstraction which propels theory toward a sub- or metapolitical status. Foucault's error in this regard is that he has helped create, without qualification of any effective kind, the reigning postmodern outlook that asserts the triumph of science over criticism, of pragmatics over intellectual authority, a "delegitimated" world in which the role of the teacher and the poet is instrumental or entertaining but not at all emancipating. But if it is true that "truth" itself, the official academic discourse as well as the general cultural framework, has always been coercive, has always stolen people's best inclinations and turned them into deceptions or merely demoted them into a marginal existence, then the time has come for intellectuals (who know about these things) to speak more boldly about justice and its obstacles.

What could such authority consist of? For one thing, it cannot pretend to be conventionally humanistic. It cannot accept a smug irrelevance in the margins and crevices of existing universities. It will have to risk irritating and motivating or harassing people who own power in administrative offices and, for that matter, in one's own department. That hardly constitutes revolution. It is not even a first step. But a critical or intellectual authority that refuses to air the predominant questions about institutional hierarchy and the "justice" of devoting university resources to military research, that pretends its main lines of work are above or somehow just out of reach of issues that join the university to daily life, will be again no authority worth heeding. It will replicate once more the delegitimated authority of the careerist professional, someone devoted to a "field" and a dossier but not to assaulting the harsh constants of capitalist society.

The institutional context of critical work today is capitalism and its dogmatically pacified theoretical enclaves. Of these, the humanities provide the great staging area for contemporary ideologies of the fettered but indignant self, a self in transit like theory itself—free to resist or rebel but only singly, in isolation from others. The resistance staged by humanist theory is the privilege granted critics to write for a thousand or so well-read people. It is the resistance of knowing history and tradition without having political or professional structures to promote group consciousness, social justice, economic equality, and all the other politically loaded, politically defeated themes and problems that theory should support. Should make possible, I think, as active political issues in the classroom, conference room, journal, and annual professional gathering. If Said is right that theory as it is practiced in academic criticism "travels" somewhat adrift, perhaps circuitously, that is surely a result of the placeless indecision that defines most theoretical work in the United States today. No one should reasonably hope for a revival of Arnoldian authority, but the critic who reads theory and finds intellectual nourishment there can do so only deliberately, cooperatively, as if theory meant something intimate about the way people live in the society such thinking and writing move through. What is missing from Foucault, as from his North American allies, is not only a concept of and commitment to justice, something wholly foreign to textualist cogitations, but a sense of the political force of theory.

The authority of the critic and the political force of theory have always moved together. They have emerged from the same institutional ground. When Foucault suggests, as he does in his debate with Chomsky, that justice is a ruling-class concept, he feeds the complacency of the conventional humanist who does not want and no doubt will never seek to test that thesis against Marx's opposing view that society is not a zero-sum game closed to structural, legal, and economic transformation, a system in which justice must be the necessary ally of the underprivileged both as a rallying point and as an objective social goal. Justice may very well be a malleable concept. But every major idea is open to the importation of fresh perspectives, new interpretations, and deforming prejudices. That realization forms the central understanding of Nietzsche's genealogical outlook. History is the record of shifting stories and revised evaluations of themes, customs, texts, and institutions whose "continuity" consists of the startlingly new uses and meanings given them in changed circumstances. To see this (and this is where Foucault initiates his skeptical detachment from immanent historical depths and transcendent human purposes that appeal to "justice" or "equality") is to understand that intellectual authority is political—a political authority in miniature which takes on the legitimacy or the illegitimacy of its institutional terrain. The critic's authority will continue to reflect the humanities' uncertainty about social aims and means unless critics themselves form part of the reconstruction of social purpose on grounds that establish a profound commitment to justice in practice at each level of society, to an expanding and radicalizing of the democratic process throughout both private and public institutional life.

One either believes that social reality can be improved by concerted political action, and that criticism can be a contributing partner, or not. If not, one looks at the work of the humanist as a docile and in all likelihood defeated enterprise. It is important to note here that Said has carefully distinguished his disagreement with Foucault, as well as his overall opposition to cultural and political domination, from current versions of Marxism, which he finds to be "an academic, not a political, commitment."[28] In this, however, he joins Foucault, who has established an extremely complex but muted relationship to Marx while distancing himself completely from contemporary French Marxisms. While Marxism may be limited as a critical position for Said because it is politically ineffective in the United States and because it reinforces pernicious intellectual divisions and ideological exclusions, in Foucault's view Marxism does not account for the control of people through the monopolistic control of information and the disciplinary power of discursive practices, "regimes" of truth below most people's awareness. Instead, Marxism depicts social control in terms of the ownership and distribution of capital, property, and labor. (Gramsci's analysis of culture, we may remember, is an instructive exception.) Foucault thus abandons Marx's notion that capital generates self-dissolving contradictions. He develops Nietzsche's method of examining interpretive habits as "systems of subjection" in their own right. These systems "are embodied in technical processes, in institutions, in patterns for general behavior, in forms for transmission and diffusion, and in pedagogical forms which, at once, impose and maintain them."[29]

Stanley Aronowitz calls the logic of this analysis into question:

> Foucault, like all historians, is caught in the contradiction between critical philosophy which refuses centers and the production of historical knowledge which requires them. And in Foucault's preoccupation with discourse, he takes sides in a long debate within philosophy and historical writing. What is very important about Foucault is that he argues (I think in this instance correctly) that speech is *doing* something. It is not reflection of something else. One sees, of course, the relationship between that and the whole project of trying to eliminate the distinction between appearances and essence. Speech is doing something, and therefore it is what is positive, it is what is visible. And for this reason it is in the complex of speech acts as well as in the constitution of the object through the ordering and the naming of objects, that we may begin to see what the object of historical investigation may be. Thus, Foucault provides a critique of ideology in a way that no Marxist has ever succeeded in doing. That is to say, he provides a microscopic analysis of the way in which discursive practices become praxes and in the bargain obliterates the Marxist distinction between the base and the superstructure.[30]

Foucault debunked the notion of ideology as a target for critical engagement many times, most notably in a 1977 interview in which he accounted for the change in his work from an earlier concern with repression to his later preoccupation with power as productive in manufacturing and shaping desire, behavior, and moral and sexual identity. That poses a difficulty in Aronowitz's nonetheless useful assessment. Another is his translation of Foucault's treatment of discourse as a "complex of speech acts." Discourse is the central term in Foucault's critical vocabulary, but he never really establishes *how* discourse functions in the ensemble of social reality.[31] It is obviously an inextricable and governing component of all social elements, suffusing the economy, law, culture, politics, business, and government—each aspect of daily life. But how does discourse cease and give way to something else—individual motivation, collective political energy, a brute and ineluctable "social logic" of some kind? Such alternative "forces" are important to Foucault, but none is reconciled as a separate but nonetheless intertwined participant in the generation and distribution of power. Aronowitz "solves" this problem by converting discourse into speech, no doubt to emphasize the positive and constitutive, practical consequences of Foucault's position (something Foucault intends to do for himself). Yet look at Foucault's diminution of ideology:

> The notion of ideology appears to me to be difficult to make use of, for three reasons. The first is that, like it or not, it always stands in virtual opposition to something else which is supposed to count as truth. Now I believe that the problem does not consist in drawing the line between that in a discourse which falls under the category of scientificity or truth, and that which comes under some other category, but in seeing historically how effects of truth are produced within discourses which in themselves are neither true nor false. The second drawback is that the concept of ideology refers, I think necessarily, to something of the order of a subject. Thirdly, ideology stands in a secondary position relative to something which functions as its infrastructure, as its material, economic determinant, etc. For these three reasons, I think that this is a notion that cannot be used without circumspection.[32]

Foucault's position here approaches and exaggerates Gramsci's notion of cultural hegemony. Their disagreement about the intellectual's role, however, derives from the significantly different models of society they work with. Foucault's model turns out to be similar to "the smooth operational surface of communication" that Baudrillard posits as our deidealizing and hyperrealizing information environment. We live in a society, Baudrillard tells us, that substitutes the sublime spontaneity of perpetually bombarding messages and their immediate cognitive and perceptual gratifications (an "incessant solicitation" to lose oneself in "pure fascination, aleatory and psychotropic") for the relative immobility of interpretation, interpersonal expression, and both political and intellectual debate.[33] Umberto Eco's figure for such a model, borrowed from Deleuze, is "rhizome": a potentially infinite interconnection between points. Such a network necessarily supersedes speech or leisurely dialogic interaction, and it threatens even to absorb entirely everything normally meant by intellectual resistance, political involvement, and critical consciousness. The issue here is the degree of openness to be found among and between institutions, within the social ensemble considered as a framework of information exchange. How much room is possible, here and now, for genuinely creative action, including the "productive" energies of dissent and revolutionary change generated by rational intentions? This is a question debated by Jürgen Habermas and his critics.[34] The crucial issue is this: The model of society any critic posits—and the model of discourse inhabiting it—will determine whether people and events appear as autonomous or submerged within larger (and largely regulatory) forces.

Precisely at this point Foucault evades Aronowitz, who imagines "the complex of speech acts" joining "the constitution of the object [of social analysis, of critique] through the ordering and naming of objectives" in a more or less representational scheme of historical investigation. But Foucault imagines that such designation, representation, and ultimately ideology all evaporate in the more predominant, historically eruptive changes in which "effects of truth"—illusions, essentially, normalizations and rule-giving procedures—"are produced within discourses which in themselves are neither true or false." Where Aronowitz finds (somewhat conventionally) the "object" of historical research to be open to ideological departures and variances, Foucault (somewhat iconoclastically) finds it to be fixed or given by the self-generative nature of discourse itself. Discourse does not "refer" to selves, writers, truths, facts, ideologies, or material regimes but, for Foucault, is in itself its own object and archive. It is a system of operations unto itself. For those who follow Foucault or borrow from his work, this is not an unproblematic assumption.

Nonetheless, Aronowitz's suspect transformation of discourse into speech acts unintentionally yet overgenerously misses the full impact of Foucault's sense of power as something that "traverses and produces things," a verbal deus ex machina that "induces pleasure, forms knowledge, produces discourse," in sum "a productive network which runs through the whole social body" without being reducible to an inherently repressive mechanism. If the discursive field is as divorced from subjectivity and creative interference as Foucault says it is, then a speech-act model of social interaction grants room to individual intentions that Foucault's vision of discursive regimes does not. Nonetheless, in his realization that Foucault "obliterates the Marxist distinction between the base and the superstructure," Aronowitz may have come upon a significant critical outcome of Foucault's position. *Base,* we should remember, is a term that denotes a realm of concrete social practice; it introduces into critical activity concern for the productive conditions surrounding objects of analytic investigation as well as surrounding, and enabling, the critical act itself. In other words, the idea of a social base promotes awareness of the material *and* cultural bonds that join the critic with a general social reality that

holds everyone's real-life possibilities in very specific social formations. It does so by revealing a discrepancy between different kinds of
labor and their rewards, a discrepancy essentially between those who
hold power and those who do not. Culture is the social space in which
values and models of behavior necessary for the reproduction of the
system as a whole are negotiated and put into play.[35] By demoting the
notion of ideology, Foucault depreciates the repressive effects of decisions, values, and people who maintain existing inequities. By dissolving the distinction between opposed realms of labor and those practices that enforce values (the ideological process at work), Foucault
dissolves the possibility that a region within the institutional order—
the humanities, for instance, ideologically conflicted but capable of
both critical and political resistance—could be available for oppositional uses. Foucault, in brief, makes resistance to the established
order not an activity of "leaders" but a dispersion of highly localized
insurgent acts throughout society: the resistance of many deauthor-
ized experts rather than of a small intellectual vanguard. This identification may be the most strategically acute outcome in Foucault's
position, but in devaluing the resistance available in socially motivated
intellectual training it risks overstating the reach and the strength of
cultural hegemony. To ascribe all intellectual action to a self-reproducing "regime of truth," as Foucault does (a world stabilized by
the impermeability of its reproductive logic), does more than evaporate revolutionary alternatives. It destroys the use of criticism.

Or it destroys criticism in the forms in which it is practiced today, at
any rate. This is where Said objects to the malleability and the ubiquity of Foucault's theory:

> The disturbing circularity of Foucault's theory of power is a form of
> theoretical overtotalization superficially more difficult to resist because,
> unlike many others, it is formulated, reformulated, and borrowed for
> use in what seem to be historically documented situations. But note that
> Foucault's history is ultimately textual, or rather textualized; its mode is
> one for which Borges would have an affinity. Gramsci, on the other
> hand, would find it uncongenial. He would certainly appreciate the
> fineness of Foucault's archeologies, but would find it odd that they make
> not even a nominal allowance for emergent movements, and none for
> revolutions, counterhegemony, or historical blocks. In human history
> there is always something beyond the reach of dominating systems, no
> matter how deeply they saturate society, and this is obviously what makes
> change possible, limits power in Foucault's sense, and hobbles the theory
> of that power. One could not imagine Foucault undertaking a sustained
> analysis of powerfully contested political issues, nor, like Chomsky him-

self and writers like John Berger, would Foucault commit himself to descriptions of power and oppression with some intention of alleviating human suffering, pain, or betrayed hope.[36]

For Said, Foucault allows no place for moral choice. While Said emphasizes "critical consciousness, which loses its profession when it loses its active sense of an open world in which its faculties must be exercised," Foucault sees criticism as "a battle about the status of truth and the economic and political role it plays" in society.[37] The difference here is most of all a difference in the individual writer's status and role. Foucault believes that we need "to think of the political problem of intellectuals not in terms of 'science' and 'ideology,' but in terms of 'truth' and 'power.' "[38] The major problem for Said in this is that it condemns the writer to a differential function within discourse itself. The critical writer is no longer free in any ethical sense, no longer capable of choosing a strategy of opposition, but instead is inscribed within a totalizing social field, part "power," part "truth."

Said holds out for moral selection and political commitment, since without the persistent possibility of choice—which the moral, as opposed to the professional or institutional, subject exercises—intellectual work becomes nothing but an element absorbed by the system it advances even as it imagines real opposition. "Resistance cannot equally be an adversarial alternative to power and a dependent function of it," Said protests, "except in some metaphysically, ultimately trivial sense."[39] In this regard Foucault turns out to be the worst victim of his theory, since, as Aronowitz points out, he "is caught in the contradiction between critical philosophy which refuses [empirical and conceptual] centers and the production of historical knowledge which requires them." This contradiction shows up in his scorn for the sovereign writer (the knowing subject) and his methodological diminution of state sovereignty, which for him is a theoretical necessity for any project that turns its "researches on the nature of power not towards the juridical edifice of sovereignty, the State apparatuses and the ideologies which accompany them, but towards domination and the material operators of power. We must escape from the limited field of juridical sovereignty and instead base our analysis of power on the study of the techniques and tactics of domination."[40]

One may wonder how Foucault can plot these techniques without some sense of research that produces useful knowledge, knowledge that works oppositionally within the dominating system that allows it to be produced.[41] In other words, Foucault is forced to depreciate both the subject-who-writes and the state-as-sovereign once he commits himself to a theoretical model that posits domination in the form of power dispersed throughout discourse (and society) disguised as sovereignties of every sort, centers of deluded freedom: "sovereignty and disciplinary mechanisms are two absolutely integral constituents of the general mechanism of power in our society."[42]

The circularity Said talks about is apparent whenever anyone tries to make political sense of Foucault's intellectual choices. What he writes, after all, records a series of choices. Note, for example, Foucault's substitution of the idea of domination-from-within discourse for a less hermetic concept of repression-from-without (from sovereign states or centers of political and institutional authority). This absolutely crucial distinction divides Said's from Foucault's understanding of the object of critical opposition. Among other things, it accounts for Said's search for affiliations between writers, and between altogether different institutional practices, as allies to erode petrified authority and false values. Foucault, on the contrary, restricts himself to an apparently centerless genealogical search through discursive "regularities" that are invisible except to the historian of disciplinary knowledge.

One must appreciate, despite this circularity, that Foucault produced one of the two most internationalist characterizations of hegemony yet. The other is Said's. Foucault's "traveling theory" may emanate from France to invade intellectual centers throughout the West (wherever critical theory is at work), but it does not circumscribe a purely nationalist area. At minimum, it is a European (and quite possibly a Western and "democratic" state-capitalist) phenomenon. For instance, what if the seductive words that Foucault uses in company with other radical intellectuals—such words as *insurgency, insurrection, subversion, revolution*—were all disempowered, rendered impotent or comic by the hegemonic ubiquity of capitalist diversity and Euro-American power, by the ability of commodity culture to satisfy the appetites of everyone with rank and influence, even the critic, too? This may be what Foucault's theory acknowledges surreptitiously. Said shows us, in his essay "Traveling Theory," that even Lukács misconceives reification as an overtotalized concept; it is a concept unable, without the critical mind that opposes it, to clarify the falsehood and repression that reifying practices impose on dulled, appropriated minds.

Similarly, here in Foucault, hegemony as discourse (knowledge as power) miscasts its own organizational strength. Hegemony may in fact be somewhere between Foucault's amorphous unities, consisting of cultural technologies and strategies of domination, and Said's focal centers. Hegemony may be structurally specific (organized somewhat eccentrically by particular administrative styles and institutional differences) rather than structurally general, as Foucault believed, and specifically sovereign, as Said suggests. This last is subject to argument, because Said has pursued the relationships that cross and recross a field of study such as Orientalism, revealing the linkage between scholarly practices and what can be thought of only as a long historical continuation of cultural and, finally, political hegemony: the way a "strong culture" invades, absorbs, and rearranges or even deforms a weaker one, making it appear quite often that this subordination is natural and preferable to any other possible order. Said has shown how this complicity between scholarship and Western state power has helped build and maintain capitalist markets, that in fact apparently "high" intellectual discourse has played a major part in the exceedingly low activity of creating a conceptual basis for political and military domination of foreign populations.

By now such information should come as no surprise to Western intellectuals, but what will remain controversial, I think, is who owns responsibility for representational systems and for traditional fields of study that essentially remain closed to the unsettling influence of work as provocative as Said's and Foucault's. Something like doctrinal rigidity, adherence to "proven" modes of writing and publication, marks large areas of textual production in every interpretive discipline. Where closure is not possible, cooptation often is. Thus the questions critics and scholars need to ask, regardless of their feelings for Said and Foucault, are those William Cain has asked: Responsibility to whom? And for what?[43] No matter how hegemony is theorized as a partly conscious but on the whole more massively unconscious event diverting (and invading) the scholar's work, every writer can look at the intellectual purpose and the political consequences of writing.

The extraordinary range of Foucault's theory has everything to do with the fact that it raises cultural and political hegemony to an even vaster "epistemological" hegemony. Any intelligent change in the structure of domination, altering the flow of power, apparently can only give way to another hegemonic regime. And yet Foucault believes that the power-knowledge complex that constitutes our intellectual reality can be resisted at the level of local activity, local knowledge. For Foucault, that resistance calls into question the prevailing system of rationality. It distresses and in some measure subverts existing language uses as they try to execute values, laws, rules, and procedures that govern a particular intellectual or social region. In other words, this "transgressive" knowledge erodes the institutional ground it stands on. It "is neither violence in a divided world (in an ethical world) nor a victory over limits (in a dialectical or revolutionary world)." It embraces, instead, "the magma of stupidity," a willingness "to think 'acategorically.' "[44] This is why Foucault's danger for the humanities, and for critical thinkers who wish to contend against injustice, seems so acute. His transgressive logic is not overtly subversive as a "representation" of good power against bad power. Foucault implicates everyone who shares in power, who enforces some corner of the social order as it stands.

That assertion brings me back to Paul Bové's critique of Said. Bové in effect turns against Said the very position Said defines: "the oppositional manner" of a critical stance that "consciously takes on the function of the left wing in politics and argues *as if* for the radicalization of thought, practice, and perhaps even of society by means not so much of what it does and produces, but by means of what it says about itself and its opponents."[45] These are Said's words, but they ironically summarize Bové's critique of Said's position. Here is Bové supporting Foucault in opposition to Said and Chomsky:

> Said advocates Chomsky who, we are told, makes difficult discriminations and supports the struggle of an oppressed proletariat when he is certain that "an ideal of justice" is its goal. Yet who measures the *truth* of this idea? Who determines that the justice pursued is an "ideal" and not "false consciousness"? Who understands how it has been made an "ideal," in whose interest, and why? By what criteria? How is it established that these criteria are not themselves part of the "regime of truth" whose function in our society leads not only to what one of Foucault's critics calls "unmitigated malignity," but to regulative authority for intellectuals who continually reestablish their identity by exercising the discourses of this regime to reposition themselves in their own interest—namely, to achieve influence and an audience?[46]

These questions indicate, I think, the seriousness of the present conflict on the critical left. Without question they constitute an assault on traditional humanist and scientific models of authority as well as an intense struggle for the right to claim a central place among members of the academic and literary radical conclave. The issues and passions that drive this quarrel have not yet broken out very far into the larger academic work force. The debate remains somewhat private. A further problem is that the essentially ungrounded nature of such theoretical exercise—ungrounded because humanists and radical theorists are not in league with any ongoing, substantial agitation or political effort (Said disproves the rule, by the way)—makes it somewhat wistful, potentially fraudulent. Further yet, one often notes a suspect urgency, an almost incomprehensible if forgivable impatience, which at its worst betrays an urge to be radical without full appreciation for "the long war of position" that must be fought as much with strategic understanding of the stakes involved, the difficult odds, as with the mutual support of clarified material and ideological interests.

Lamentably, everything Bové says about Said's self-promotion can be turned against Bové also. His accusation that "Said's image of critical consciousness is essentially a legitimation of the *status quo* of intellectual life"[47] comes teasingly close to a charge of collaboration with ruling class interests, an indictment that would include everyone involved with the humanities. Surely Bové cannot mean that, but it remains to be seen who does and who does not advance the status quo, or whether the single writer is in fact capable of the kind of social impact both Said and Bové, in different ways, desire. For anyone working "in that potential space inside civil society"[48] which allows criticism to extend democracy by opposing tyranny of many kinds, accommodation to the banalities of capitalist culture is lessened only by the clarity of a strategy for resistance. That is why Bové is right to worry about Said's notion of "critical consciousness" and Said is right to expose the vagueness and the covert textuality of Foucault's notion of power.

What joins these writers and makes their views compatible though uneasy allies is their opposition to cultural and political closure. Said arrives at this position through Gramsci, Bové through Foucault, and Foucault through Nietzsche. Yet while the images of containment they work from are dissimilar, all three pose the problem of the intellectual as a problem of critical strategies confronting an actual world. Each defines a world that can be tested by critical work. My sense here is that the figure of a Gramscian or "organic" intellectual who is allied with emergent classes need not be utterly divorced from Foucault's model of "specific" intellectuals who work "at precise points where they are situated either by their professional conditions of work or their conditions of life (housing, the hospital, the asylum, the laboratory, the university, familial and sexual relations)."[49] These two intellectual identities are not irreconcilable, because the kind of work they perform is affiliated politically even though they are strategically at odds. Both Said's oppositional critic and Foucault's transgressive intellectual question their own institutional frameworks and challenge organizational principles that perpetuate domination. The difference, strategically, is the level at which that challenge operates and the scope of its possible strength.

Thus to say, along with Bové, that Said reinforces or in some crucial way supports the prevailing cultural order is to miss Said's important contribution to an awareness that the power of hegemonic institutions (and practices) cannot be resisted only "from below" or "from within" but necessarily must be opposed in between, in alliances between professional groups. For radical professionals, the fight against the smug, self-serving practices of people "at the top" demands others, similarly placed, who commit themselves to egalitarian values by joining as directly as possible with those who are locked out. In turn, to overlook the fact that Foucault, willingly or otherwise, stands apart as a "leading intellectual" is also foolish. Regardless of his attempt to position himself as a humbly placed theorist and scholar, Foucault was and will continue to be a world-class figure in the West. His discourse has been assimilated precisely as Said says it has. It is now and for the immediate future a master discourse within critical theory. Not to see this is to miss the academic assimilation that neutralizes oppositional writing in a society that provides room for intellectual battles but little for the uses of theory as an ally of actual political resistance. The reason is clear. Intellectuals have no concrete reasons to seek solidarity beyond their own professional ranks. Even there, in the exclusive professional circle, "solidarity" (such as it is) culminates in enhanced status for the well-educated few who project sympathy for the many.

Because the institutional context of criticism today is obscured by knowledge that is fractured into separate regions, disciplines, and intellectual niches, Foucault's notion of attacking the concept of truth itself seems to offer the most effective current strategy of anti-hegemonic power. Yet one must question the degree to which a global "truth" operates through these divisions. No matter how much intellectual (and all other) discourse is officiated by experts—inhabited, monopolized, and in some sense invented by the consensus that emerges out of professional arguments, a consensus that is, as Fish shows, the basis for those arguments to begin with—one of the most significant reversals of the claim to impartial objectivity is forged by writers who widen the area of any intellectual discipline so that it includes, and erupts within, public debates about the political force of specialized knowledge. The great function of critical analysis is not to clarify some nook within the existing scholarly order but to demystify the myth of privileged insight, which obfuscates intellectual practices. The most radical power of critical work is not its authority to win converts to interpretive agendas but its ability to make public the antidemocratic habits of expert knowledge. It is therefore a political task in a political setting. The effort of criticism is always, if it is committed to public welfare, a public act. It escapes by deviance and devious self-assertion from the purr of consensus.

With enduring clarity, C. Wright Mills grasped this fact. "It is in connection with the legitimations and the representations of power and decision," he wrote in 1955, amid the rubble of McCarthyism, "that the intellectual—as well as the artist—becomes politically relevant."

> Intellectual work is related to power in numerous ways, among them these: with ideas one can uphold or justify power, attempting to transform it into legitimate authority; with ideas one can also debunk authority, attempting to reduce it to mere power, to discredit it as arbitrary or as unjust. With ideas one can conceal or expose the holders of power. And with ideas of more hypnotic though frivolous shape, one can divert attention from problems of power and authority and social reality in general.[50]

Foucault advances one of the myths of our present intellectual consensus by remaining ambivalent in his challenge to authority and to ruling interpretive modes, attacking the epistemological unity but not the hegemonic complexity (embracing education, the economy, the military, and numberless bureaucratic forms) by which the state employs knowledge. That myth is the belief that expertise is private or, if not trapped entirely within professional regions, then essentially, effectively private, since expert knowledge and expert activity are exploited systematically by those who have access to them. Thus Foucault attempts to undo state power and expert authority by undermining the institutional coherence knowledge carries with it as its motive and raison d'être. Thus the philosopher becomes dangerous again. Thus, too, the humanist is apparently in a difficult position because there seems to be no audience for literary and critical debate beyond the classroom, the journal, and the professional conference. Thus literary critics do not debate the prospect of a nuclear winter with physicists. Or if they do, the exchange is harmless, another academic event closed to the world. If the physicist's ways of imagining scientific knowledge were to become an object of critical interest, if scientific discourse as it is torn from the theoretical physicist's vision of a mysterious but knowable universe by the intervention of the military, by the engineer's acquiescence to state power: if these were to be of as much interest to the best interpretive minds as the rich world of literature always has been, and rightly so, then the physicist and the critic and the public would have more in common and more ways of seeing knowledge function politically.[51]

As things stand now, the public has a glancing interest in the deep unease that troubles conscientious scientists about the misuse of science for military advantage. Only when a large public issue such as the Vietnam War ignites general protest do the bonds of citizenship between specialists and the uninitiated majority override the gulf that divides them. And so, also, consumers of the nightly news do not see the developing rage of oppressed peoples throughout the world until it explodes in revolutionary violence or mere frustration directed at television cameras. It appears in North American homes with sustained intensity only if Americans are involved directly. Otherwise it is peripheral to the day's events, a blip between commercials. The job of the radical critic is not so much to make these realities known as to challenge the conceptual basis for maintaining such ignorance. The radical's job is to prepare intellectual access for anyone who wants to comprehend the actual conditions—including the institutional conditions of authority and power—that separate people from the democratic control of their environments.

The critic's task is not only to question truth in its present guises. It is to find ways of putting fragments of knowledge, partial views, and separate disciplines in contact with questions about the use of expert labor so that the world we live in can be seen for what it is. Thus the virtue of defining critical work in terms of opposition to the state rather than (or at least alongside) transgression of intellectual norms is that it offers the possibility of defining criticism as an ally of demoted people and of an intensified political process. Critical analysis cannot be relegated to text-bound labor unless critics insist upon fighting among themselves for purely professional authority. That, ironically, is what Foucault's transgressive strategy calls for. The larger authority of the democratic enterprise—to put public needs and general human welfare into open conflict with the depoliticized mystique of Western institutions (the professionalization of expert knowledge in government, science, technology, law, and education)—can be fought for, nevertheless, by critics who work against the authorization of existing power by technical and professional elites. Such work requires not just negational suspicion, rampant skepticism, but proposals and concepts from which more just institutions may emerge. Justice requires that everyone have access to all information in a political system that develops the organized energy of once excluded interests and identities. This access is not wholly a matter of illuminating previously invisible discourse; it depends on the emergence of previously invisible people and political positions.

The critic's role here is to read texts and their contexts with an awareness of how interpretive practices guarantee or oppose the political neutrality of intellectual authority. More, the radical critic has to work to arouse students, colleagues, and everyone else within reach to think about justice and democracy as concrete problems. Everyone who works in some way contributes not merely mental or physical labor to the state's perpetuation but political labor too. Everyone impedes or accommodates reality as it stands. The state goes on as its policies do, as its complicated coordination of purportedly separate social areas constrains dissent or unleashes it. Foucault's purpose here is, among other things, to call attention to the way "truth" (the image of Truth, specific practices of "truthful" discourses) inhabits professional work of every kind and becomes an ally of domination. Truth, in this sense, appears as the tacit justification of an "open" scientific-minded society that promotes order at the expense of life. My objection is that by restricting political struggle to professional combats, Foucault enhances divisions between experts and nonexperts. He assumes the unassailable strength of the bureaucratic state.

Foucault is helpful nonetheless in showing how subtly and how insidiously an incomplete or superficial "democracy" relies on both policing and subjugation in their least opposable, most unconscious forms. This danger does in fact, as he believed, place responsibility on those who have the technical skill to contest it. Still, the questions critics must ask are how far that responsibility extends and what model of professional conduct is to guide it. In large measure these questions bear on the issue of the critic's audience. Whom do critics address? What should they promote as valuable and worthy of intellectual commitment? In what way? Said, we can see, encourages a more confrontational strategy than Foucault does. He means to protect the literary institution and the profession of critical scholarship, but he aims to do so by opening criticism to the world of political power. Specifically, he intends to confront those forms of power that do not hide but occupy privileged places in the institutional order, enforcing their organizational authority within accepted limits that work against the hope for human community. His work, therefore, struggles to reconcile humanist textual practices with an anti-elitist search for democratic cultural diversity. The term *humanist,* he tells us, is "a description for which I have contradictory feelings of affection and revulsion."[52] This ambivalence leads him to a strenuous exploration of the critic's responsibility and limitation. I would say that the major tension in Said's writing, a tension formulated variously in such books as *The Question of Palestine, Covering Islam,* and *Orientalism,* is the problem of crisis, which he looks on as the "form of experience that concretely represents the essence of reification as well as its limitation."[53]

Critical consciousness for Said is "consciousness that is given rise to by crisis." Under the unique stresses of social turmoil and both cultural and economic tension, such consciousness gains understanding of its class status and class affiliations. In moments of crisis, history is not an affair of the schools. It is no longer narrated and closed like a story well rehearsed. In moments of crisis, history is vulnerable to influence, open to people's choices and resistances and to the immediate persuasiveness of charismatic and rational speech. It is open to accidents, too, with their brute illogic. The determining feature of *critical* as opposed to reactive or reductively assertive consciousness, for Said, is that it disputes its own theoretical framework in order to comprehend the historical facts it must deal with. Critical consciousness does not live in purely meditative space. It is an element in a larger struggle not for theoretical clarity alone but for the right to make statements, render judgments, exercise choices, and create social and political partnership with the dispossessed millions left to hardship, deprivation, and injustice in ordinary circumstances. The struggle for critical consciousness is the struggle to build political structures against inhumanity.

Thus it is that critical consciousness works in the wider world as persuasion. This is where traditional academic criticism flounders, unable to agree (as a collection of diverse intellectual habits) about what to construct, which values and indispensable knowledge to work for. This is also where radical critics come apart, emphasizing theoretical differences at the expense of the larger, more profound possibility of intellectual and political partnership that could work persuasively in a world that agrees about such things as the need for hierarchy, patriarchy, commercial growth, marketplace logic, ideological combat, and authority of every kind but the one that speaks for and with the oppressed.

I agree with Said: the immediate hope for critical work is to increase its commitment to informed moral choice among the widest possible audience. Criticism will begin to promote human power when it finds access to achievable social goals and when it becomes less enchanted by theoretical enclosures, including such ingeniously ambivalent theories as Foucault's, which abstracts the political object of intellectual energies, immobilizing their public force. Merely stating such a hope does not help much. The impediments within professional criticism are not unlike those all around it. Critics who want to intensify the political use of critical consciousness will have to convince members of their profession that such activity is valuable and possible. Those who believe it is will have to show their students and intellectuals in adjacent disciplines, as well as professionals in different areas altogether, what options they actually have as specialists and as citizens.

Right now and for the imaginable future we have no intellectual, professional, or political base for alliances between radical theorists and dispossessed people. Both the theoretical and the social groundwork needed must be laid. The belief among liberal humanists that they have no "liberation strategy" to direct their steps is a vivid reminder of the humanities' class origin. Yet intellectuals always have something to fight for more important than their own professional position. North American intellectuals need to move beyond theory, tactics, and great dignified moral sentiments to support, in the most concrete ways possible, people harmed or endangered by the guiltless counterrevolutionary violence of state power. Humanists might focus on this side of global terrorism to expose the forces at work there. Since those in the North Atlantic circle who run one of the two colossal war machines, who sometimes circulate casual disinformation, are our students—people who have traveled through high school and college literature and writing courses—"we humanists" have our task and target perpetually before us: the next generation of leaders and the critical culture that breeds democratic citizenship.

Of course that task both simplifies and postpones the critic's partnership with the violated many, making it seem wholly a long war of position among normal operations. But it does not have to. The major intellectual task today is to build a political community where ideas can be argued and sent into the world of news and information as a force with a collective voice, a voice that names cultural distortions and the unused possibilities of human intelligence.[54] Were enough tough-minded humanists (and scientists, lawyers, journalists, writers of any sort) to circulate among themselves a problem-specific set of arguments that not only negotiated the technical diversity of established intellectual discourses but spoke from the normally unadmitted, unarticulated viewpoint of society's victims, the sheer difficulty of bridging both conceptual and ideological differences would demand clear statements about issues as close as the purpose of public education, as distant as the impact of commercial television on Third World children.

In the meantime, criticism on the left remains an anomalous effort of a few scattered theorists and socially conscious writers tucked here and there within the professional critical establishment. Their work covers a variety of objectives, from the effort to demystify literary history to the making of a specifically Marxist hermeneutics to the aim Said and Foucault share: to retard the unthinking acceptance of the still-seductive image of an independent, apolitical intellectual out of range of the powerful cultural realities that drive knowledge to dehumanizing uses. No one can easily portray literary studies and the literary intellectual as self-evidently imperialistic or as breeding small legions of colonialist ideologues, tyrants of a new intellectual police state. But the fact stands clear for anyone's inspection that most of what is produced as literary and critical scholarship enhances the polite but rather dogmatic insistence that things literary stay free of pressures, institutions, and contradictions that define political opportunities in our lifetime. The work of the critical left must be, as always, to remind its less radical colleagues of the importance of such issues as the intellectual's role in a military superstate, the political consequence of a steadfastly depoliticized critical identity, and the neglected social and historical basis of professional intellectual authority. The immediate strategic prospect for the radical critic, therefore, is to stimulate critical solidarity among the few critics who agree to such goals.

The problem beyond this task can be found in many forms at many levels of the social hierarchy. It is the problem of human fears and human hatreds. It is the problem of misunderstanding as well as disagreement that follows differences of heritage, ethnic and racial identity, political combat, and religious principle. Putting the political problem that faces the critic who seeks to advance justice as a problem of historical blockage (a story of traditional limitations of monumental proportions) almost stops critical consciousness in its tracks. But this impasse is not merely given, a factual certainty closed and unmovable, a fatality. People not only conform to the homogenizing logic of cultural orders but express creative energies, stylistic and interpersonal deviance. These differences are means, unique to each region and neighborhood, of evading dominant cultures. They are the grounds for *human* as opposed to *systematic* power. Despite miscomprehension, disagreement, and overt hostility, people of diverse interests, abilities, and traditions cooperate in concrete ways that can be strengthened by active political involvement. Therefore the struggle for a human community beyond the domination of manipulative images and exploitive policies resides in the political process and can only culminate in a political process more rigorously inclusive.

In the United States, community identities and political attitudes are kept in a reified form that denies class consciousness and thus the possibility of revolutionary alliances. Humanist education and traditional critical practices have played a major role in maintaining that stalemate. They have consistently depoliticized their work, or pretended to, and insisted upon a severe separation from social and political reality. As a consequence, thousands of humanists and millions of students in the world's wealthiest nation have been convinced that serious intellectual work is uncommitted, value-neutral. Whatever communally creative efforts criticism might have produced— promoting arguments and knowledge that enhance democracy, for example—disappeared in the contemplative historical outlook literary study has exercised. It has been an institution, uniquely placed in the culture, more interested in reproducing its own political obedience to the ethic of professional good sense (obedient to a market that does not want cultural and political differences let loose) than in charging itself and its students with the passion to act intelligently, morally, on the evidence of exclusion, intolerance, pacification, and injustice.

My question for Said, then, one to which I hold myself also, is this: How, given the self-defined impotence and actual political obstruction of the humanities as an institution (a fact that creates not just uncertainty on the left but repeated professional retrenchment by liberals), will radical critics "reopen the blocked social processes ceding objective representation (hence power) of the world to a small coterie of experts and their clients"? What disruptive conceptual and institutional force could stimulate largely self-absorbed intellectuals "to consider that the audience for literacy is not a closed circle of three thousand professional critics but the community of human beings living in society"? This effort involves "the recovery of a history hitherto either misrepresented or rendered invisible," as Said suggests. That is the history of people and cultures left out of daily Western awareness. It is, simultaneously, a history of the Western cultural system, its forms of capturing, describing, and finally incapacitating those people and their ways of being human. Still, the active interference Said proposes, "a crossing of borders and obstacles, a determined attempt to generalize exactly at those points where generalizations seem impossible to make,"[55] will need intellectual affiliation—critical solidarity with specifically political aims—of a kind to this point unimaginable among humanists and, for that matter, among members of the critical left.

In this regard Bové is helpful when he recognizes that "radically critical intellectuals must understand the historical specificity of the cultural practices of their own period with an eye to bringing their own practice and discourse in line with other oppositional forces in a society struggling against hegemonic manipulation and state violence."[56] Magali Sarfatti Larson's *Rise of Professionalism,* Thomas L. Haskell's essays ("Professionalization as Cultural Reform" and "Professionalism *versus* Capitalism"), and Burton J. Bledstein's *Culture of Professionalism* provide some of that history.[57] Nonetheless, despite a considerable amount of writing by Marxists, Foucauldians, feminists, and other intellectuals contributing to that work, this effort threatens to remain a romance of the left. It will not become a politically or theoretically effective practice, a "struggle" in any viable sense of that term, until oppositional critics of various sorts create a collective strategy, a genuinely shared pedagogical and theoretical activity that puts them in contact with one another in more restlessly experimental, more strategically decisive formats than intellectual work now possesses. How can the nostalgic notion of an "intellectual community" become something forceful, no longer a sentiment gusting through books and journals, unless oppositional critics share intellectual energy in social forms that persuade less radical teachers and critics to join work that has constructive goals and objective content? There is room for disagreement within such a union. But the effort to reveal the institutional context of critical activity as a political realm with political responsibilities that are wholly public is necessary to educate those who do not see that interpretive practices are unavoidably political acts that in themselves, within their diversity and competition for authority, create a politics of knowledge in which social justice or injustice is the final result.

Said is right. "Consciousness goes beyond empirical givens and comprehends, without actually experiencing, history, totality, and society as a whole—precisely those unities that reification had both concealed and denied."[58] Foucault is also right. "Humanism is based on the desire to change the ideological system without altering institutions; and reformers wish to change the institution without touching the ideological system. Revolutionary action, on the contrary, is defined as the simultaneous agitation of consciousness and institutions; this implies that we attack the relationships of power through the notions and institutions that function as their instruments, armature, and armor. Do you think that the teaching of philosophy—and its moral codes—would remain unchanged if the penal system collapsed?"[59]

Foucault's provocative question recalls the beginning of the French Revolution and poses the unthinkable possibility of disbanding the carceral network that, too lenient, too punitive, divides the general populace just as the issue of a political role for criticism divides humanists. The ratio in each case is stable. Nonetheless, unlike Foucault and Bové, perhaps unlike Said too, I think the humanities offer the least coercive (if also one of the least likely) places in our society where cultural differences and opposition to state tyranny could join intellectual practices that work for international human solidarity. That is my Utopian aim. What remains, for anyone who seeks artistic skill where militarism and the free market reign, is to make each argument that fosters such fragile light. Not at all clear, still, is the degree to which the self-contestation of critical writing will continue to perpetuate theory without political commitment to exploited peoples who sustain intellectual work by their labor, and their poverty, while remaining without political representation. In this respect Gramsci has outthought his critics. If professional intellectuals relinquished just that self-concern which prolongs insularity and spoke to one another as people who have power to challenge violent authority and authority's violence (which they do), demoted people everywhere would have representation in the only culture capable of changing the world's material order.

Notes

1 On the Road to Work: Introduction

1. Anthony Giddens points out that the "institutional separation of the 'economic' from the 'political' has long been treated as a major characterization of capitalism by many authors, both Marxist and non-Marxist." But in truth there is "a definite sense in which economic and political relations are more closely integrated in capitalism than they ever were previously" in any form of society. One of my major points in this book is that literary critics, theorists of criticism, and teachers of various kinds of textual study all play a part in the political organization of democratic state capitalism—"our" form of political and economic social integration. The relation their work has to the economy and to the state as a whole needs clarification, but most of all it needs recognition and attention by literary intellectuals who have been "contained" by this separation of politics from the economic realm, which, as Giddens notes, "is best described as one of *insulation*" and which, more disturbing yet, keeps critical writers (concerned with cultural realities) distant from the central social, economic, technological, and political problems of our time. See Anthony Giddens, *A Contemporary Critique of Historical Materialism*, vol. 1 (Berkeley: University of California Press, 1981), pp. 125–28.

Note, with regard to the concept of work, Marx's statements in the *Paris Manuscripts:* "Private property has made us so stupid and one-sided that an object is only *ours* when we have it—when it exists for us as capital, or when it is directly possessed, eaten, drunk, worn, inhabited, etc.—in short, when it is *used* by us." Marx's seminal insight, his nearly (and ironically) Emersonian stress, is that all labor under the appetite of capital's abstraction drains the possibilities of communal exchange in favor of private, reductive exchanges both mediated and supervised by the conditions of ownership and possessive individualism. Work is thus sedimented in each act and item, in the scholar's text and the poet's song no less than in the market's open exploitation of

197

people kept from radical forms of collective action by the drudgery of manual labor and the hegemonic tyranny of cultural images celebrating the freedom of those who do not work so painfully or unrewardingly.

2. I have in mind an emphasis much like William Greider's in his discussion of the North American press:

> I still hold an old-fashioned faith in the democratic process, a corny belief that public opinion can still govern the governors in this great nation. If the public is adequately informed, that is. The news media are the essential fulcrum in that equation.
>
> When the press uses its freedom heroically, as did Bob Woodward and Carl Bernstein in the Watergate scandal, the public finds its way to the truth and the republic is literally saved from degradation. If the press is timid or intimidated, the public dialogue becomes clouded and confused, and empty promises pass for truth.
>
> Today, my impression is that the press is in retreat. It seems to be pulling in its lances, taking fewer risks, avoiding the hard and the nasty confrontations it would have zealously pursued five or ten years ago. Yes, on some days, the press still infuriates the government, exposes larcenous politicians or directs its beam at social injustices. And that's just what its critics (and the politicians) are always complaining about: Why doesn't the press quit making trouble and just report the news? [Greider, *Boston Globe,* January 14, 1984, p. 11]

My sense is that the humanities also have been in retreat for some time and that the social function of critical theory is in doubt if not in ruins. One sign of that retreat is the instant rejection of a figure as striking as the one Greider celebrates. The image of the heroic critic at war with social injustice (or for that matter at war with interpretive vertigo) does not sell. It is as foreign to the current critical ethos as it is to journalists, apparently. But what role are critics to play in the absence of any agreed-on model of intellectual purpose? The one thing that most defines the humanities today is intense competition for critical authority and intellectual legitimacy, an ever-widening combat that makes it less likely that any person or any position will emerge victorious. The resulting pluralism that defines the status quo also generates dissent. The cumulative effect is comic or tragic institutional disablement, a scene that is humorous for its intensified normality or lamentable because of energies and opportunities wasted. I think the courageously embattled figure is unpersuasive whether it is cast in the imagery of political warfare or in that of textual combat and the clash of authorial wills, as Harold Bloom's domesticated version of ideological strife projects.

The path that critics and teachers might now take is as unclear as the muddled standoff between Greider's confrontational position and Edward Jay Epstein's opposing sense of critical defeat. For Greider, "there is an antidote to the news media's new passivity: public pressure. Those voices of political dissent and contradictory analysis must bang on the door and raise a holy stew, demanding attention. It's not easy to do, but editors and reporters do respond to a lot of noise. They hate to discover that there are vast events under way in society that they as professional observers did not perceive." Contrast this with Epstein's somewhat gloomy conclusion:

> If the version of the news presented on network television is fixed to a large extent by organizational requirements, the prognosis for change is severely limited. The systematic distortions of events which journalistic critics, conservatives, radicals and social scientists point to will not be remedied by more enlightened executives, the education of journalists, different personnel, the politicization of recruitment—which, ironically, both conservative and radical critics advocate—or the availability of data from the academic world. As long as the requisites remain essentially the same, network news can be expected to define American society by the problems of a few urban areas rather than the entire nation, by action rather than ideas, by dramatic protests rather than substantive contradictions, by rhetorical dialogues rather than the resolution of issues, by elite news makers rather than economic and social structures, by atypical rather than typical views, and by synthetic national themes rather than disparate local events. [Edward Jay Epstein, *News from Nowhere* (New York: Random House, 1973), p. 272]

3. The notion of critical work, of intellectual usefulness, should not overlook objections that writers as different as Jürgen Habermas and Jean Baudrillard pose to vocabularies emphasizing (or depending upon) the useful, productive energies of intellectual endeavor. Specifically, the language of work or productivity carries an immanent danger of reinforcing either the technological rationality that drives and divides our society (Habermas's critique) or the petrified utilitarianism that miscomprehends the actual symbolic density and irrationality of a media-saturated society (Baudrillard's critique).

Note, for example, Baudrillard's charge that a production or work model is essentially nostalgic, an outlived reference within our contemporary reality, a world he sees as organized by the law of structural value. In brief, the "natural law" of value—the use of nature and the use of things in nature—which Marx overturned in his critique of the "commodity law" of value that arose with industrial capitalism's expanding markets, has been displaced one stage higher or further from its apparently concrete ground. Today, Baudrillard asserts, we live within neither the first nor the second order—neither in natural law nor in commodity or exchange law, the realm of political economy. Today we live under the law of simulation in a world of endlessly changing *codes*—a law of structural value that creates a social order of hyperrealistic images disconnected from any determinate use-value. This move away from realistic and representational vocabularies not only enlarges the extent of the new cybernetic order but dimishes the fact of ideological and institutional (for that matter of international) conflicts. Baudrillard feels that "we need a symbolic violence more powerful than any political violence" if critical activity is to be genuinely oppositional (i.e., effective). The paradox of this position should be fairly evident. See Jean Baudrillard, "Forgetting Foucault," *Humanities in*

Society 3, no. 1 (1980), and "The Structural Law of Value," in *The Structural Allegory*, ed. John Fekete (Minneapolis: University of Minnesota Press, 1984).

Habermas's position, in contrast, separates work from communication (or from communicative "competence"). Habermas's essentially productivist and reductive definition of work neglects the interactive and transformative possibilities of workers' resistance. First, although his position is still evolving, to this point he has embraced a concept of reason, of communicative rationality, that stands outside the technocratic and productive institutional field. Intellectual effort, work no less than any other, is thus divided from the putatively more submerged, less communication-oriented forms of work that drive our society. In sum, we find a representationist definition of reason and of communication in much of Habermas's writing. In that scheme creativity, imagination, invention, and the power of intelligently transforming the social order all reside in the noninstrumental world: work and communication are separate areas of social domination. Thus the "solution" for the endemic (and repressed) crises of capitalism will be found in undoing the deformed communication structure we all live with. The similarity with Baudrillard here is not without problems, but one of them is not their deep agreement about the depoliticized status of work in the present configuration of critical activity.

These positions make clear, perhaps inadvertently, that a rhetoric of critical work needs to place itself within a critique of knowing—its pragmatic, tactical, and political emphasis needs an epistemological clarity that examines the conditions of knowledge and the actual limits on and of thinking, reading, and writing—if it is not to recreate an invisible but nonetheless fatal idealism even as it pushes, polemically or otherwise, for a de-idealized dedication to name the institutional context of intellectual authority. Here Derrida's work can help, even though, too heterogeneous and complex to be confronted as a whole, it has been shown to carry the "autonomization of the formal principle" that is possibly "the dominant cybernetic paradigm" in what John Fekete and others are beginning to call a "structural allegory"—structuralism's and poststructuralism's fascination with "an anti-foundationalist language paradigm" that excludes "foundational factors extrinsic to the text." This perspective of endlessly generated texts and interpretations without sufficient reference, grounding, or oppositional force (without adequate conceptual density of an interinstitutional capacity) picks up Baudrillard's understanding and turns it upon academic criticism as it stands. No term, gesture, vocabulary, or critical program is going to relieve the inherent turbulence of this general cultural situation. Thus my emphasis on critical *work* accepts its indeterminate fate as an ideological accent that means to direct analytic energies toward examining the actual outcomes of intellectual practices.

We are, as Fekete realizes, left then to work with texts in order to get beyond them, to work toward "a multiparadigm anti-foundationalist program" that could change the way critical work is done (as well as what it could achieve). That sobering realization brings us back to Baudrillard's account, which now can be reframed from a perspective such as the one Derrida opens up. Since Baudrillard, as Charles Levin has pointed out, seems to have recourse to a regressive anthropological primitivism, a buried human or social liberation lurking beneath rational sign structures and beneath contemporary circulations of codes (a deposited semantic plenum waiting to be regained by nihilistic excavations of the commodity/sign logic of commercial culture), Derrida seems to offer a nonanthropological way to extract critical speculation and analytic creativity from the infinite production of words and texts that (from Baudrillard's view) merely reproduce abstract, coded relations: social closure. Yet Derrida, as Fekete shows, reifies the language paradigm into an ontotheological principle—a strange surplus for the writer who makes ontotheological stability his own target. Thus what for Derrida is a *theoretical* model, the deconstructive antifoundationalist rationality that attempts to produce gaps or openings in an otherwise closed linguistic/social field (somewhat ironically bringing with it a nihilistic metaphysics that grounds its own effort), Baudrillard in turn sees as the *social* model—in fact as social *activity*—itself: abstract reproduction of signs that, to the extent they assert openings possible within cultural reality, maintain the existing structure of economic, cultural, and social reproduction *as if* it were semantically (rationally) productive and not, as Baudrillard sees it, empty of everything but noise and a repressively, tautologically omnivorous sociality of codes feeding on themselves. It is in this airtight linguistic space, theoretical or actual, that the notion of critical work seeks to draw breath. As later pages of this introduction will show, Derrida's work has placed itself in fact, and quite clearly, on concrete ground. See John Fekete, "Modernity in the Literary Institution," in *Structural Allegory,* pp. 228–47; Charles Levin's introduction to his translation of Baudrillard's *For a Critique of the Political Economy of the Sign* (St. Louis: Telos Press, 1981), pp. 5–28. Also, for Habermas's shifting position, see Martin Jay, "Habermas and Modernism," *Praxis International* 4, no. 1 (1984): 1–14; John Keane, "On Tools and Language: Habermas on Work and Interaction," *New German Critique* 6 (Fall 1975): 82–100; Ron Eyerman and David Shipway, "Habermas on Work and Culture," *Theory and Society* 10, no. 4 (July 1980): 547–66; Richard Winfield, "The Dilemma of Labor," *Telos* 24 (Summer 1975): 115–28.

4. Marcus Rediker's fine piece in *Radical History Review* 26 (1982) captures the warmblooded moral intelligence that E. P. Thompson brings to his work: "Thompson writes with continual human reference," Rediker points out, "affirming certain values over and against others, and he tries to make his readers active valuing agents as they think about history and politics." In this effort he "speaks to the historical profession," but more important perhaps, "he speaks to many outside the formally-defined Left and the academy" (p. 128). Thompson's work is well known in the United States. I need not list his significant publications here, but I might note that the body of his writing is of particular usefulness not only as an embodiment of writing strategies and historical practices that cut across (in many ways against) the hierarchical boundaries of both scholarship and activist critical consciousness, but in helping to make a materialistic historical awareness widely available.

I think Thompson is a writer whose ability to talk with (and, as Rediker says, "perhaps more crucially, to learn from") nonacademic audiences has given his work an urgency and a scope that often fade into dreary in-house debates with more orthodox academic writers. To respond to readers of my argument who would remind me that what I seek to accomplish by "resituating" humanistic effort is already largely done in the best historical scholarship, I will agree if they, for their part, offer Thompson's writing as one of their models. The point is not to create a political advocacy program but to establish contexts for reading that allow intellectual debate to gain its lived and vital framework in the world of human conflict. Perhaps the central impediment here is the combined (*a*) disciplinary segregation of knowledge; (*b*) textual enclosure (as if scholarship and learning were essentially to be kept distant from public discourse); and (*c*) disregard for the shaping, formative value—the social force—of a culture still ongoing, still evolving contradictorily but massively within and around the critic's and teacher's work. In that work the idea of a cultural past, of tradition(s), is crucial, and Thompson, among others, leads us to examine how present cultures inherit texts and values from past cultural formations. The important emphasis here is not on the Marxist inclination in Thompson's vision but on his ability to widen our understanding of the materiality of the cultural field we inhabit. Specifically, he shifts attention from what I believe to be a misguided emphasis on the "scientific" status, accuracy, or usefulness of historically materialistic analyses to an institutional emphasis without pretensions to decontaminated insight. Teaching and scholarship are at their best when they devote themselves to the largest possible range of inquiry. Thompson is a writer in that splendid tradition of writers (Jonathan Swift is another, as is John Milton) who, despite ideological differences, orient intelligence to its finest acuity as moral sense politically clarified.

5. Evan Watkins has written a powerful essay on the development and maintenance of critical authority, "Conflict and Consensus in the History of Recent Criticism," *New Literary History* 12, no. 2 (Winter 1981): 345–64. He points out that "criticism at its very center embodies what has become in the United States perhaps the most powerful means of [cultural and, eventually, political] control: the authority of instruction." The classroom, he says, "is a situation where students learn the sociopolitical power of instruction as a central and organizing activity in the shaping of adult relationships, and thus it is not an exaggeration to say that the meaning of 'dominant' and 'subordinate' comes to them as a relation of instructor and instructed."

Duncan Kennedy's essay "Legal Education as Training for Hierarchy," in *The Politics of Law,* ed. David Kairys (New York: Pantheon, 1982), offers a detailed examination of the institutional and ideological pressures on students to "behave in ways that fulfill the prophecies the system makes about them and about that world" of scholarship and professional training they feel forced to accommodate. The most socially aware students at any level of professional study are concerned with just this structural formation. They are quite aware of the hierarchical nature of student–teacher relationships, as of the hierarchy that exists within the university and within the professional work world generally; many seek out critiques and articles that help them make sense of impersonal inflexibility in the educational process. Such students, in contrast to those whom Harold Bloom would defend against "facticity" and the wildness of the cultural past (a superego-like "spirit of revenge," as he calls it), desire to defend themselves against the contemplative hermeneutics of pedagogical authority which turns solely to the past and often against student creativity. Those students, strong readers all, want to know how to read texts to gain access to the future by constructing an achievable *social* (unmystified, antihierarchical) freedom.

6. Paul Solman and Thomas Friedman's *Life and Death on the Corporate Battlefield* (New York: Simon & Schuster, 1982) is a clear and instructive account of the Darwinian forces at work in business competition and how people win, fail, and mostly just survive there. The book in many ways shows the distinctly untheoretical, wholly practical pressures facing students in the "real" world of work. It is a useful introduction to the kind of thinking and acting that leads many nonacademic people to scorn humanist (that is, literary, philosophical, and theoretical) training.

7. That student is a critic in the making, someone who has come alive to something more important than the professional credentials dispensed by graduate schools. If "credentials" are involved at all, they are the questions and concepts that allow analytic discourse to begin.

8. The constructed and contested nature of all human statements—and of the authority that directs and maintains institutional order—begins to appear there. The student's own critical awareness begins there, too. People at work seriously within the competition of university environments will feel no inclination to make intellectual discriminations unless they are offered the chance to determine which styles and methods and questions (which forms of intellectual management) seem significant and for what reasons. It seems to me that criticism and literary teaching today, despite enormous theoretical and critical capacities, do not oppose or in any sustained, curricularly elaborated way challenge the dominant form of our culture. Richard Ohmann's *English in America* (New York: Oxford University Press, 1976) remains the best single statement on the self-limited truncation of critical education within a widely shared consensus forged from an essentially technocratic, wholly meritocratic ideology that constantly reproduces hierarchical institutional organizations.

9. Any reader interested in the issues this book raises may already be well aware of Perry Anderson's steadfast assessment of the tasks of historical materialism in our deeply "post-Marxist" era. One model of the sort of critiques I have in mind may be found in his book *In the Tracks of Historical Materialism* (London: Verso, 1983), especially those sections concerned with post–World War II French theory, somewhat overcharged as they may finally be. A no less compelling account of "problems involved in considering the total 'set' of contemporary British culture" can be found in his brilliant long essay "Components of the National Culture," in *Student Power/Problems, Diagnosis, Action,* ed. Alexander Cockburn and Robin Blackburn (Baltimore: Penguin, 1969), pp. 214–84. Anderson attempts a conjunctural analysis that

means to place its own effort and the objects it investigates at the intersection of specific cultural, political, and economic coordinates, and to do so with the greatest historical detail relevant to clarifying concrete intellectual and social practices. Stanley Aronowitz, *The Crisis in Historical Materialism* (New York: Praeger, 1981), provides another model of institutionally specific critiques. That text outlines the current and genuinely distressed mood of the entire ensemble of commitments my text intends to support. One outcome of such a difficulty is the deep uncertainty about *which* problems and what *particular* strategy will be most helpful to reversing this situation. Thus we find, now more than at any time "since Marx's death," as Ronald Aronson sees it, not only abandonment of the dedication and courage that traditionally formed an oppositional nucleus faithful to the vision of general human improvement, but a retreat to an entrepreneurial Marxism among its scattered advocates. From that perspective, Aronson finds even a writer of Anderson's extraordinary resolve to lapse into an intellectual tour de force that is open to the charge of a dehistoricizing "personal" authority. I will leave it to those who read Anderson's texts to imagine alternatives to the position he carries forward. See Aronson, "Historical Materialism, Answer to Marxism's Crisis," *New Left Review* 152 (July/August 1985): 74–94.

10. Note Régis Debray's pursuit of the ideological grounds of political practice:

> Given that political practice can only exist 'in and under an ideology' (Althusser), knowledge of the political order is to be sought not within the political itself, but within ideology. By the same token, knowledge of the ideological order is to be sought within the religious order.... The general question for political anthropologies—namely, the conditions of possibility for group survival—immediately takes us on to the ground of religious anthropology. 'Practical' is not, as Marx thought, the opposite of 'religious,' for the mysteries of religion translate the mysteries of human practice. Erecting practice into a shibboleth can ultimately become an excuse for theoretical laziness and its by-product: obscurantism.... Observation of modern societies shows that the structures of political behaviour are not radically modified when one mode of production is replaced by another [since such] structures impose themselves on societies and, if need be, against them. [*Critique of Political Reason* (London: Verso, 1983), pp. 35–36]

11. Fredric Jameson, *The Political Unconscious* (Ithaca: Cornell University Press, 1981), p. 3.

12. Even more specific as a problem is the difficulty, perhaps the impossibility, of theorizing the present moment. What is the nature of our contemporary cultural and historical milieu? Is it, as Jameson has found (along with others similarly aware of the pastiche and parodistic self-reflection of commercial culture), a "postmodernist" logic that in effect supersedes the revolutionary agant-gardism that once seemed latent in monopoly capitalism? Contemporary North American culture, from that point of view, corresponds to the homogenizing commodity logic of a later or putatively "third stage" of capitalism—postmonopolistic, culturally and economically dominant across

much of the earth's surface, and now given to the socially integrating seduction of mass spectacles as well as to the efficiency of advanced technologies. In some sense such an environment seems to have transformed (and deflected attention from) the grotesque impersonality of immense capital formations. Jameson follows Ernest Mandel's *Late Capitalism,* trans. Joris De Bres (London: New Left, 1975; first published 1972). As I noted above in n. 3, Jean Baudrillard's writing provides another point of access to a vision of the seemingly widespread collapse of critical reflection. There it is seen to be brought about by a culture that circulates signs and overloaded commercial images as commodities in their own right (especially of interest here is *The Mirror of Production,* trans. Mark Poster [St. Louis: Telos, 1975]). Although Baudrillard does not agree with Mandel's assumption that our contemporary, "third" phase of capitalism is a "purer" stage in the evolution of capital interests or capital accumulation, he does approach some kind of agreement by finding the essential logic of capitalism to be an increasingly intense abstraction of all signifying processes (in which, by the way, the commodity itself is one form of abstraction). A pure form of semiological evaporation is thus created in our culture, absurd maneuverings that reveal, to Baudrillard at any rate, the original arbitrariness in the Marxist distinction between sign and commodity, between the exploitation of labor and alienation through false consciousness (ideological distortion).

I'll not comment further on what must be recognized as a complicated and vexed issue; but I will say that such perspectives, regardless of their own abstractions and abstractness, provide points of departure for an investigation of relations between the logic of culture and the logic of capital. The danger, of course, is the tendency of such strong thesis building to enclose too much too quickly or, at minimum, to suggest a summarized reading of the social field, which is, in the end, not reducible to its images, its communications networks, its economic orders, and its institutional regularities. To make this assertion is not necessarily to fall into the obscurantism Debray warns against, but it is to notice the untotalizable complex of forces, interactions, and events that we face as critics. Among the organizing structures that no doubt close off desirable social change, that close us in, fomenting crises, economic and political, segmenting cities, dividing populations by new and old class pressures, an unsummarizable remainder perseveres—those forms of response, armed with knowledge, undominated by culture's reigning logic. That surd is criticism's life.

13. Fredric Jameson, *Marxism and Form* (Princeton: Princeton University Press, 1971), p. 372.

14. Debray, *Critique,* p. 26.

15. Fredric Jameson, "Postmodernism, or the Cultural Logic of Late Capitalism," *New Left Review* 146 (July/August 1984): 57.

16. See Lyotard's "Capitalisme énergumène," in *Critique* 306 (November 1972), for a sophisticated rejection, along with Deleuze and Guattari, of the concept of totality.

17. Foremost, perhaps, see André Gorz's important long essay *Farewell to*

the Working Class, trans. Mike Sonenscher (Boston: South End, 1982). Erik Olin Wright has carefully discussed the separation of labor's exploitation from the general, somewhat autonomous authoritarian domination that Anthony Giddens's *Critique of Historical Materialism* (see n. 1, above) develops. A similar inclination, as Wright points out, can be found in the work of Barry Hindess and Paul Hirst (Wright points to their volumes, in league with Anthony Cutler and Athar Hussain, *Marx's Capital and Capitalism Today* [London: Routledge & Kegan Paul, 1979, 1980]; look also at sec. 1 of their *Pre-capitalist Modes of Production* [London: Routledge & Kegan Paul, 1975], pp. 21–78). Wright's essay on Giddens is in *New Left Review* 138 (March–April 1983): 11–35.

18. Jameson, *Political Unconscious,* p. 95.

19. I should note here Jameson's splendid essay "Periodizing the 60s," which, among other things, takes explicit account of the "antipolitical 'social contract' between American business and the American labor unions" which was forged in the mid-1950s "and created a situation in which the privileges of a white male labor force take precedence over the demands of black and women workers and other minorities" (p. 181). This essay goes some way toward overcoming "the difficulty of articulating cultural and informational commodities with the labor theory of value" as that difficulty appears in the work of the Frankfurt critics and in such writers as Guy Debord (see Jameson's foreword to Jean-François Lyotard, *The Postmodern Condition: A Report on Knowledge,* trans. Geoff Bennington and Brian Massumi [Minneapolis: University of Minnesota Press, 1984], p. xv). "Periodizing the 60s" appears in *Social Text* (Spring/Summer 1984): 178–209.

20. The virtually simultaneous publication of Miliband's and Poulantzas's major works on the state should not in the least obscure the real differences that separate them. Poulantzas, for one, has taken account of those differences in his review of Miliband's *State in Capitalist Society* (London: Weidenfeld & Nicolson, 1969) in *New Left Review* 58 (November/December, 1969). Poulantzas's *Political Power and Social Classes* was first published in Paris in 1968.

21. See Miliband, *State in Capitalist Society,* chap. 3.

22. Poulantzas, *State, Power, Socialism,* trans. Patrick Camiller (London: New Left, 1978), p. 256.

23. See n. 3 above and Joseph Valente's review, "Hall of Mirrors: Baudrillard on Marx," in *Diacritics* 15, no. 2 (Summer 1985): 54–65. "Acategorical or non-reductive thought is a chimera," Valente writes, "the pursuit of which can lead only to the compulsive self-erasure of a negative science (such as grammatology), a pitfall Baudrillard fortunately avoids, or the random resistance of a negative politics (sixties anarchism) which he does not" (p. 65).

24. Lyotard, *Postmodern Condition,* p. xxiv.

25. In his attempt to work out the interrelations of the state, mass movements, and organized political parties, Poulantzas somewhat pessimistically predicts a perpetually marginal or external position for feminism and ecolog-

ical consciousness, a pessimism that seems to imagine (for very enigmatic reasons) that, for example, there "must be a feminist movement outside the most ideal possible party because the most ideal party cannot include such types of social movement even if we insist that the revolutionary party must have certain conceptions of the woman question" (p. 72). Apparently the desirable aspect of this exclusion, for Poulantzas, is that it expresses the necessary autonomy of various resistance movements that cannot—and for current political struggle within recent "authoritarian statism" should not—be absorbed within a centralizing party mechanism. The accommodating aspect of this position, unstated though it remains, seems to be that such issues as feminism and ecological opposition are somewhat to the side of the absolute struggle for power between a now-fractured working class and the concentration of forces (or more specifically the "condensation" of those relationships of force) that construct the state's ruling order.

The state, in Poulantzas's view, is first of all necessarily a *site* of social conflict (of class conflict) and also an amalgamation of the continuing tension between dominated groups and the dominant interests. Thus, the state is not a functional instrument of ruling class power, and class conflict reverberates throughout society as a whole. State policies that hold social fractions together therefore become the crucial means of maintaining social cohesion and class dominance. At the same time, those policies need to divide parties and groups dominated or excluded from power so that they may not mass together in resistance. Two immediate items are of interest here. First, Poulantzas sees the capitalist welfare state as caught in a crisis no less severe than the crisis traditional Marxism has been suffering, a crisis of state legitimacy deriving from the greater visibility of contradictions exposed between elements (and interests) within its hegemonic coalition. Second, unlike André Gorz, who sees what Alvin Gouldner calls "the new class" of managerial labor—that is, of mental work and intellectual workers—as somewhat distinct from the traditional working class but positioned now to "lead" that class toward self-management, Poulantzas sees such white-collar workers as possible allies of the proletariat but in no way their potential vanguard force. This role Poulantzas has reserved for the traditional if also essentially "privileged" position of Eurocommunism, a position that makes any North American sympathy with Poulantzas's theoretical models somewhat strained.

I think it is true that Poulantzas remained, nonetheless, steadfast in seeking intellectual means to advocate a widespread enlargement of democratic socialism, a democratic enhancement within contemporary social possibilities (a move toward reform rather than revolution). His position presents, in short, "the question of rupture . . . . what democratic socialism requires is a deepening and an extension of liberties, of representative institutions and so on. This cannot occur without a deep transformation of social and economic conditions. This is the conclusion that I draw: that you cannot struggle to expand political rights and liberties in a defensive position against the authoritarian tendency of today's capitalism. But I believe that we cannot save political democracy any more without profound modifications of the social and economic structures of capitalism itself" (p. 70). Poulantzas's ambivalence is very much like an ambivalence within the theoretical model he inherits from Althusser, where, in terms of causality (or of determination "in the last instance"), the state's relative independence of the economy and of the culture that it organizes becomes a "superstructural" ensemble that more or less creates its own "base," while, in terms of political consequence as the site of social struggle, the state contradictorily holds (and withholds) a potential to enhance the liberty of both individuals and classes in the very political action it impedes. This ambivalence in part, but only in part, accounts for E. P. Thompson's rejection of Althusserian models and strategies. See *The Poverty of Theory and Other Essays* (London: Merlin, 1978). For the Poulantzas quotations above, see his interview with Stuart Hall and Alan Hunt in April 1979, some six months before his death, in *Socialist Review* 48, vol. 9, no. 6 (November/December 1979): 57–74, first published in *Marxism Today*, July 1979, pp. 194–201.

26. Clifford Geertz, *Local Knowledge* (New York: Basic Books, 1983), p. 222.

27. Georges Bataille, "The Notion of Expenditure," *Raritan* 3, no. 3 (Winter 1984): 62. This essay is from January 1933, originally published by Gallimard.

28. Jacques Derrida, "The Principle of Reason: The University in the Eyes of Its Pupils," *Diacritics* 13, no. 3 (Fall 1983): 17. Derrida finds a complicity in positions adopted by Walter Jackson Bate in "The Crisis in English Studies," *Harvard Magazine*, September/October 1982, and by William J. Bennett in "The Shattered Humanities," *Wall Street Journal*, December 31, 1982, each of whom appears to want to close off discussion of the sort Derrida advocates. Less militantly, Stanley Fish, whom I will examine later (in chap. 5), carries forward some of these energies Derrida decries.

29. See Derrida's essay on Bataille, "From Restricted to General Economy: A Hegelianism without Reserve," chap. 9 of *Writing and Difference*, trans. Alan Bass (Chicago: University of Chicago Press, 1978). See, too, Derrida's "preface" to *Dissemination*, trans. Barbara Johnson (Chicago: University of Chicago Press, 1981), the section called "Outwork" (pp. 1–59).

30. Jacques Derrida, *Positions*, trans. Alan Bass (Chicago: University of Chicago Press, 1981), p. 67. Derrida's forceful clarity about the dynamics and inclusive space of "texts" receives a strong emphasis, precisely in the direction I mean to underline in this introduction, in his response to two critics of his essay on apartheid "Racism's Last Word" (*Critical Inquiry* 12 [Autumn 1985]: 290–99). Noting that his essay "is an appeal, a call to condemn, to stigmatize, to combat, to keep in memory" everything that the word *apartheid* denotes, Derrida asks his detractors not to "separate word and history!" But, more than that, he reminds them that an appeal such as the one he has made "is still strategically realistic because it refers to a massively present reality, one which no historian could seriously put in question." Since he is accused of sliding from his own understanding of textual inclusiveness—in which or by which nothing is apparently "outside" or "beyond" texts and textuality—Derrida points to a distinction he has repeated throughout his writing: "*text*, as I use

the word, is not the book . . . it is not limited to the *paper*" of published objects. "It is precisely for strategic reasons," Derrida notes, "that I found it necessary to recast the concept of text by generalizing it almost without limit, in any case without present or perceptible limit, without any limit that *is*. That's why there is nothing '*beyond* the text.' That's why South Africa and *apartheid* are, like you and me, part of this general text, which is not to say that it can be read the way one reads a book. That's why the text is always a field of forces: heterogeneous, differential, open, and so on. That's why deconstructive readings and writings . . . are also effective or active (as one says) interventions, in particular political and institutional interventions that transform contexts without limiting themselves to theoretical or constative utterances even though they must produce such utterances." Putting to rest the misreading that accuses deconstructive practice of reinforcing textual enclosures, Derrida reminds us that "deconstruction *begins by* deconstructing logocentrism, the linguistics of the word, and this very enclosure itself." Ironically, adherents of the political left and right equally fail to see that "these practices are perhaps more radical and certainly less stereotyped than others, less easy to decipher, less in keeping with well-used models whose wear and tear ends up by letting one see the abstraction, the conventionalism, the academism, and everything that separates . . . words and history." The misconstruction of Derrida's concept of *text* leads his critics to deny or simply misunderstand that he is capable of making an appeal concerning an issue as important as that of apartheid and its future, an appeal that is "strategically realistic" and aware of contradictions within the logic of a state apparatus such as the one South Africa mounts against its own population. His appeal is no less aware of contradictions in political acts and gestures that mean to protest tyranny. Alert to "the economy of necessarily ambiguous motivations" in rhetorical appeals and political dissent, alert also to the distinctly unmonolithic nature of states and cultures, Derrida is faced with the amusing but sometimes troublesome fact that "people get impatient when they see that deconstructive practices are also and first of all political and institutional practices." See Jacques Derrida, "But Beyond . . . (Open Letter to Anne McClintock and Rob Nixon)," *Critical Inquiry* 13 (Autumn 1986): 155–70.

31. Quoted in Samuel Weber, "The Limits of Professionalism," *Oxford Literary Review* 5, no. 1 (1982): 60.

32. In this regard, Lyotard tells us that "an institution differs from a conversation in that it always requires supplementary constraints for statements to be declared admissible within its bounds. The constraints function to filter discursive potentials, interrupting possible connections in the communication networks: there are things that should not be said. They also privilege certain classes of statements (sometimes only one) whose predominance characterizes the discourse of the particular institution: there are things that should be said, and there are ways of saying them. Thus: orders in the army, prayer in church, denotation in the schools, narration in families, questions in philosophy, performativity in businesses. Bureaucratization is the outer limit of this tendency." And yet, Lyotard continues, "the limits the institution imposes on

potential language 'moves' are never established once and for all (even if they have been formally defined)" (*Postmodern Condition*, p. 17). Michel de Certeau's comments on *la perruque*, all those tricks, tactics, dodges, feints and/or subversions that allow people to make do in normal institutional arrangements (thereby opening closed discursive space), are to the point here: see chap. 3, especially, of *The Practice of Everyday Life*, trans. Steven F. Rendall (Berkeley: University of California Press, 1984).

33. Derrida, "The Conflict of Faculties," in *Languages of Knowledge and of Inquiry*, ed. Michael Riffaterre (New York: Columbia University Press, 1982).

34. Derrida goes on to say that the "censoring" devices of these "prohibiting limitations function through multiple channels that are decentralized, difficult to bring together into a system. The unacceptability of a discourse, the noncertification of a research project, the illegitimacy of a course offering are declared by evaluative actions: studying such evaluations is, it seems to me, one of the tasks most indispensable to the exercise of academic responsibility, most urgent for the maintenance of its dignity. Within the university itself, forces that are apparently external to it (presses, foundations, the mass media) are intervening in an ever more decisive way" ("Principle of Reason," pp. 12–13).

35. Ernest Mandel makes the classical contemporary definition of state-organized capital disaccumulation in vol. 2 of his *Marxist Economic Theory*, trans. Brian Pearce (New York: Monthly Review Press, 1968), pp. 522–23:

> The great economic crisis of 1929–1932 was really overcome in heavy industry only through German rearmament, bringing in its train rearmament on the international scale. . . . The replacement market is, essentially, a new purchasing-power created for the purchase of products of heavy industry by the state. . . . Its only source is a *redistribution of the real national income*, a redistribution which can, of course, lead to an increase in production, that is, in overall real income, which thus becomes an extra source of new purchasing power. . . . The role of replacement market played by the arms economy is indispensable for making possible profitable use of the capital of heavy industry and the 'overcapitalised' big monopolies. But the arms economy makes the state the chief customer of this industry. The special ties between the state and monopoly capital . . . thus assume a more specific form.

And it is here—in the making, enlarging, and proliferation of all the technologies and forms of knowledge that now are creating not only a global militarism (by North Atlantic and Soviet bloc pursuits) but a globe-engirdling military surveillance and weapons deployment—that the present-day university is gaining its new face and most desperate compromise with "extraintellectual" forces.

For these and related reasons, therefore, Mike Davis is correct is revising the too-general notion of hegemony. "Conventional definitions of American postwar 'hegemony' have focused on the sheer preponderance of economic and military power concerted through an atomic-military monopoly, monetary sovereignty, overseas investment, and historic differentials of productivity and mass consumption." But this "balance of power" viewpoint flattens the complex relationships between economic power (and competition) and both political and military power. "A better methodology" for charting the actual interrelations between sometimes paradoxical inversions among economic cycles and political/military strength "is to define 'hegemony' not as a single, all-embracing power relation—radiating through various instances—but as a dynamic system which unifies accumulation, legitimation and repression on a world scale." Precisely at this point "It is necessary to take into account that the special position of the United States in the world division of labour, attributable to its hegemonic status, involves such phenomena as the head-quartering of so much transnational production in the United States or the unusually large scale of its research and higher educational establishments," a fact that alone will continue to maintain and reproduce North American predominance in international organization—in the systematic integration of markets and of populations within an increasingly homogenizing culture-and-information network. See Mike Davis, "The Political Economy of Late Imperial America," *New Left Review* 143 (January/February 1984): 6–7, 23.

36. Derrida, "Principle of Reason," p. 11.

37. Even at the conclusion of an early section in *Of Grammatology*, "Of Grammatology as a Positive Science" (a defense in advance of such charges as Valente's, above in n. 23, that grammatology is a "negative" science), Derrida stakes out a somewhat sketchy but nonetheless historically grounded context for pursuing *arché-writing*, or what he calls "the complicity of origins":

> The fact that access to the written sign assures the sacred power of keeping existence operative within the trace and of knowing the general structure of the universe; that all clergies, exercising political power or not, were constituted at the same time as writing and by the disposition of graphic power; that strategy, ballistics, diplomacy, agriculture, fiscality, and penal law are linked in their history and in their structure to the constitution of writing; . . . that economy, monetary or pre-monetary, and graphic calculation were co-originary, that there could be no law without the possibility of trace (if not, as H. Lévy-Bruhl shows, of notation in the narrow sense), all this refers to a common and radical possibility that no determined science, no abstract discipline, can think as such. [*Of Grammatology*, trans. Gayatri Chakravorty Spivak (Baltimore: Johns Hopkins University Press, 1974), pp. 92–93]

See Anderson's critique of Derrida, *In the Tracks of Historical Materialsim*, pp. 46–47 and 53–54; and see Gayatri Spivak's defense of Derrida's "counternarrative," which runs across the grain of "good theory" by undoing the oppositions at work in the establishment of "principles of the concrete struggle, leading to efficient understanding" (a charge that could be brought against any explicitly political position). Spivak finds a "moral outrage against Derrida, which ranges from the conservative to the radical in literary criticism," among diverse "academic critics [who] share a belief, in the last instance, in the adequate subject of the critic and his company, in the adequacy of theory (that will allow the critic to have the privilege over 'mere practice' and guaran-

tee him the sense of a controlling role in culture or politics, in cultural politics), a faith in the availability of an analyzable reality purged of its relationship with the sexed subject" (Spivak, "Love Me, Love My Ombre, Elle,"
Diacritics 14, no. 4 [Winter 1984]: 21–22).

These observations invite much closer inspection of several issues, one of
them the critic's regulative authority. As Spivak suggests, a major element in
that authority is the field of professional and cultural practices that sustain
social and sexual stereotypes. The irony of ironies here, I think, is the necessary assertion of authority on the part of any revolutionizing, deconstructing
critic. Spivak's assertion falls victim to the same dilemma as a recent Carnegie
Commission's report on the future of teaching in the United States. In calling
for greater teacher effectiveness and expanded authority for the nation's
teachers, the report overlooks the tension between the two. This is a built-in
paradox of sorts—an inevitable source of friction, at any rate—whenever
significant institutional or social changes are projected. On one side, a person
or group invested with considerable authority is required to push against the
structure of habits and practices that, on the other side, need critical attention
(and transformation) while providing the leverage for the authority brought
against it. In sum, increased authority (for critics, for teachers) may be
no more compatible with the critic's attempts to battle "the sexed subject"
than it is with the teacher's efforts to be an empowering, not an enforcing, influence. And yet the rivalry involved there forms part of an unavoidable
staging.

I am suggesting that strong critical practices—even those that seem to undo
or erode traditional rivalries of politically stalemated scenes—become part of
the stage and framework they pretend to circumscribe. This is a ratio Spivak
is aware of; nevertheless, given the passion and cool intelligence of her concern, that dynamics is underplayed for the sake of a more polemic attack.
What should anyone say about positions as strong as the one Spivak gives us
but that they offer an effective demonstration of understanding (of theoretical discourse, of institutional practices, of writing strategies, etc.) which
attempts to reorient the way texts are read and the way teaching methods
situate readers and writers within stereotypes generated partly through the
literary and philosophical tradition, including that of the adequate critic battling the rigid enforcement of sex roles and identities—battling, also, the
inadequacy of rational authority as a guarantee of critical insight? The critic's
authority is thus caught in a paradoxical and self-undermining logic where
the "undecidable" element in sending and receiving messages/themes/signs/
statements cannot be thought of as the determining fact of critical reading
and writing.

I think Spivak approaches such an awareness when she finds that, as "Derrida analyzes philosophical or theoretical texts, however canny they might be,
'the scene of writing' is seen to be betrayed rather than declared. When he
reads literary or visual texts, on the other hand, the scene of writing seems
more directly 'thematized' in what is being read" (p. 25). Something like this
stabilizing of a momentarily or more persistently privileged field of texts and

themes, of writers too, takes place almost inevitably within any writing practice that discriminates between alternative positions and thereby tries to put its judgment into circulation. This is not just a ranking and hierarchical ordering that seeks to exert itself, but a foregrounding of operations, concepts, and positions that at once carry forward the writer's desire to name in a certain way and to exert intellectual (and perhaps political) force or authority on a dominant field of practices. Derrida has found room to exert his complex analytic practice in its double scheme of *undoing* the philosophical and theoretical heritage and of interpreting or *reading* the field of forces (textual and contextual, entangled as they are) that constitute the scene of writing. The adjacency of these operations in his work, separate enough to be pointed out as distinguishable modes or moments in his writing, as Spivak suggests, does not leave them indeterminate or undecidable but makes them part of the habit by which Derrida "constructs interpretations of what's going on" in a text or scene under scrutiny which can easily "seem wildly fantastic by the rules of reason" (p. 29).

In some sense here, Derrida, the demystifier of reading who shows how the work of reading resembles dreamwork, becomes an adequate practitioner in a world of texts, problems, and institutionally authorized operations that he can finally name. And it is precisely in this sense that Spivak is right in insisting that "the tradition that [Derrida] is thus 'feminizing' or opening up has been the most prestigious articulation of the privileging of man. . . . It is surely significant that, even today, the men who take to him take everything from him but his project of re-naming the operation of philosophy with the 'name' of woman" (p. 35). That name, as Derrida inherits it from Nietzsche, at the close of the second (the fall 1886) preface to *The Gay Science*, "Baubo," presents an irony overt enough to be an obscene comic challenge to everyone and every text that acts as if "truth" and/or philosophy were open to inspection.

38. Edward Said, "Criticism between Culture and System," in *The World, the Text, and the Critic* (Cambridge: Harvard University Press, 1983), pp. 178–225.

39. Marshall Berman, *All That Is Solid Melts into Air* (New York: Simon & Schuster, 1982).

40. Dominick LaCapra, *Rethinking Intellectual History* (Ithaca: Cornell University Press, 1983), p. 35.

41. Ibid., p. 63.

42. Anderson, *In the Tracks of Historical Materialism*, p. 24.

43. Jameson's foreword to Lyotard, *Postmodern Condition*, p. xv.

44. Anderson, *In the Tracks of Historical Materialism*, p. 79.

2   The Role of the Critical Intellectual

1. The issue of intellectual and critical authority is most often looked at in terms of the normal (and normative) activity of academic writers, which in turn puts the question of authority as a matter of intellectual paradigms. In

brief, the exercise of intellectual authority appears as a fairly stable event within culture, and from that point of view it is a self-defining activity that changes its epistemological models and its outstanding problems or questions in response to the various arguments and outlooks that come to the fore in academic debate. Deeper, epochal shocks to the role or place of intellectual activity—to the function of rationality itself—present far graver threats to the authority that writers normally call on. And just how such destabilizing social events are to be assessed (their causes, their possible longe-range outcomes) presents intellectual debate not only with its most anxious moments of self-examination but, as we have seen in the argumentative turmoil during and after the Vietnam War, with its most internally disruptive (potentially institution-altering) challenge. A tendency in all assessments of intellectual authority—in its stable, legitimated operations as well as in its self-contesting, deeply unsettled moments—is to assume a more or less lasting place for the constructive value of intellectual work, since it occupies such a central structural position within our society. The paradigm-assessing models of inspecting intellectual authority, therefore, focus on the normal and the continuing (the traditional and the self-reproducing) aspects of academic rationality without assessing changes in the structure of social organization itself. The recent debate about "postmodernism," however, is now beginning to focus on the apparent shifts in cultural dynamics and between long-standing institutional areas that may very well change the *function* of intellectual work if not quite so much its position or the professional autonomy that allows it to create and alter its ruling paradigms.

In addition to the anthology edited by John Fekete, which I have already cited above, let me cite Hal Foster's anthology, *The Anti-aesthetic: Essays on Postmodern Culture* (Port Townsend, Wash.: Bay Press, 1983), and the fifteenth-anniversary issue of *Telos*, which contains a very provocative symposium on "the role of the intellectual in the 1980s" (*Telos* 50, vol. 14, no. 4 [Winter 1981–82]). Several other texts, somewhat to the side of literary critical awareness, deserve attention, also: *Social Science as Moral Inquiry*, ed. Norma Haan, Robert Bellah, et al. (New York: Columbia University Press, 1983); *Reinventing Anthropology*, ed. Dell Hymes (New York: Pantheon, 1972); Alan Brinkley, "Writing the History of America: Dilemmas and Challenges," *Daedalus*, Summer 1984, pp. 121–41; Robert F. Berkhofer, Jr., "The Two New Histories: Competing Paradigms for Interpreting the American Past," *OAH Newsletter*, May 1983, pp. 9–12.

2. Gouldner's trilogy is composed of *The Dialectic of Ideology and Technology* (1976), *The Future of Intellectuals and the Rise of the New Class* (1979), and *The Two Marxisms* (1980). The first two are published by Oxford University Press and the third by Seabury Press. "Prologue to a Theory of Revolutionary Intellectuals" appeared in *Telos*, Winter 1975–76, pp. 3–36.

Chomsky's *American Power and the New Mandarins* (1967) and *Towards a New Cold War* (1982) are both published by Pantheon Books. I should point out also that Chomsky's detailed arguments in *The Fateful Triangle* (Boston: South End, 1983) not only continue his exploration of American foreign policy and its misguided power but have stirred characteristic critical disagreements. See, for example, the August 16, 1984, *New York Review of Books* for a fairly typical exchange. For anyone interested, Chomsky's article "US–Israeli Rejectionism—an obstacle to Peace" in the *Boston Globe*, January 16, 1984, provides an overview of his latest efforts.

3. Gouldner, *Future of Intellectuals*, pp. 7, 8.

4. This is an important and complex position. It is challenged as well as reformulated by Manuel Castells's brilliant book *The Economic Crisis and American Society* (Princeton: Princeton University Press, 1980): "*The United States economy relies on a very small number of large corporations that concentrate and centralize capital, labor, and resources,*" Castells writes (his italics), and this means that "control over the means of production [throughout society] is exercised by corporate monopoly capital. . . . Capitalism is a society where corporate capitalist interests are the basis of the social structure" (pp. 142–43).

Gouldner's belief that the new managerial class is breaking away from the ruling capitalist class is based on his sense of the autonomy that specialized knowledge (education, in brief) gives to the managers of corporations and large capital interests. But that reading is disputed by Castells and by Maurice Zeitlin, who, Castells notes, shows us that the managerial class is in effect a more efficient extension of "old" capitalist dominance. In sum, the "ruling class dissolves itself into a process of managerial organization in search of rationality and technological development" (p. 146). Alongside the weakness of the working class in the United States, we need to add the weakness of the managerial class—a group that does not "undermine" capitalism's traditional values, as Gouldner believes, but identifies its own interests and behavior in terms of the reigning values and professional norms evolved by the capitalist establishment. This is the subject of a valuable study by Leonard and Mark Silk, *The American Establishment* (New York: Basic Books, 1980). See, in addition, G. William Domhoff, *Who Rules America Now?* (Englewood Cliffs, N.J.: Prentice-Hall, 1983), p. 40 and, especially, chap. 3.

5. Gouldner, *Future of Intellectuals*, p. 3.

6. Ibid., p. 34.

7. Gouldner, "Prologue," p. 18. I might note here, as an aside, that Wittgenstein approaches an explicit concern with the philosophical basis of intellectual authority in two adjacent manuscript entries collected in *Culture and Value*, ed. G. H. von Wright (Chicago: University of Chicago Press, 1980): "Nothing we do can be defended absolutely and finally. But only by reference to something else that is not questioned. I.e. no reason can be given why you should act (or should have acted) *like this*, except that by doing so you bring about such a situation, which again has to be an aim you *accept*." He goes on: "Perhaps what is inexpressible (what I find mysterious and am not able to express) is the background against which whatever I could express has its meaning" (p. 16e). In contrast to thóse statements of 1931 (post-*Tractatus*), Wittgenstein's notions of "families of resemblance" and of "language games" in *The Philosophical Investigations* (New York: Macmillan, 1976) are attempts to get around the problem of authority—of "reference to something else that is

not questioned"—in the operation of language. This detour is encapsulated in his comment that "every sign *by itself* seems dead. What gives it life?—In use it is *alive*. Is life breathed into it there?—Or is the *use* its life?" (p. 128e). Dilemmas about the authorizing capacity of language show up repeatedly throughout Wittgenstein's writing as figurative characterizations, vivid, sometimes metaphoric descriptions of language structures. For example, early in the *Investigations* he writes: "Our language can be seen as an ancient city: a maze of little streets and squares, of old and new houses, and of houses with additions from various periods; and this surrounded by a multitude of new burroughs with straight regular streets and uniform houses" (p. 8e). The whole of the *Investigations* is an extended meditation on the impasse of seeking access to the authority of discourse, to its empowering devices. The fantasy and ideological motivation of this project are caught nicely by Wittgenstein himself: "What is your aim in philosophy? [he asks himself]—To shew the fly the way out of the fly-bottle" (p. 103e). We may see in all of this that, contrary to Gouldner's thesis, intellectuals *must* and also *can be* "conceptualized rigorously" in a more concretely social and historical framework than the "language games" they adopt.

8. For a particularly instructive look at the debate about the purpose as well as the status of theory in literary criticism (in the academy on the whole), see the Summer 1982 issue of *Critical Inquiry* (vol. 8, no. 4, pp. 723–42) with the astonishingly reactionary essay by Stephen Knapp and Walter Benn Michaels, "Against Theory," and the subsequent rejoinders by E. D. Hirsch, Jr., Daniel O'Hara, and others in the issue of June 1983 (vol. 9, no. 4).

9. Gouldner, *Future of Intellectuals*, p. 28.

10. Gouldner, "Prologue," pp. 20–21.

11. Noam Chomsky and Edward S. Herman, *After the Cataclysm* (Boston: South End, 1979), p. 24.

12. Gouldner, "Prologue," p. 34.

13. Chomsky, *American Power*, p. 23.

14. Gouldner, "Prologue," p. 34.

15. Ibid., p. 32.

16. Gouldner, *Future of Intellectuals*, p. 40.

17. Ibid., p. 83.

18. Ibid., pp. 85–90.

19. Michel Foucault, *Power/Knowledge: Selected Interviews and Other Writings, 1972–1977* (New York: Pantheon, 1980), p. 146.

20. Gouldner, *Future of Intellectuals*, p. 105 (n. 28). Gouldner continues: "As the proportion of government funding for universities and colleges increases, university policy increasingly becomes a political question rather than being governed by private trustees" (p. 106, n. 28). What Gouldner seems to miss is the structural affiliation between people who sit on boards of trustees—many of them, by no means all—and the working of capital throughout society and especially in the making of government budgetary and bureaucratic policies. This is a connection well mapped in David N. Smith's *Who Rules the Universities?* (New York: Monthly Review Press, 1974), which includes extremely

interesting observations on the working of the trustees of the University of California during Ronald Reagan's governorship. Let me just say, in summary, that Smith (along with G. William Domhoff in *Who Rules America?* [Englewood Cliffs, N.J.: Prentice-Hall, 1967]) finds that the interference into "America's leading universities by members of the American business aristocracy is more direct than with any other institution which they control" (this is Domhoff's statement quoted by Smith, p. 55).

21. David F. Noble, *America by Design: Science, Technology, and the Rise of Corporate Capitalism* (New York: Knopf, 1977); Leonard Silk and Mark Silk, *The American Establishment* (New York: Basic Books, 1980); Herbert I. Schiller, *Who Knows: Information in the Age of the Fortune 500* (Norwood, N.J.: Ablex, 1981); Christopher Lasch's comments are included in his foreword to Noble's book, pp. xii–xiii.

22. Richard Rorty, *The Consequences of Pragmatism* (Minneapolis: University of Minnesota Press, 1982), pp. 61–62.

23. Gouldner, *Future of Intellectuals*, p. 88.

24. Two books of genuinely immediate usefulness address this inadequacy: James O'Connor, *The Corporations and the State* (New York: Harper & Row, n.d.), and Michael Useem, *The Inner Circle: Large Corporations and the Rise of Business Political Activity in the U.S. and U.K.* (New York: Oxford University Press, 1984).

25. Régis Debray, *Teachers, Writers, Celebrities* (London: New Left Books, 1981), p. 79. Debray provides a sobering institutional analysis of the rivalry and interrelationship of the media (mostly television news) and university intellectuals. It would be impossible to summarize his position without distorting and reducing it; suffice it say that the book offers a strong alternative to Gouldner's idealizations.

26. Ibid., pp. 21, 22. Additionally, for perspective on Gouldner's position, see the important essay by Stanley Aronowitz, "The End of Political Economy," *Social Text* 2, no. 1 (Summer 1979): 3–52, for a complex but extremely clear presentation of three theories of capitalist crisis. Look especially at pp. 39–40, on the public sector and arms expenditures, and at the section on Lenin's theory of imperialism, pp. 8–20. This essay can also be found as chap. 7 of Aronowitz's *Crisis in Historical Materialism* (New York: Praeger, 1981), pp. 139–201.

27. Gouldner, "Prologue," pp. 12–13.

28. Leo Braudy, "Succeeding in Language," in *The State of the Language*, ed. Leonard Michaels and Christopher Ricks (Berkeley: University of California Press, 1980), p. 491.

29. John Fekete, *The Critical Twilight: Explorations in the Ideology of Anglo-American Literary Theory* (London: Routledge & Kegan Paul, 1977), is a valuable examination of the movement toward, through, and beyond the "New Critical" aesthetic ideology that has produced more than one generation of critical readers. The continuity that Fekete exposes has led to the metaphysically vaporous "secular religion" of Marshall McLuhan and to the insistent formal aridity of structuralism, which, Fekete shows us, is "an epis-

temological strategy of technocratic rule," part of the profoundly *un*critical habit of North American critical theory. This unconscious stress on technocratic manipulation and what Fekete calls an ethic of "creative" consumption (extending into the ostensibly "critical" mentality itself) provides the reigning coherence of humanist criticism.

30. Frederick Crews, "Do Literary Studies Have an Ideology?" *PMLA* 85 (1968): 426.

31. Ibid., p. 424.

32. Rorty, *Consequences of Pragmatism*, pp. 69–70.

33. Randolph Bourne, *The Radical Will: Selected Writings, 1911–1918* (New York: Urizen, 1977), p. 342.

34. Ibid., p. 339. Frank Lentricchia makes a distinction between the radical democratic force of pragmatism and the very different "scientific side of pragmatism" in his opening remarks to *Criticism and Social Change* (Chicago: University of Chicago Press, 1983). Lentricchia finds pragmatism to be "the quintessential American point of view . . . a rejection of hierarchical structure itself, of the stabilizing (kingly) forces of structure, which would always stand safely outside structure—outside the game, but ruling the game." And so pragmatism "at its critical best may underwrite the radical democrat," but "the scientific side of pragmatism—its desire to control and plan our relations to our social and natural environments—history has proved to be problematic," since pragmatism argues in "behalf of the lone existential individual and against the collective." It turns out, as Lentricchia sees it, that "the pragmatist implies that education can stand in pure opposition to society, directing its critique and would-be transformation from somewhere 'outside' the social space of its scrutiny, 'free' from the contaminating things it would change" (pp. 3–4). Such a perspective, of course, assumes that knowledge and intellectuals are both beyond the production process of capitalist culture.

We can look at the Dewey/Bourne debate as a classic version of the confrontation between intellectuals supporting (Bourne) and abandoning or even undermining labor (Dewey). Dewey's elitist pragmatism is more problematic than Lentricchia thinks it is. Dewey's position is not merely "undecidable" or torn between a gross hope to save the individual from authority's repressive pressures and a "mostly uncritical celebration of the uncontextualized individual"; like Rorty's suave outlook in the decade preceding Reagan's imperial presidency, it argues for the surveillance function and managerial usefulness of intellectuals in the capitalist state—a support, in particular, for the ideological consolidation of America's destiny as "a rallying point for the nations" (as Rorty puts it). This debate, new or old, represents the longstanding antagonism in North American intellectual discourse between a choice to support labor (and the working class) and a choice to support the ever-enlarging sphere of capital-intensive strategies of domestic and global domination. The failure of critical intellectuals to support labor at the very least affirms the central capitalist tactic of eroding or suppressing labor militancy. It also blunts any chance of developing bonds of solidarity with and political support for people who are struggling to free themselves from exploitive practices of international capitalism, a "movement," political, cultural, and social as well as economic, which gains considerable, often unwitting, help from intellectuals.

35. Rorty, *Consequences of Pragmatism,* p. 70.

36. Ibid., p. 67.

37. Stanley Karnow has recently summarized the Congressional Research Service's documentation of the United States' leading position in the world as exporter of arms and munitions. See "The Arms Peddlers," *Boston Globe,* August 4, 1984.

38. Rorty, *Consequences of Pragmatism,* p. 61.

39. Chomsky, *Towards a New Cold War,* pp. 5–6.

40. Chomsky, *American Power and the New Mandarins,* p. 313.

41. Chomsky, *Towards a New Cold War,* p. 80.

42. Ibid., pp. 80–81. I think it is useful to note Leonard and Mark Silk's observation that a cultural establishment—composed of numerous influential universities, several powerful foundations (such as the Brookings Institution and the Ford Foundation), the *New York Times,* the Museum of Modern Art (and, I would add, the major television networks)—of extraordinary persuasive power serves as a "third force" both mediating and joining the interests of American big business and the government bureaucracy. The "democratic" character of the ideological consensus evolved by that interaction is the subject of their book *The American Establishment.* One of their points is that these entangled institutions and interests have created something on the order of a secular state church with historical ties to an actual church, the "liberal" Christianity of the Unitarian church in Massachusetts. The emergence of the new radical right on the foundations of a resurgent Christian Evangelicalism can be seen as an attempt to seize the "old" establishment for more virulently capitalist purposes.

43. Gouldner, *Future of Intellectuals,* p. 41.

44. Chomsky, *Radical Priorities,* p. 224.

45. Ibid., p. 228.

46. See the 1975 report of the Trilateral Commission, *The Crisis of Democracy* (New York: New York University Press, 1975), for a stunning example of what C. Wright Mills has called "the engineering of consent." The Trilateral writers (M. J. Crozier, S. P. Huntington, and J. Watanuki) are worried that value-oriented intellectuals have gained too much ground from the more "responsible" and democratically stabilizing "policy-oriented," technocratic intellectuals, who will not, unlike their more radical colleagues, foment popular unrest and thus create difficulty for those who must govern America. Also, Henry A. Giroux's essay "Mass Culture and the Rise of the New Illiteracy," *Interchange* 10, no. 4 (1979/80): 89–98, argues that the relationships "between the various modes of communication and the existing socio-political forces that dominate this society" need to be made objects of critical analysis.

47. Chomsky, *Towards a New Cold War,* pp. 104–5. Chomsky goes on to write that "one cannot accept the view that state censorship is the answer to the distortion and deceit of intellectual servants of ruling groups. Just as

surely, we cannot pretend that there is freedom of opinion in any serious sense when social and cultural taboos shield the formation of policy from public awareness and scrutiny."

48. We should remind ourselves of the historical conditions that led to mass public education, as Stanley Aronowitz does: "When the productivity of labor, combined with the increased frequency of the periodic crises [in capital's stability], reached a point when children could no longer be employed in factories and workshops without dire social consequences, the public education system was developed to absorb this new surplus labor force." Such a perspective provides a materialistic account of educational practices to supplement the somewhat idealistic model of cultural hegemony in Gramsci. See Stanley Aronowitz, "The End of Political Economy," *Social Text* 2, no. 1 (Summer 1979): 41–52.

49. This aversion is corrected by Mark Poster's and Martin Jay's justifiable caution against any reductionist, wholly undialectical rush to subsume or "totalize" a putatively given context. See Poster's concern for the presentist stance in Baudrillard's *Mirror of Production*, pp. 13–15 (cf. chap. 1, n. 12, above), and the epilogue to Jay's *Marxism and Totality* (Berkeley: University of California Press, 1984).

50. Anyone interested in this issue should look at the discussion of Marx and Gramsci (pp. 70–74) in Richard Johnson, "Histories of Culture/Theories of Ideology: Notes on an Impasse," in *Ideology and Cultural Production*, ed. Michele Barrett et al. (New York: St. Martin's Press, 1979).

51. Chomsky, *American Power and the New Mandarins*, p. 125. William A. Williams, Martin Sklar, and others have repeatedly demonstrated that the "liberal" or "welfare" state has been prompted by disequilbriums in American society which only state intervention could alleviate. Such intervention has served the economic and general social interests of the corporations. Gramsci's investigations into cultural hegemony allow us to explore the role of intellectuals and the intelligentsia in preserving or revising such fundamental concepts as the "just" order of the democratic state. Williams's *Empire as a Way of Life* (New York: Oxford University Press, 1980) provides extremely useful historical information to frame this issue.

52. When the social order weakens and starts to break down, an "organic crisis" develops. "According to Gramsci," Thomas R. Bates writes,

an "organic crisis" involves the totality of an "historical bloc"—the structure of society as well as its superstructure. An organic crisis is manifested as a crisis of hegemony, in which the people cease to believe the words of the national leaders, and begin to abandon the traditional parties. The precipitating factor in such a crisis is frequently the failure of the ruling class in some large undertaking, such as war, for which it demanded the consent and sacrifices of the people. The crisis may last a long time, for, as Gramsci wryly observed, "no social form is ever willing to confess that it has been superseded." In combatting the crisis, the intellectuals of the ruling class may resort to all sorts of mystification, blaming the failure of the state on an opposition party or on ethnic and racial minorities, and conducting nationalistic campaigns based on irrational appeals to patriotic sentiment. This is a very dangerous moment in civic life, for if the efforts of the mandarins fail, and if the progressive forces still fail to impose their own solution, the old ruling class may seek salvation in a "divine leader." This "Caesar" may give the old order a "breathing spell" by exterminating the opposing elite and terrorizing its mass support.

That post-Vietnam, post-Watergate America shows signs of such an elaborated organic crisis, with the ascension of a luminous state steward more adept than his rivals at masking the tensions and underlying contradictions, should be obvious. Two questions seem paramount here. What intellectual strategy would be capable of undoing the hegemonic partnership between "old" liberal institutions (such as the university) and the "new" conservative ethos? What role should radical critics play in a culture, momentarily stabilized by a charismatic "leader" and unresponsive to the values of the left, now poised to continue its inherently contradictory coherence by increasingly obtuse and potentially violent means? A culture in crisis, especially a prolonged and innately unsolvable crisis (a structural and institutional as well as "ethical" crisis of competing values), offers intellectual and political opportunities that are often obscured. See Bates's "Gramsci and the Theory of Hegemony," *Journal of the History of Ideas* 36 (1975): 351–66.

53. Antonio Gramsci, *Selections from Political Writings (1910–1920)*, ed. Quintin Hoare (New York: International Publishers, 1977), p. 179.

54. Peter Nettl, "Power and the Intellectuals," in *Power and Consciousness* (New York: New York University Press, 1969), pp. 26–27.

55. See Carlos P. Otero's introductory essay in Chomsky's *Radical Priorities*, pp. 11–56. The romantic genealogy entangling creative freedom with and against free enterprise involved here has led one reader to see this moment (in my text and in Chomsky's position) as "a perfect instance of how useful Jameson's dialectic of 'ideology and utopia' can be." I agree and direct any reader interested in exploring the subject to read carefully Jameson's concluding chapter in *The Political Unconscious* and, by way of useful clarification, chaps. 5 and 6 in William C. Dowling's *Jameson, Althusser, Marx* (Ithaca: Cornell University Press, 1984). Let me note here, too, my commentator's reminder that Chomsky's civic conscience came to the fore only after he gained prominence and authority "as the person who reinvented linguistics for our time," someone who (in addition), "by teaching at MIT, the heart of the technocratic empire, . . . provides living, legitimating proof that the American liberal way of life works." I should add that two essays that bear on the issue of romantic genealogies are Habermas's "Consciousness-Raising or Redemptive Criticism," *New German Critique* 17 (Spring 1979): 30–59, and Michael Lowy's "Revolution against 'Progress,'" *New Left Review* 152 (July/August 1985): 42–59, each dealing with mixed elements—romantic, Marxist, mystic, surrealist—in Walter Benjamin's critical practice.

56. Nicos Poulantzas, "The Problem of the Capitalist State," *New Left Review* 58 (November/December 1969).

57. See also Gar Alperovitz, *Atomic Diplomacy* (New York: Simon & Schu-

ster, 1962), and Gabriel Kolko, *The Politics of War: The World and United States Foreign Policy, 1943–1945* (New York: Random House, 1968).

58. Chomsky, *Towards a New Cold War*, p. 5. I might note here the appalling statistic offered by the National Coalition on Television Violence: the average American sees 18,000 murders of various sorts on television by age 18.

59. Bourne, *Radical Will*, p. 310.

3   Intellectual Authority and State Power

1. Hayden White's brief essay on intellectual protocols, "Conventional Conflicts," *New Literary History* 13, no. 1 (1981): 145–60, suggests that the "professionalization of criticism was required, in large part, by the relative freedom accorded to artists and scientists in liberal societies." In the ordinary operations of renewing professional culture and its theoretical standpoints, "an attack on this or that convention is fully consonant with the critic's traditional role as arbiter between conservative and innovative forces within any given area of cultural practice, [but] an attack by critics on convention per se undermines the very authority of the *profession* of criticism" (p. 146).

White seems to imply without quite saying so that Derrida's brand of deconstructive interpretation erodes, or at any rate defers and suspends, the professional critic's institutional authority. In a well-known essay, "The Absurdist Moment in Contemporary Literary Theory," *Contemporary Literature* 17, no. 3 (Summer 1976): 378–403, White finds that Derrida's "endless series of metaphorical translations from one universe of figuratively provided meaning to another" empty out the world and leave the professional critic without any concrete (or for that matter any conventional) vocation. This is a theme that Gerald Graff has picked up. "The moral that Derrida tends to enforce if not preach," he tells us, "is that insofar as the structures of sense making are inescapable, they are *transpolitical* in character." But for Graff the radically fictional nature of this arrangement gives way (somewhat ambiguously) to, on one hand, "political conflict, [which] . . . presupposes a common inventory of objects over which different and warring factions compete for control," and, on the other, the possibility that "objectivity is merely an enabling assumption that makes intellectual activity possible" with no "guarantee of infallibility." Graff is certainly right, I think, in believing that "interpretations depend on some assumed point of reference," but his objection to what he calls "textual leftism" seeks a clarified professional and social context that his own writing leaves vague. A good deal of what Graff omits can be found in an excellent article on Derrida, Trilling, and the inadequacy of the academic left by Adam Gussow, "Joseph Epstein & Company: The Rise of the Literary New Right," *Boston Review* 9, no. 2 (April 1984): 7–10. Graff's essay "Textual Leftism" is in *Partisan Review* 49, no. 4 (1982): 558–75.

2. This is a vast subject with an immense bibliography. For the sake of brevity I am going to cite five texts that clarified my thoughts (or initiated them) at an early moment in this project: Frank Kermode, "Institutional

Control of Interpretation," *Salmagundi*, no. 43 (Winter 1979), pp. 72–86; Edward Said, *Beginnings* (New York: Basic Books, 1975); Lewis A. Coser, *Men of Ideas* (New York: Free Press, 1965); Richard Sennett, *Authority* (New York: Knopf, 1980); and John P. Diggins and Mark E. Kann, eds., *The Problem of Authority in America* (Philadelphia: Temple University Press, 1981), an expanded version of an issue of *Humanities in Society*, 3, no. 2 (Spring 1980).

In addition, I want to call particular attention to the work William Spanos has been doing. See, for example, "The End of Education: 'The Harvard Core Curriculum Report' and the Pedagogy of Reformation," *Boundary 2*, 10, no. 2 (Winter 1982): 1–76. Barry O'Connell's essay "Where Does Harvard Lead Us?" *Change*, September 1978, pp. 35–40, 61; George Levine, "Notes toward a Humanist Anti-Curriculum" *Humanities in Society* 1, no. 3 (1978): 221–43, and especially Michael W. Apple, ed., *Cultural and Economic Reproduction in Education* (London: Routledge & Kegan Paul, 1982), offer significant appraisals of the current condition of humanist schooling, as do a number of essays in Jerome Karabel and A. H. Halsey, eds., *Power and Ideology in Education* (New York: Oxford University Press, 1977)—David K. Cohen and Marvin Lazerson's "Education and the Corporate Order" and Marzio Barbagli and Marcello Dei's "Socialization into Apathy and Political Subordination," for instance.

3. White, "Conventional Conflicts," p. 146.

4. Richard Ohmann, *English in America: A Radical View of the Profession* (New York: Oxford University Press, 1976), p. 86.

5. Ibid., pp. 297, 299.

6. Ibid., pp. 301, 302.

7. Ibid., p. 332.

8. Stanley Karnow, "The Arms Peddlers," *Boston Globe*, August 4, 1984.

9. See Marx's introduction of August and September 1857, "The Method of Political Economy," which initiates an approach to the relation (not always contradictory) between intellectual work and cultural hegemony. The key to Marx's ontology in this portion of the *Grundrisse* is clearly "the active subject" and not "objectified activity," a distinction that reinforces his thoughts on labor and its sytematically depreciated value in capitalist economies. As I noted earlier, Stanley Aronowitz's important essay "The End of Political Economy" carries this analysis forward and allows us to think more clearly about (1) the Utopian or counterlogical resistance of oppositional criticism within the institutional framework of capitalist logic; (2) the relation between criticism as a form of work and the global (both national and international) structure of cultural, economic, and political power—that is, of capitalism and its expanding communications networks, which carry inherent resistances that are consistently left undeveloped or blocked; and (3) the political force of intellectual work, which resides, in large part, with powerful and accurate descriptions of our actual conditions, descriptions that separate need from desire by showing how social formations are built by people constrained by cultural, political, and economic limitations. Part of what I have in mind in looking at outcomes not "wholly favorable" to capitalism is addressed in

Michel de Certeau, "On the Oppositional Practices of Everyday Life," *Social Text* 3 (Fall 1980): 3–43.

10. Jürgen Habermas's recent writing in his *Theory of Communicative Action,* vol. 1 (Boston: Beacon, 1984), gives an elaborate—and frequently persuasive—account of the emergence of modern rationality as distinctly beset by crises of self-doubt which prevent critical energies from gaining socially useful leverage. Habermas sees what he calls our "life-world" as structured by three predominant areas: strategic action (the economy), communicative action (bureaucratic institutions), and affective action (culture and everything that now, in the wake of the Frankfurt analysts, is often known as the "culture industry"). Culture, in this assessment, is the final area in which capitalism's full colonization is to be won. Having triumphed in the economic and institutional organization of "late capitalist" societies, culture now provides a last area of struggle between capitalist and non- or anticapitalist forces. This understanding of an emerging "cultural domination," among other things, follows from Habermas's disagreement with Max Weber's emphasis on a "purposive" rationality throughout modern society which historically has deprived culture of access to meaningful and regenerative beliefs while it has increased the tendency of each aspect of public and private life to conform to bureaucratic and instrumental control (an anti-Enlightenment cultural rationality). The disagreement here is about the amount of open space still available within culture for liberation and the sort of creativity that is distinctly "critical" in opposition to bureaucratic and instrumental reason. Weber's analysis influenced the early Frankfurt theorists to project a pessimistic and, finally, contemplative model of critical energy. Habermas argues for a view of retrievable "communicative" action that names and opposes rational obstructions to general human interests.

For two readings of the cultural homogeneity and the political consolidations actually possible within contemporary "postmodern" culture—the degree to which it can be thought of as open to counterhegemonic political energies or in some large sense closed or blocked—see Fredric Jameson, "The Politics of Theory: Ideological Positions in the Postmodernism Debate," *New German Critique,* no. 33 (Fall 1984): 53–65, and Fred Pfeil, "Makin' FlippyFloppy: Postmodernism and the Baby Boom PMC," in *The Year Left: An American Socialist Yearbook, 1985,* ed. Mike Davis, Fred Pfeil, and Michael Sprinker (London: Verso, 1985). Jameson's reading is quite sympathetic to Habermas's position. Pfeil argues for a greater inspection of "organic movements" and the conjunctural facts of our complex social evolution. Habermas's political suggestions remain somewhat sketchy and, regardless of differences between the German Federal Republic and contemporary North America, also unarticulated to a degree that renders them enigmatic. Since *The Theory of Communicative Action* restricts itself, self-consciously, to sociological and epistemological analyses, it stops short of naming the radical implications teasingly posed at its own reflective horizon.

11. Jameson, "Periodizing the 60s," *Social Text* 3, no. 3, and 4, no. 1 (Spring/Summer 1984): 178–209, esp. 194.

12. Ibid., p. 195.

13. Hal Foster, ed., *The Anti-aesthetic: Essays on Postmodern Culture* (Port Townsend, Wash.: Bay Press, 1983); John Fekete, ed., *The Structural Allegory* (Minneapolis: University of Minnesota Press, 1983).

14. Such an effort demands that several kinds of materialistic and historically specific critique come together, an economically and politically delineating format such as the one to be found in the writing of Mike Davis (cf. n. 35 in chap. 1, above) along with a more dialectically inclined theoretical project for the reading of texts and global cultural formations (establishing historical "periods" in terms "of what is historically dominant or hegemonic" so that "the exceptional—what Raymond Williams calls the 'residual' or 'emergent'—can be assessed") such as Jameson's. Here I think Ohmann's nearly classic text on teaching the English curriculum in North America provides an institution-specific (a professional) critique that "frames" the actual circumstances in which critical positions of any sort, for whatever use, take hold. One issue that Ohmann has clarified is how critical consciousness is formed in our culture and how it is also blocked and diverted. This problem, somewhat less "theoretical" than those Jameson deals with, is no less important for the present and future of critical teaching in this country; it also gains a good deal of clarity when framed by Davis's and Jameson's hegemonic critiques. The mistakenly external context of cultural dominance and cultural interaction (with its various forms of resistance, heterogeneity, and cross-cultural mixing) and the similarly mistaken notion of an internal professional context must be joined together as the mutually interacting, mutually supporting arenas they are.

15. Jameson, "Periodizing the 60s," p. 190.

16. Ibid., p. 205.

17. Ibid., p. 207.

18. In a statement of some concrete usefulness in the current climate of antiterrorist hysteria, Jameson notes the "objective coincidence between a misguided assessment of the social and political situation on the part of left militants [in the 1960s] (for the most part students and intellectuals eager to force a revolutionary conjuncture by voluntaristic acts) and a willing exploitation by the state of precisely those provocations." This coincidence, he continues, "suggests that what is often loosely called 'terrorism' must be the object of complex and properly dialectical analysis. However rightly a responsible left chooses to dissociate itself from such strategy (and the Marxian opposition to terrorism is an old and established tradition that goes back to the 19th century), it is important to remember that 'terrorism,' as a 'concept,' is also an ideologeme of the right and must therefore be refused in that form" (ibid., p. 203).

19. Edward W. Said, *The World, the Text, and the Critic* (Cambridge: Harvard University Press, 1983), p. 224.

20. Richard Ohmann, "The MLA and the Politics of Inadvertence," *PMLA* 83 (1968): 989–90.

21. See Fred Halliday's reading of the "contradictory unity" in the cultural

and political aftermath of the decade of protest prompted by the civil rights movement and the Vietnam War. Halliday feels that little of permanent social value resulted ("The Conjuncture of the Seventies: Reply to Ourgaard," *New Left Review* 147 [September/October 1984]: 76–83).

22. Eugene Goodheart, *Culture and the Radical Conscience* (Cambridge: Harvard University Press, 1973), pp. 154, 73.

23. Ibid., p. 154.

24. Ibid., pp. 154–55.

25. Ibid., p. 85.

26. Elizabeth Drew's closing statement in *Politics and Money* (New York: Macmillan, 1983) provides a more sober assessment of the contemporary "democratic experience":

> We have allowed it to become increasingly difficult for the good people who remain in politics to function well. What results is a corrosion of the system and a new kind of squalor—conditions that are well known to those who are in it and to those who deal with it at close range. The public knows that something is very wrong. As the public cynicism gets deeper, the political system gets worse. Until the problem of money is dealt with, the system will not get better. We have allowed the basic idea of our democratic process—representative government—to slip away. The only question is whether we are serious about trying to retrieve it. [P. 156]

Drew's point is that in the decade since Nixon's campaign-financing scandals, the concentrated power of big-business interests has surged dramatically into political dominance by the skillful use of political action committees (PACs), which pump enormous amounts of money into the "democratic" process. This development is treated clearly in Thomas B. Edsall, *The New Politics of Inequality* (New York: Norton, 1984). We might remember here that Ronald Reagan became president on the strength of 27 percent of the possible voting public

27. Goodheart, *Culture and the Radical Conscience*, p. 157.

28. White, "Conventional Conflicts," p. 146. White goes on to say, "Modern interpretation thrives as much on the question, 'Who shall have the authority to determine what is a proper question to put to a text?' as it does on the question, 'What does this text mean?' In the deliberative disciplines especially, every claim to knowledge is also a claim to power. And interpretation has as much to do with establishing the legitimacy of a particular exercise of interpretive power as it does with the establishment of the validity of a given interpretation of a text" (p. 155).

29. Zbigniew Brzezinski, "Moving into a Technetronic Society," in *Information Technology in a Democracy*, ed. Alan F. Westin (Cambridge: Harvard University Press, 1971), pp. 165–66.

30. Ibid., p. 167.

31. Armand Mattelart, *Multinational Corporations and the Control of Culture* (Atlantic City, N.J.: Humanities Press, 1979), pp. 294–95.

32. Wayne Booth, "Freedom of Interpretation: Bakhtin and the Challenge

of Feminist Criticism," *Critical Inquiry* 9, no. 1 (September 1982): 48–49. Booth continues: "We may soon be freed of that most debilitating of all inhibitions for the critic—the fear that if we find the artist's self-expressions spiritually empty or socially futile or politically destructive or otherwise repugnant, we should not say so, because to say so reveals us as philistines and bourgeois nincompoops." This is essentially, Booth finds, "the fear that I find expressed whenever I have talked about the possibility of a revived ethical and political criticism." It is very much the same kind of professionally enclosed, self-blinding fear that can be seen so clearly each day in the American press as ostensibly "objective," wholly scrupulous reporters and editors follow one another through hyped stories chosen for public drama (regardless of their minimal content or lasting interest) while the deeper, larger issues of central American values in domestic and foreign policy go unexamined. More subtle perhaps, the consensus about what is "allowable" as humanist critical work is no less influenced by distaste for professional reproach and personal embarrassment than is the more overt consensus that shapes the news. Take a look at Ithiel de Sola Pool and Irwin Shulman, "Newsmen's Fantasies, Audiences, and Newswriting," *Public Opinion Quarterly* 23 (1959).

33. Booth, "Freedom of Interpretation," p. 71. Jonathan Culler has noted that "Booth, that great contemporary champion of understanding," creates a rather polarized notion of understanding as one mind "entering another mind" (Booth's phrase). As Culler points out, in "Booth's terms, misunderstanding is simply negative, a failure to enter or to incorporate something which is there to be entered or incorporated" (Culler, *On Deconstruction* [Ithaca: Cornell University Press, 1982], p. 177).

34. Booth, "Freedom of Interpretation," pp. 48–49. Booth's account might gain force and focus by a careful examination of Culler's similar concern in his text, just cited (see pp. 43–64), an analysis not without risks of its own. And it might gain a particular cogency in regard to the professional and institutional as opposed to a more detached and global cultural sphere if it responded (perhaps via Bakhtin's discussion of Rabelais) to Elaine Martin's "Power and Authority in the Classroom: Sexist Stereotypes in Teaching Evaluations," *Signs* 9, no. 3 (Spring 1984): 482–92.

35. Steven Lukes, "Power and Authority," in *A History of Sociological Analysis*, ed. Tom Bottomore and Robert Nisbet (New York: Basic Books, 1978), pp. 663–64.

36. Antonio Gramsci, *The Modern Prince and Other Writings* (New York: International Publishers, 1959), pp. 119–20.

37. Lukes, "Power and Authority," pp. 664–65. Anyone interested in Weber's concept of power, especially in contrast to Gramsci's, may find Poulantzas's discussion in *Political Power and Social Classes* (London: New Left, 1973) of some use; see pp. 99–156.

38. Lukes, "Power and Authority," p. 665.

39. Gramsci, *Modern Prince*, p. 124.

40. Ibid.

41. Said, *World, Text, and Critic*, p. 171.

42. Ibid., p. 175.

43. For a strong analysis of intellectual hegemony in twentieth-century British culture, see Perry Anderson, "Components of the National Culture," in *Student Power/Problems, Diagnosis, Action,* ed. Alexander Cockburn and Robin Blackburn (Baltimore: Penguin, 1969), pp. 214–84. Anderson shows that the idea of the social whole, of an institutional and cultural totality, has been systematically suppressed by all of the dominant strains in British intellectual practices, which have thereby produced a culture "operating against the growth of any revolutionary Left. It quite literally deprives the Left of any source of concepts and categories with which to analyze its own society" (p. 277). A similar condition has taken shape in the United States, and the work of exposing it has just begun, in journals such as *Cultural Critique.*

44. Paul Mattick, *Marx and Keynes* (Boston: Porter Seargant, 1969); Michel Aglietta, *A Theory of Capitalist Regulation: The U.S. Experience* (London: New Left, 1979); Ernest Mandel, *Late Capitalism* (London: New Left, 1975); Roman Rosdolsky, *Making of Marx's "Capital"* (London: Pluto, 1977); and Harry Braverman, *Labor and Monopoly* (New York: Monthly Review Press, 1974). For an opposing view that sees the foundation of capitalist power in the imperialist domination of foreign territory and markets (and not in the organization and control of labor), see Paul Baran and Paul Sweezy, *Monopoly Capital* (New York: Monthly Review Press, 1964).

45. Noam Chomsky and Edward S. Herman, in their opening remarks in *The Washington Connection and Third World Fascism* (Boston: South End, 1979), point out how deeply true the opposite of that coordinated paranoia is: "The United States has organized under its sponsorship and protection a neo-colonial system of client states ruled mainly by terror and serving the interests of a small local and foreign business and military elite. The fundamental *belief,* or ideological pretense, is that the United States is dedicated to furthering the cause of democracy and human rights throughout the world, though it may occasionally err in the pursuit of this objective" (p. ix).

Kenneth Burke, alost alone among literary critics, shows a passionate interest in such orchestrations of rhetoric and social scenery. In the third section of *The Grammar of Motives* (Cleveland: World, 1945), Burke takes aim at the constitution of society for and by means of war: "When there is much preparation being made *for* war, we might at least aim to prepare with equal zest *against* it. . . . An anecdote shaped about war would be designed not so much for stating what mankind *substantially is* as for emphatically pointing out what mankind is *in danger of becoming*" (p. 330). Burke is often elaborate and to some degree evasive, but one of the qualities that should commend him to humanist intellectuals is the boldness with which he has sought to attach his writing to its actual social circumstance as a critical antagonist to the unironic and aggressive facts we all live with.

46. Irvine Alpert and Ann Markusen have studied the institutional pressures that create blatant contradictions between the stated "independence" of writers doing research and making policy at the Brookings Institution and the political conformity that actually results. They reveal the strength of both the

professional motivations (the desire to perform in ways that do not conflict with institutional orthodoxy) and the intellectual subservience of the brokerage function that think tanks play as they mediate between private capital and state agencies. Deviance and dissent are soon discouraged if not weeded out by peer pressure or outright termination. One might hope to think such sterilization takes place less frequently in universities and colleges, although there is ample evidence that such hope needs caution. See "The Professional Production of Policy, Ideology, and Plans: Brookings and Resources for the Future," *Insurgent Sociologist* 9, nos. 2–3 (Fall 1979/Winter 1980): 94–106. See also, for an examination of the suppression of dissent in historical scholarship, Jesse Lemisch, *On Active Service in War and Peace: Politics and Ideology in the American Historical Profession* (Toronto: New Hogtown Press, 1975).

4 *Intellectual Territories*

1. See Charles Newman's courageous and very provocative attempt to break free of antiseptic critical perspectives in his book-length essay "The Post-modern Aura," *Salmagundi*, nos. 63–64 (Spring/Summer 1984): 3–199.

2. If C. Wright Mills's *Power Elite* (New York: Oxford University Press, 1956) did not demolish the notion of an unstratified society free of cultural rule, then G. William Domhoff's *Who Rules America?* (Englewood Cliffs, N.J.: Prentice-Hall, 1967) is a worthy supplement. The work of the Frankfurt school, especially that of Horkheimer and Adorno, veers away from explicit concern for the situated nature of ruling-class interests. Instead, it generally seeks an understanding of the authoritarian personality as an institutional event, as a product of family indoctrination in the midst of repressive social norms. Their ambivalence about ruling interests and values as a product of hierarchical domination (i.e., as a political reality that cannot be subsumed by rationality or the dispersion of false consciousness) comes to a head to some extent with Claus Offe's "Political Authority and Class Structures—An Analysis of Late Capitalist Societies," *International Journal of Sociology* 2, no. 1 (1972): 73–105. The advantage of Gramsci's analysis of culture over that of the Frankfurt writers, it seems to me, is that it advances Marcuse's aborted attempt to place the critic in a confrontational role as someone who can "negate" (or counteract, somehow modify) the reigning social and political imperatives—especially those that foster military solutions to democratic issues. For a description of Gramsci's position which comprehends his understanding of the complexity of ruling interests, see Norberto Bobbio, "Gramsci and the Conception of Civil Society," in *Gramsci and Marxist Theory*, ed. Chantal Mouffe (London: Routledge & Kegan Paul, 1979), pp. 21–47.

3. Literary critics, no less than other professionals, often avoid confronting a sometimes hostile and at best indifferent public reality. Much of that retreat appears in the form of institutional disagreements about what humanist work should produce in the first place. I can understand, then, how even sympathetic readers of this book may fear that, if its views were more firmly

entrenched within the curriculum (or within its pedagogy), humanist effort as it stands, as a plurality of interpretive and textual activities, might be threatened. That fear is, of course, based on not at all unreasonable assessments of the misappreciation for scholarship and critical thinking that surrounds the humanist's work. A saving counterargument might therefore stress such a reading of professional combat as Stanley Fish's, a reading or argument that emphasized the "merely" self-adjusting, wholly in-house nature of these debates about what criticism and scholarship do and can hope to accomplish. That is not an argument I want to adopt. Instead, I believe that a result like the one I envision for this text would help critics and teachers to overcome their embarrassment about dealing with issues and knowledge outside small areas of insulated expertise. It might at least lend support to efforts that are under way in nearly every scholarly field to increase interdisciplinary research and dialogue and, wherever possible, to illuminate the world that such knowledge is now building all around us.

Let me quarrel here with a critic whose intelligence I admire. Charles Altieri has made what I believe is a strong defense against working out a shared public agenda for criticism:

> The rhetoric of crisis for contemporary criticism contains within itself a basic source of criticism's problems. On the one hand the critic expects and is expected to spell out the contradictions, failures, and achievements of a culture. But each of his or her assessments depends on invoking standards that are usually problematic—partially because of the difficulty of securing authority but even more perniciously because of the inevitable self-staging and self-idealizing that go into positing standards of judgment. Thus to describe conditions of crisis is usually to stage oneself as ennobled both by one's perceptions and by one's courage to live with those perceptions. Critical ideals then can easily appear as primarily disguised statements of need and mirrors not of the society but of the critic's self-regard. [*Boundary* 2, 9, no. 3/10, no. 1 (Spring/Fall 1981): 389]

Altieri is a shrewd worrier, but he is worried (in my estimation) about the wrong issue. The critic's narcissism is a problem worth the effort required to contain or reverse it. However, the source of that excessive self-regard is not an ennobled critical posture—a courageous singularity or personal identity— but an inordinate interest in professional authority, anxiety about being heard among the clatter of competing critical voices. Without question, any published statement can be interpreted as an attempt at recognition. The fact that the elementary law of professional life requires everyone to attempt to gain some measure of recognition only partially counters that accusation. Once we see that anyone who joins the professional academic enterprise must sooner or later try to be heard, must attempt to persuade a difficult and diverse audience, it becomes quite clear that narcissism in the form Altieri worries about is controlled (or sobered) by professional reception: by the very intellectual exchange Altieri appeals to at the end of his argument, by "the quality of a community's [in this case, the humanist community's] discourse about images" (p. 410). My objection to the repeated suspicion about the critic's self-staging is not that such suspicion is unwarranted but that it is consistently directed to writers and writing that are polemically assertive.

I agree with Altieri that we should "accept the partial, tentative nature of both propositional and expressive criteria." Yet if we are "to find a shared stage for assessing what [narcissism] leads us to produce" as critical writers, we will need to account for the professional and historical conditions of accepted models of self-staging on which humanists rely to assert authority. We cannot overlook the self-promotion of the politically committed or politically aroused writer. But we also cannot overlook the creation of crises in the language, in the imaginative activity, and in the professional and social work conditions of humanists. Immanuel Wallerstein has suggested that in moments of crisis (of economic contraction or of mounting intellectual combat during social upheavals short of all-out class warfare, i.e., short of revolution) the cultural temperature rises."At such moments, it has usually been the case that a political quarrel *internal to the bourgeoisie* becomes quite acute."

> It is often defined terminologically as the fight of 'progressive' elements versus 'reactionary' ones, in which the 'progressive' groups demand that institutional 'rights' and access be defined or redefined in terms of performance in the market ('equality of opportunity'), and 'reactionary' groups lay emphasis on the maintenance of previously acquired privilege (so-called 'tradition').

With some adaptation, this model accounts better for the ongoing turbulence about critical self-staging and the perpetual squabble for humanist authority than Altieri's idealistic appeal to refurbished discourse (better, also, than what we saw earlier in Rorty or will see later in Fish). Wallerstein leads us to think about the class interests that join intellectuals despite their ideological differences. He points to the economy, in distinction to culture and the political realm, as the central social area determining behavior and attitudes for the majority of well-established people. In moments of economic and social crisis, we can expect cultural crisis to ensue. We can expect both the cultural and the political right and left to create a great deal of friction, outright battles over intellectual and social territory. Such conflict enlarges disputes about professional as well as moral authority. At that point it is difficult, if not impossible, to assert convincingly (as Kenneth Burke once seemed to) that " 'humility' is the proper partner of irony"—and this inability follows, no doubt, along the lines Altieri maps out. But the intrabourgeois conflict that Wallerstein addresses is not only about the priority of such ideals as Tradition and Equality (of *result* more than of "opportunity"). It is about who and what values will define the dominant practices of a society: What policies, what accomplished ruling interests?

Humanist disputes participate in larger skirmishes and bear on wider terrain than the critic's self-love and professional authority, although these things are crucially involved with one another—and with everything else critical writers do. As long as the economy is stable, as long as the political process seems sound and functions smoothly, academic disagreements about securing authority (or about foreign policy, or about the role of the Federal

Reserve Bank in solving fiscal crises) provide "part of the mechanism of renewing and revitalizing the essential motor of the system," as Wallerstein suggests. Those segments of the population whose rewards and authority are not so great—whose material and social interests are not so directly served by the economic and cultural order—will continue to depend on political shifts that define their access to a system they do not control or have much leverage in. See Immanuel Wallerstein, *The Capitalist World-Economy* (Cambridge: Cambridge University Press, 1979), p. 288; Kenneth Burke, *Grammar of Motives*, p. 513. And see Evan Watkins's review of Altieri's *Act and Quality* (Amherst: University of Massachusetts Press, 1981) in *Boundary* 2, 12, no. 1 (Fall 1983): 235–41.

4. The immediate fact of our social environment is the "growing militarization of political authority," whose costs are assessed by the Sivard Report, *World Military and Social Expenditures*, at $660 billion worldwide for 1982 and $595 billion for 1980. Those figures are projected to be close to $800 billion for 1983 and approaching the staggering amount of $1 *trillion* for 1984. The costs go higher. The Pentagon alone plans to spend $1.96 trillion during the five years between 1985 and 1989 (these numbers come from the "Fiscal 1985–89 Five Year Defense Plan," a classified Pentagon budget report that has been excerpted for publication in *Defense Week* (December 19, 1983). This expansion of the United States military budget and of spending for weapons all around the world is intimately connected to the acceleration of monopolistic growth in the international marketplace. Arms sales mean big business. James Cypher's essay, "Ideological Hegemony and Modern Militarism: The Origins and Limits of Military Keynesianism," *Humanities in Society* 5, nos. 1/2 (Winter/Spring 1982): 45–65, demonstrates the global reach of a militarized economy in which the "*primary* purpose of postwar military spending in the U.S., through the late 1970s, was the *legitimation* of capitalism" (p. 49). Under Reagan, military spending has realized an overtly imperialist intention.

"Economic prosperity in the United States during the decades since World War II has increasingly depended on military expenditures and overseas expansion," James O'Connor reminds us. Such dependency jeopardizes every human need and social priority by creating absurd imbalances such as this: the "annual budget for US military bands is larger than the federal budget for all civilian art programs—music, dance, painting, drama, etc." (James O'Connor, *The Corporations and the State* [New York: Harper & Row, n.d.]). The less absurd but no less startling consequence of the systematic cooperation between private capital and research institutions (including, most of all, the contemporary research university) appears in the enhanced power of scientific and technological disciplines. That power shows up in both monetary and symbolic terms. It appears in political influence as well as in a general aura of prestige, much of it at the expense of critical and evaluative disciplines. The result of this alignment is an essentially symbiotic relationship between *corporate interests* (and influence, including direct cash contributions and the sponsorship of university programs), government and private *surveillance* (often subtle but nonetheless a permanent intervention within the scholarly world), and *the educational process.* In sum, the autonomy of the university is truly compromised by its partnership with state and corporate capital. The famous "objectivity" of university and academic procedures is eroded by arrangements that put the university in the middle of a process that develops research (especially the extremely sophisticated research needed for advanced weapons) whose costs are transferred to the social realm—that is, paid for by tax revenues directly or indirectly. One of the sacrifices here is critical analysis (moral as well as logical clarity), since many people in many areas of the university must pretend that this affiliation of knowledge, the university budget, and both state and corporate capital is not so immediate and so consequential for the life of the university (for the life of dispassionate scholarship too) as in fact it is.

We can go further here. Manuel Castells has recently called attention to the fact that the economic crisis that has redefined institutional interrelationships in the post-Vietnam era has been "caused by a general process of social disruption in most capitalist societies." In short, the dynamics of capital accumulation have been altered by cultural and social upheavals. Traditional structures of exploitation gave way for a time, or shifted, creating strains on the ideological unity of dominant interests. "During the decade 1967–1977," Castells writes,

> most of the advanced capitalist societies went through a period of turmoil, social innovation, and political conflict. In the United States the social movements of the 60s profoundly affected the consciousness of millions of Americans. Civil rights movements, black protest, student revolts, antiwar activities, community and social welfare demands, public workers' struggles, increased union organizing, wildcat strikes, women's liberation—all of these movements undermined the social hegemony of the corporate elite, notwithstanding the political innocence of the participants (which prevented them from becoming a revolutionary challenge in the short term).

Castells's point is that despite challenges to the stability of the capitalist state, Western culture "has developed very powerful mechanisms of social control and economic regulation that prevent major transformations of the system *as long as the political factors remain unmodified.*" The military, the economy, education, research, and culture as a whole form an integrated network that perpetuates the conditions of political conformity. See Manuel Castells, *The Economic Crisis and American Society* (Princeton: Princeton University Press, 1980), pp. 3–75.

5. Paul Fussell, *The Great War and Modern Memory* (New York: Oxford University Press, 1975), p. 35.

6. Robert Anchor, "War and the Social Order," *Humanities in Society* 5, nos. 1/2 (Winter/Spring 1982): 25–26. Robert M. Maniquis is even more direct in naming this circumstance. "Contemporary academic criticism is usually considered in isolation from the surrounding culture of the Bomb," he argues. "The Bomb embarrasses the historian," yet, more problematic, it is "self-defeating to exaggerate the weakening of political will under the sign of the

Bomb, but it may also be naive to underestimate it" ("Pascal's Bet, Totalities, and Guerrilla Criticism," *Humanities in Society* 6, nos. 2/3 [Spring/Summer 1983]: 259, 263).

7. Richard Falk, *A Global Approach to National Policy* (Cambridge: Harvard University Press, 1975), pp. 2–3.

8. O'Connor, Castells, Aronowitz, and others argue that imperialism or national defense and national paranoia (and aggression) constitute only one source of motivation for military growth. Since World War II, military expansion has been an economic policy: "military spending as disaccumulation is at least as significant as its actual use in relation to wars and other interventions abroad." In brief, its "significance in relation to employment, investment, and many other economic indices is not circumscribed by U.S. foreign interests." The outcome of such fully rationalized and structurally integrated military preparations (military hardware, military planning, military logic) can only be continued state violence and territorial conflict. One of the central unaddressed questions for humanist intellectuals in the United States is what strategy they will adopt to confront that violence. Is pacifism a viable stance? Does it challenge (or can it be made to challenge) state violence? Does it overlook distinctions that need to be made: the justice, for example, of wars of liberation, or the necessity of armed resistance to large and small coercions that exploit and oppress enormous parts of the world's swelling population? See Stanley Aronowitz, "The End of Political Economy," in *The Crisis in Historical Materialism* (New York: Praeger, 1981), p. 19; see also "Towards a New Strategy of Liberation," chap. 6 in the same volume.

9. Philip Rahv, *Essays on Literature and Politics, 1932–1972* (Boston: Houghton Mifflin, 1978), p. 292.

10. Mark Poster, "Mode of Production, Mode of Information: Toward a Critique of the Critique of Political Economy," *Humanities in Society* 5, nos. 3/4 (Summer/Fall 1982): 228, 223.

11. We might look at the normalization of intellectual work to which Hayden White pointed earlier and which Lewis Coser, following Isaac Rosenfeld, characterizes as "a shrinkage of extremes." The demise of unattached intellectuals, people who worked without formal affiliations with universities or publishers or research institutes, reflects the same set of forces that narrows the ideological spectrum. Coser writes:

> In contemporary America [1965], though not in the rest of the world, critical left-wing ideologies have lost much of their appeal among intellectuals: the disillusionment of left-wing intellectuals with Russian gods; the prosperity of American society; its apparent ability to hobble along on a pragmatic mixture of free enterprise, government intervention, and defense spending; the whole climate of the Cold War, with its polarization of the world into two camps—all these have played their parts. In any case, radicalism and socialism as ideologies have markedly declined in contemporary America, and most intellectuals who once subscribed to or sympathized with these movements have by now found havens in one or another position on that wide spectrum that in America is called "liberalism." [Lewis Coser, *Men of Ideas* (New York: Free Press, 1965), p. 265]

Daniel Aaron puts this pattern of assimilation succinctly in *Writers on the Left* (New York: Oxford University Press, 1977): "Literary radicalism never seems to be sustained over a long period, and the writer is gradually absorbed again into the society he has rejected. The aftermath of his revolt is sometimes tragic, sometimes pathetic or ludicrous. Often the disenthralled writer becomes embittered or ashamed after his adventure in nonconformity, or he becomes tired as his idealism flags and the prison-house of the world closes upon him" (p. 4). Another force, beyond futility and fatigue born of social impossibility, is the relative affluence established intellectuals can count on. The rewards for cooperating with the system mobilize intellectual energies, contain dissent, and minimize the chance that any kind of widespread serious antagonism to reigning norms and values will ever take root.

12. This territory has increasingly been inhabited by Stanley Fish, whose notion of an "interpretive community" has become part of common critical parlance. I look at this not altogether unproblematic concept in chap. 5. See also sec. 3 of Mary Louise Pratt's essay "Interpretive Strategies/Strategic Interpretations: On Anglo-American Reader Response Criticism," *Boundary* 2, 11, nos. 1/2 (Fall/Winter 1982/83): 221–29. Pratt has additional useful comments about Jonathan Culler's rather antiseptic concept of "literary competence," an idea designed to steer criticism away from the political and social context of intellectual work and toward professionally supervised interpretive efforts.

13. Raymond Williams, *Culture and Society, 1780–1950* (New York: Harper & Row, 1958), p. 319.

14. Edward Said points out that Williams is a "reflective" critic "rather than a committed revolutionary" (like Georg Lukács). Nonetheless, Williams takes criticism outside its professional cloisters to place theorists and interpreters in the actual world of lived experience and ideological combat:

> The theoretical model which I have been trying to work with is this. I would say first that in any society, in any particular period, there is a central system of practices, meanings and values, which we can properly call dominant and effective. This implies no presumption about its value. All I am saying is that it is central. Indeed I would call it a corporate system, but this might be confusing, since Gramsci uses 'corporate' to mean the subordinate as opposed to the general and dominant elements of hegemony. In any case what I have in mind is the central, effective and dominant system of meanings and values, which are not merely abstract but which are organized and lived. That is why hegemony is not to be understood at the level of mere opinion or mere manipulation. It is a whole body of practices and expectations . . . we can only understand an effective and dominant culture if we understand the real social process on which it depends: I mean the process of incorporation. The modes of incorporation are of great social significance. The educational institutions are usually the main agencies of the transmission . . . at the true level of theory and at the level of the history of various practices, there is a process which I call the *selective tradition:* that which, within the terms of an effective dominant culture, is always passed off as '*the* tradition,' '*the* significant past.' But always the selectivity is the point. . . . If what we learn there

were merely an imposed ideology, or if it were only the isolable meanings and practices of the ruling class, or of a section of the ruling class, which gets imposed on others, occupying merely the top of our minds, it would be—and one would be glad—a very much easier thing to overthrow. [Raymond Williams, "Base and Superstructure in Marxist Cultural Theory," in *Problems in Materialism and Culture* (London: New Left, 1980), pp. 38–39]

See also Edward Said, "Traveling Theory," in *The World, the Text, and the Critic* (Cambridge: Harvard University Press, 1983), pp. 237–41.

15. Williams, *Culture and Society*, p. 328.

16. Nicos Poulantzas, *State, Power, Socialism* (London: New Left, 1978), p. 215.

17. Sacvan Bercovitch, "The Rites of Assent: Rhetoric, Ritual, and the Ideology of American Consensus," in *The American Self*, ed. Sam B. Girgus (Albuquerque: University of New Mexico Press, 1981), p. 19.

18. Ibid., p. 29. Bercovitch makes a strong statement of "the process of Americanization," which has carried a powerful counterrevolutionary force from the very founding of "the Puritan venture" to contemporary middle-class culture. See his essay "New England's Errand Reappraised," in *New Directions in American Intellectual History*, ed. John Higham and Paul K. Conkin (Baltimore: Johns Hopkins University Press, 1979), pp. 85–104.

19. Bercovitch, "Rites of Assent," p. 33.

20. Herbert Schiller, *Who Knows: Information in the Age of the Fortune 500* (Norwood, N.J.: Ablex, 1981).

21. The good news about computer literacy and computer-assisted learning is summed up in an article in the *Boston Globe* by Muriel Cohen: students are "drawn to computers because their responses, unlike those of many teachers, are not judgmental." Not only does the student have more "control" over the interaction, but the learner is the one who is active rather than the teacher ("Computers Altering Student-Teacher Relationship," January 9, 1983). The bad news is offered by Douglas Noble. Not only is computer literacy an effective way to sell computers; it has the means "to transform the workplace, the home, the school, and the functions of government into an efficient, highly controlled, and easily monitored technological marketplace." In addition, "the makers of the Information Society, those who would transform our world to suit their needs, have perpetuated CL [computer literacy] in order to ensure public acquiescence in their grand design." First of all, "CL mystifies in the name of demystification." Second, it disarms skepticism and critical suspicion by producing "computer-friendly" people. Third, it "is used to psychologize dissent." Fourth, it tends "to stifle debate and to depoliticize discussion" by restricting the absolute numbers of choices commonly available or readily apparent. And it is, as Noble shows, an extension of a militarized framework in which information is more easily controlled, restricted, censored, selected, and classified if everyone is plugged into a technologically sophisticated (technologically manipulated) system where reading and thinking can be narrowed to fit newly manufactured assumptions about *what*

should be known, *who* should know it, and *how* it ought to be used. See Douglas Noble, "The Underside of Computer Literacy," *Raritan* 3, no. 4 (Spring 1984): 37–64.

22. This restriction on scholarship and scientific research, a restriction on the exchange of knowledge in particular, has been strongly protested by enlightened members of the academic community. But the increased funding of academic work by government and industry—a 90 percent rise in industry support and a 41 percent rise from the government between 1979 and 1983—makes the intervention, oversight, and control of knowledge by those extra-academic forces more likely and less stoppable. The lamentable withdrawal of the United States from UNESCO in 1984 is immediately related to (among other things) restriction of both access to and use of information that can be turned against capitalist state power. The "threat" UNESCO poses is essentially in providing literacy to Third World nations: the charge, of course, is that UNESCO has strayed from the objective neutrality of Western democratic cultural and economic assumptions. The National Science Foundation figures on the increased funding of basic research which I cite here are for nonmilitary research in the basic sciences. I might note also that in 1982 M.I.T. entered into a five-year, $7 million contract with W. R. Grace & Co. and Yale signed one with Bristol-Myers for $3 million over five years and another, spread over three years, with Celanese for more than $1 million. Harvard Medical School and its teaching affiliate, Massachusetts General Hospital, signed two contracts in 1981 for $76 million spread across five- and ten-year periods. Such whopping amounts of money create a very close partnership, which Donald Kennedy, president of Stanford, suggests could change the fundamental conditions of intellectual production: "without some care, we may find one day that 'scientific objectivity' has become an oxymoron, a self-contradiction" (*Boston Globe*, November 7, 1983, p. 43). It may already have done so.

23. Alvin Gouldner's depiction of innate tension between technical and humanist intellectuals, which we looked at in chap. 2, makes sense to a point. Universities are influenced by the critical intensity of their faculties—an intensity that often comes from scientists rather than humanists—as the resistance to the Reagan administration's policy of state censorship over basic research in several areas of military production and computer encoding has proved. Harvard, Stanford, Cal Tech, and M.I.T. have all begun to draft policies against such infringements of scholarly freedom. What remains for the most part unexamined is the overall framework of private funding and public access. The lines of cooperation, "partnership," and restriction (even censorship) are well in place and, regardless of university resistance or objection, will continue to allow the authority of money and of "national security" to exert pressure if not full dominance.

24. The fact that intellectual authority is derived in a very real way from its institutional affiliation with the state can be seen as soon as we recognize that society (any nation, every government, each cultural system) is the construction of human choice and judgment. The crucial decisions that perpetuate

social order are, as Raymond Williams says, beneath awareness in the incorporating energies of a "selective" tradition that appears as the only set of viable terms and cultural practices. Thus it is that decisions that mold and reproduce society are influenced by the way people who hold power at important moments of social formation (or reformulation) "read" the world, make sense of their cultural heritage, and finally legislate laws and policies that shape behavior. The role of the intellectual is never wholly visible in that work, nor is it ever suspended. It is exercised in the classroom, where students learn what educators and politicians deem desirable and necessary knowledge. It is exercised in the training of lawyers and clergymen and bureaucrats, all of whom exert pressure on political judgment and political activity. In other words, the intellectual's role is derived from the state because the position of intellectual work is inserted well within the cultural and institutional system of state power. The intellectual articulates values by interpreting texts, framing questions, and choosing a perspective from which to define the way those questions and interpretations fit into reality. But most of all, the political impact of intellectual work shows up in assumptions about the kind of world we are to address in the first place.

The prevailing liberal humanist view has the force of a long tradition behind it. A good deal of what many well-meaning, somewhat politically inclined humanists believe to be trailblazing critical effort falls squarely in the ever-protean liberal accommodation—a way of lending sympathy to radical causes without lending political support. In other words, much newly minted criticism is a freshening, updating, and revising of liberal depoliticization. Given the state rivalries that dominate the world's natural and human resources, given the nature of capitalism (which, as John Gurley shows, "is not receptive to freedom" in underdeveloped countries but "is always hospitable" to more capitalism), and given the inability of humanists to create much enthusiasm for reading the great canonical texts even among the educated class in North America, a larger revision than liberal critics now offer will be needed if the humane uses of intellect and literacy are to break free of theory. Take a look at "The Combahee River Collective: A Black Feminist Statement," in *Capitalist Patriarchy and the Case for Socialist Feminism*, ed. Zillah Eisenstein (New York: Monthly Review Press, 1979).

25. Jean-François Lyotard, *The Postmodern Condition* (Minneapolis: University of Minnesota Press, 1984).

26. Richard Rorty has mapped an anti-Nietzschean account of the neoconservative or "sublime" left intellectual in his essay "Habermas and Lyotard on Post-modernity," in *Praxis International* 4, no. 1 (April 1984): 32–43, which can be read as an introduction to the complicated current debate about "postmodernism" and postmodern culture. Let me call attention here to Habermas's essays on Benjamin and on Horkheimer and Adorno in *New German Critique*, no. 17 (1979), pp. 30–59, and no. 26 (1982), pp. 13–30; and his "Modernity versus Postmodernity," no. 22 (1981), pp. 3–14.

27. Michael W. Apple, *Ideology and Curriculum* (London: Routledge & Kegan Paul, 1979), p. 11.

28. See Michael W. Apple, *Education and Power* (London: Routledge & Kegan Paul, 1982), and Harold Entwistle, *Antonio Gramsci: Conservative Schooling for Radical Politics* (London: Routledge & Kegan Paul, 1979). For a lucid examination of Althusser and his relation to intellectual events in France that have had strong influence in England and the United States, chap. 7 of Arthur Hirsh, *The French New Left* (Boston: South End, 1981), is useful. A reading of schooling in the United States can be found in Stanley Aronowitz and Henry Giroux, *Education under Siege* (South Hadley, Mass.: Bergin & Garvey, 1985).

29. Gerald Graff, "The University and the Prevention of Culture," in *Criticism in the University,* ed. Gerald Graff and Reginald Gibbon (Evanston, Ill.: Northwestern University Press, 1985), pp. 70, 65.

30. Samuel Weber, "How Not to Stop Worrying," *Critical Exchange,* no. 15 (Winter 1984), p. 22. Let me call attention here once more to the neglected but instructive long essay by Charles Newman, "The Post-modern Aura: The Act of Fiction in an Age of Inflation," *Salmagundi,* nos. 63/64 (Spring/ Summer 1984), pp. 3–191. Newman moves toward a critique of cultural dynamics as immediately material and institutional energies produced within an explicable and wholly concrete international context (see secs. 23 and 24, for example) which critical writers now must pursue to its maturity.

5   Theory and the Interpretive Community

1. Stanley Fish, *Is There a Text in This Class?* (Cambridge: Harvard University Press, 1980), p. 171. Kuhn writes that "the most striking feature of the normal research problems" with which scientists regularly deal "is how little they aim to produce major novelties, conceptual or phenomenal," because "the results gained in normal research are significant" only to the extent that "they add to the scope and precision with which the paradigm [of normative scientific work] can be applied" (Thomas Kuhn, *The Structure of Scientific Revolutions* [Chicago: University of Chicago Press, 1962], pp. 35–36). For a comparison with Habermas's thesis that "truth" consists of consensual understanding(s) among speech communities, see the appendix to *Knowledge and Human Interests* (Boston: Beacon, 1971).

2. Fish, *Is There a Text,* p. 173.

3. Ibid., pp. 303–4.

4. Ibid., p. 320.

5. Stanley Fish, "Professional Anti-professionalism," *Times Literary Supplement,* December 10, 1982, p. 1363.

6. Stanley Fish, "Interpretation and the Pluralist Vision," *Texas Law Review* 60, no. 3 (March 1982): 496.

7. Critical debate, as we see here in Fish's model, continues to find new ways of aggrandizing rhetoric without situating it within the institutional framework where rhetoric lives, so that it speaks (or signifies) from settings wider and more conflicted than the normative rivalries of professional disputes.

When, for example, the specialized languages of a domesticated deconstructive practice can appear as a way to free academic readers from their depoliticized lethargy, the field of literary studies is subject to more disciplinary regulation than it knows how to adjudicate. Thus from the vantage of American deconstructors, Philip Lewis says, the only hope is "to hold out for the conditional against the doctrinal," "to philosophize a-theoretically, a-critically," "to assume the pagan mask of the poet-raconteurs whom Plato banished from his republic"; "it is to assume, to put into play, the notion that philosophy's burden is not to achieve proof, but conviction, and thus that the philosopher's task is as much a matter of rhetoric—style or tone—as it is of argument." This evasion of evidentiary contexts, like Fish's embrace of them, amounts to arguing within the realm of accepted constraints or, in contrast, dismissing all constraints for the privilege of a playful postmodern paganism. Either way, the academic writer inflates the value of his or her position as an authorized interpreter, someone who "knows" what can and cannot be asserted (Fish) or who asserts "a position with respect to the institution that surrounds and seeks to contain" its destabilizing playfulness (Lewis). In both models interpretation is seen as embedded within an academy shut off from the world, an academy that additionally resists assessing its own relation to the social whole, a whole that deforms (and constrains) language professionally in order to meet competing commercial or institutional intentions, each self-authorized, self-interested, and self-enclosed. In what way will academic critical authority be strengthened by remaining faithful to the rule-making arguments and rule-breaking games of professional debates?

8. Fish, "Interpretation and the Pluralist Vision," p. 505.

9. Contrast Fish's words with Robert Chianese's sense that there are "constructive forms of social action available to academic humanists":

> We can organize and serve on forums for debate of public policy. . . . We can articulate positions on issues of the day through professional organizations. We can employ our skills directly in political and social movements off campus that cry out for clear analysis and creative solutions. . . . We have already realized the need to form a national organization to promote the humanities—the American Association for the Advancement of the Humanities. Such a group or one similar to it can begin to study and formulate policy about particular social crises that concern us most. . . . There is another task for the humanities that needs to complement an organized movement of social criticism and reform: the involvement of the humanities in the formulation of a new, emerging order of ideas. [Robert Chianese, "Humanities and Social Action," *Humanities in Society* 3, no. 4 (Fall 1980): 359]

What also might be debated is the form of organization, as well as the ideas, that such political commitment should pursue. Is the goal of that effort reform, as Chianese suggests, or something more thoroughly opposed to the professional and institutional structures that now impede political vision and social justice?

10. Fish, *Is There a Text*, p. 365.

11. Ibid., p. 356.

12. Ibid., p. 368.

13. Perry Anderson, "The Antinomies of Antonio Gramsci," *New Left Review* 100 (November 1976/January 1977): 6. Gramsci shows us that a culture is, among other things, a system of values and practices that produce authority, authorized speakers and writers, people who maintain and sometimes extend the fictional coherence of national identity.

14. Duncan Kennedy's *Legal Education and the Reproduction of Hierarchy* (Cambridge, Mass.: Afar, 1983) provides a cogent statement of the challenge to traditional legal training, and *The Politics of Law*, an anthology of "progressive" essays edited by David Kairys (New York: Pantheon, 1982), is a useful companion volume. Kennedy's volume has a brief reading list (as well as an invitation to request a free bibliography of Critical Legal Studies) at the end of his text. Fish, by the way, has attacked the Critical Legal Studies movement in his essay "Anti-professionalism."

15. Armand Mattelart, *Multinational Corporations and the Control of Culture* (Atlantic City, N.J.: Humanities Press, 1979), p. 295. See chap. 3 above.

16. Fish, "Interpretation and the Pluralist Vision," p. 563.

17. Ibid., p. 564.

18. Ibid., p. 562.

19. Gayatri Chakravorty Spivak, "The Politics of Interpretations," *Critical Inquiry* 9, no. 1 (September 1982): 278.

20. Thomas Haskell has shown that the "institution-building enterprise" of the humanities in the last two decades of the nineteenth century consciously emulated the establishment of a national professional scientific community, a community of self-defining, self-regulated competence in differentiated fields of study which could thus assume collective instead of individualistic authority. "Men of science were so successful at this institution-building enterprise," Haskell writes, "that by the end of the century the word 'scientific' seemed to epitomize the very essence of well-founded intellectual authority" ("Professionalization as Cultural Reform," *Humanities in Society* 1, no. 2 [Spring 1978]: 103–13). The general authority of the university in North American and international life is directly tied to the demonstrated competence in problem solving and in the accumulated professional solidarity of various academic disciplines developed through the past eighty to one hundred years. The authority of scientific inquiry has appeared less absolute recently, as a result of such work as Thomas Kuhn's, which shows the importance of paradigms and paradigm making in scientific research (a kind of storytelling activity of its own) and as a result, also, of increased concern about the relation between science and both corporate and government financing. Science, in brief, can now be seen as an enterprise like others, work that rests on values and assumptions that are not wholly methodological or conventional but contain conscious or subliminal awareness of the larger human environment, values and assumptions that bear on the entire social world. In other words, conventional norms and the notion of rationality increasingly look like a group narrative, a set of rules and vocabularies to generate prob-

lems and to orient agreed-upon procedures to represent and investigate those problems. It follows, too, that in the humanities, where storytelling is at the heart of the scholarly and critical effort, the idea of a mode of intellectual authority that could derive from correspondence with real events in a preexisting order of meaning and value has given way to the wilder, more unsettling relativity of competing interpretations, each with terms and analytic conclusions that demand additional scrutiny, more discourse, endless critical controversy. The old-fashioned self-assurance that we find in such an essay as E. D. Hirsch's "Theory in Humanistic Studies," *Daedalus* 99, no. 2 (1970), is skewed by its misplaced hope for external authority. "There is a supra-individual and timeless contribution in the humanist's professional work," Hirsch concludes, "that resides in its authentically scientific aspect. We humanists give up everything if we make this cognitive aspect a mere hostage to our ideological concern for relevance and value" (p. 354).

The plaintive tone of this appeal is heard most in that curiously ambiguous word *aspect*. Richard Rorty, following Kuhn, reminds us that "scientific breakthroughs are not so much a matter of deciding which of various alternative hypotheses are true, but of finding the right jargon in which to frame hypotheses in the first place." In fact, he goes on, "it has become obvious that *whatever* terms are used to describe human beings *become* 'evaluative' terms," so that any attempt to constitute interpretive activity (the study of texts and the framing of stories in which to situate those texts) on a scientific basis of nonideological self-evidence or self-verification is doomed to nonsense, disrespect, or dismissal (Richard Rorty, *The Consequences of Pragmatism* [Minneapolis: University of Minnesota Press, 1982], pp. 195, 193).

For a brief but intelligent discussion of Fish's contribution to the evolving notion of an interpretive community, see John Fekete, "Modernity in the Literary Institution: Strategic Anti-foundational Moves," in *The Structural Allegory*, ed. John Fekete (Minneapolis: University of Minnesota Press, 1984), pp. 228–43, esp. 239–43.

21. Fish, *Is There a Text*, p. 14. The "bottom line" of Fish's position amounts to a rigorous professional pragmatism: interpreters are "embedded within a practice" and inherit an "already at work notion of practice" in their field, Fish reminded his audience at UCLA at the October 1986 meeting of the Humanities Institute. "Act as you think you're supposed to act in the institution where you work!" is advice Fish gives his graduate students, advice that places pragmatic emphasis on the rhetorical as opposed to the theoretical basis of interpretive work. In response to Hayden White's objection that Fish might well be contributing to the anti-intellectual habits of North America's commercial pragmatism, Fish defended his attack on theory—his charge that all uses of theoretical arguments and positions are rhetorical devices instead of substantial discriminations between values and epistemologies—by stressing that his sense of its irrelevance is designed to motivate arguments to "decenter Theory" from its privileged status in the contemporary humanist curriculum. Aside from the irony that Fish relies on a quasi-deconstructive vocabulary to undermine critical theory, his forthright defense has the merit of

admitting that it wants to drive critical writing to the self-conscious awareness of its slumbering ambition to be something that Fish believes it cannot be. "Theory wants only one practice, philosophy." Instead of a lame philosophical practice, Fish would like to see critical writers attempt to accomplish practical results within the rules of the game they play. I agree that a change in the institutional enterprise where teaching and writing most often take place is in fact the first priority of critical writers; I do not agree that to change such an enterprise (or, as Fish puts it, "to do something") "you do not need the theoretical account of it." My response, even as I admire Fish's aim to promote active and polemical critical energy, is to note that uninteresting and unconvincing critical writing follows the neglect of theoretical accounts and theoretical positions. It does so, today especially, for reasons very similar to those Fish cherishes: since professional criticism is now largely devoted to discriminating between theoretical paradigms, devoted also to creating an enlarged and possibly more productive critical framework of questions and interpretive operations, no one can take an active part in it who is not also able to understand a complicated set of theoretical vocabularies. Such critical activity is not, as Fish believes, merely "theory talk." It is one way to stimulate intelligent intellectual behavior. It is only one way, but it is crucial in preparing rational political energies among critical writers. The work of converting theory and criticism to practical public uses still remains. Fish may, inadvertently or otherwise, help create the dialogue necessary for that work.

22. Ibid., pp. 17, 16. Note Michel de Certeau's inquiry into the dialectic of exchange within a network of professional activity in *The Practice of Everyday Life*, trans. Steven F. Rendall (Berkeley: University of California Press, 1984), pt. 2.

23. The "humanizing" or "civilizing" force of literary study is a central assumption (as well as goal) of the university humanities curriculum. It can be found powerfully articulated in the Harvard Core Curriculum Report that William Spanos and others have scrutinized. The report tells us, for example: "We assume that in dealing with such questions [intrinsic to literary studies] students will be exposed to a variety of critical approaches, *but the primary purpose* of the Core Literature courses is to show how *great authors* have contrived distinctive statements about *timeless and universal aspects of human experience*" (Spanos's insertion and emphasis; *Boundary 2*, 10, no. 2 [Winter 1982]: 13). This notion of the "timeless" and "universal" quality of human experience as it is rendered in great literary masterpieces overlooks everything that is distinctively historical in such texts and smuggles into literary studies the ideology of a positivist recovery of unproblematic truths, an ideology designed to diminish critical interest in cultural differences and social conflicts.

24. Frank Lentricchia, *Criticism and Social Change* (Chicago: University of Chicago Press, 1983).

25. Martin Jay, *Adorno* (Cambridge: Harvard University Press, 1984), provides a starting point here.

26. The critical force of humanist work is theoretically opposed to the belligerent constants of contemporary capitalist practices (of authoritarianism

and totalitarianism of all forms), but such opposition and its analytic subtlety are likely to remain dormant—a set of instruments for potentially precise knowledge, a poignant and powerful art of interpretive judgment—unless critics make an unusual effort to reach toward neglected yet politically awakened groups on the margins of our dominant culture. The maturing political consciousness of native Americans, of black women, of Hispanic peoples is motivated not only by their economic plight but by the exclusion (or at best the ambivalent acceptance) of their cultures by the reigning humanist culture. Literary studies and literary critics have everything to gain and nothing of value to lose by deepening their understanding of these cultures, by understanding the process of exclusion that demotes some cultures as "foreign" or antagonistic to central Western values. The greatest benefit of that expanded knowledge could be the contact generated between those on the "inside" and those on the "outside"; that contact could strengthen the intellectual bonds needed for social cooperation across cultural divisions. The purpose of this cooperation is not solely to "legitimate" demoted cultures, and not at all to "enlarge" the humanities, but to foster intellectual and cultural affiliations that promote the political energy to fight elitism, racism, sexism, and their dehumanizing legacies.

27. Paul de Man, "The Resistance to Theory," *Yale French Studies* 63 (1982): 18.

28. Paul A Bové, *Destructive Poetics* (New York: Columbia University Press, 1980), p. 46.

29. Ibid., p. 44.

30. De Man, "Resistance to Theory," p. 19.

31. Paul de Man, *Allegories of Reading* (New Haven: Yale University Press, 1979), p. 204.

32. Ibid., p. 98.

33. De Man, "Resistance to Theory," p. 20.

34. Ibid. It is worth noting here de Man's conscious shriveling of the concept of ideology. Midway through the essay on theory de Man writes, "What we call ideology is precisely the confusion of linguistic with natural reality, of reference with phenomenalism. It follows that, more than any other mode of inquiry, including economics, the linguistics of literariness is a powerful and indispensable tool in the unmasking of ideological aberrations, as well as a determining factor in accounting for their occurrence. Those who reproach literary theory for being oblivious to social and historical (that is to say ideological) reality are merely stating their fear at having their own ideological mystifications exposed by the tool they are trying to discredit. They are, in short, very poor readers of Marx's *German Ideology*" (p. 11).

No one who comprehends the situated and partial awareness of all human thought and writing will confuse linguistic with "natural reality" (whatever de Man may have meant by that term), nor is ideology reducible to such confusion wherever it occurs. Ideology is not "precisely" anything; but it occupies everyone's thinking and haunts spoken and written statements in the numerous guises that the shaping, positioning, and limiting of human consciousness (and of knowledge) are forced to assume in order to make defendable interpretations—a workable argument, a credible understanding—in the first place. Ideology is not confusion that literary comprehension of de Man's, or anyone's, sophisticated variety can depose and somehow evaporate. De Man's own ideological purpose in this passage is clear: to elevate critical theory of the rigorously self-enclosed self-consciousness he prefers (a choice, after all, of a certain kind of world, essentially textual) over all other intellectual and critical perspectives, especially over those that seek to clarify what can be *known* in order to improve personal, social, and political choices.

35. Frank Lentricchia, *After the New Criticism* (Chicago: University of Chicago Press, 1980), p. 284. In fact "truth" in any sense that might stabilize awareness or help people to comprehend the facts of their world is the very notion de Man most challenges and tries to undermine. Since "the historical impact of twentieth-century literary discussion" is "so slight" (an opinion that ignores the role of literary study in the shaping of dominant cultural attitudes), de Man leads theory and the theorist away from social responsibility and historical knowledge. "Literary theory can be said to come into being when the approach to literary texts is no longer based on non-linguistic, that is to say historical and aesthetic, considerations or, to put it somewhat less crudely, when the object of discussion is no longer the meaning or the value but the modalities of production and of reception of meaning and of value prior to their establishment—the implication being that this establishment is problematic enough to require an autonomous discipline of critical investigation to consider its possibility and status" ("Resistance," p. 7). This is a polemic and not a descriptive passage, as de Man pretends it to be. It is written with a carefully modulated urgency and deliberative forcefulness that suggests the exact sense of crisis that his 1967 essay "Criticism and Crisis," in *Blindness and Insight* (New York: Oxford University Press, 1970), warns us to beware of. Apparently the crisis in literary studies, which in the late 1960s seemed to be generating interest in de Man's chosen writers and methods, had passed beyond disengaged reflection and threatened to overwhelm linguistic suspicion and neatly delineated aporias by the early 1980s. One wonders, however, if the literary establishment (which de Man felt called on to defend for its value-neutral professional purity) were truly under siege, whether the optimistic assertion of exploding, unstoppable theory that he projects would resolve or exacerbate the crisis.

36. James O'Connor, *The Corporations and the State* (New York: Harper & Row, n.d.), p. 111.

37. R. P. Blackmur, *The Lion and the Honeycomb: Essays in Solicitude and Critique* (New York: Harcourt, Brace, 1955), pp. 293–94. Blackmur's remarks were anticipated in a capsule comment by Charles Francis Kettering in 1946, which William Appleman Williams uses as a headnote for *The Roots of the Modern American Empire* (New York: Random House, 1969): "A man must have a certain amount of intelligent ignorance to get anywhere."

38. John H. Schaar, *Loyalty in America* (Berkeley: University of California Press, 1957), pp. 160–67. Schaar's account of Oppenheimer's treatment by

the government is, as he says it is, an "example of the emergent tendency to equate loyalty with conformity" whenever the fear of communism without and subversion within overrides respect for constitutional rights and all other political values.

39. A Walton Litz's moving tribute to Blackmur in his essay "Literary Criticism," in *Harvard Guide to Contemporary American Writing*, ed. Daniel Hoffman (Cambridge: Harvard University Press, 1979), comprehends the astute command of both the early and late essays Blackmur wrote, an appreciation that escapes some readers. The earlier Blackmur was and still is widely admired for the grace of his analytic tact, an ability to move within the complexity of literary texts and find the unuttered motive or the unnoticed shift of rhetorical strategies. The later Blackmur, more concerned with the social costs and political consequences of culture, has gained adherents who now see him as capable of nudging criticism toward "other forms of knowledge" with a socially alert intellectual voice. Evan Watkins, Cornel West, and Daniel O'Hara have expressed renewed interest in Blackmur's last work. William Cain has made a useful (I think accurate) assessment of Blackmur's writing and of the controversy that divides the early from the late Blackmur: *The Crisis in Criticism: Theory, Literature, and Reform in English Studies* (Baltimore: Johns Hopkins University Press, 1984), pp. 146–62.

40. Blackmur, "Toward a Modus Vivendi," in *Lion and Honeycomb*, pp. 28–29.

6   *Intellectual Identity*

1. In a splendid essay, "Deconstruction and Radical Teaching," *Yale French Studies* 63 (1982): 45–58, Michael Ryan points out that "radical teachers and business technocrats" both "hold the same view of the university," radicals arguing that "the university services capitalism by providing it with trained manpower, technology, and new knowledge" that the technocratic community agrees to, depends on, and does "all [it] can to foster." In this regard, "opposition" to admitting the political reality of interpretive and pedagogical work comes not from "conservative" business people (who merely disagree about the virtue of revamping institutional arrangements) but from "liberal" academics who disagree with the notion that intellectual work is grounded on inherently political facts of life that are not amenable to "bracketing" or epistemological neutrality. David L. Schalk, *The Spectrum of Political Engagement* (Princeton: Princeton University Press, 1979), explores some of the central writers in the post-Benda debate about "engagement."

2. Paul Bové, "Intellectuals at War: Michel Foucault and the Analytics of Power," *SubStance*, nos. 37/38 (1983): 45; Frank Lentricchia, *Criticism and Social Change* (Chicago: University of Chicago Press, 1983), p. 6.

3. Let me briefly address three issues that emerge from this terrain. First, I want to make clear that good politics and good morals cannot become a program for scholarly activity. As one of my readers has pointed out to me (a

position I agree with), the critic's and the scholar's job is to speak the truth as they see it. The need to underline this fact follows from the miscalculation some may make of my sense that teachers and critics today more than ever must help students gain a critical intellectual identity. Just as I was at pains in my long introduction to this book to spell out how self-defeating and ultimately anticritical and anti-intellectual any method resembling one-sided overemphasis in classrooms or in critical conversation must be (and always is), I want to make it plain here that the obligation to situate students within both theoretical and institutional contexts carries with it, from my perspective, the absolute necessity to admit every conceivable fact and angle of analysis bearing on the work of illuminating (defining, inspecting, adjudicating) texts of all kinds and the problems they present.

Second, in reverse, another kind of reading may find my sense that many young readers are vulnerable to pacification in contemporary culture a position that underplays the split between high and mass culture, which a good number of students internalize with considerable social pain (especially in relation to their families) as they identify with the academic as opposed to the local terms they leave behind. I believe that much of the second part of my introduction and its notes (see n. 12 to chap. 1, for example) counteract any inclination to aestheticize defenses that literary teachers and critics may be tempted to erect. My overall point in raising the issue of contemporary culture is to establish it as an unavoidable ground for critical inspection, as part of the live context within which readers deal with texts and all things intellectual.

Third, and finally, the specific implication for critical pedagogy here is, among other things, the need to address the professional norms and circumstances that create a determinate (though not always fully visible) context for student and teacher/critic/scholar alike. As I noted earlier, the particular pedagogical methods of pursuing questions of context along with the problems of reading texts themselves need to be elaborated.

4. See Gramsci's comments on the formation of intellectuals and on education in his late writing: pp. 5–43, for example, in *Selections from the Prison Notebooks*, ed. Quintin Hoare and Geoffrey Nowell Smith (New York: International Publishers, 1971). Harold Entwistle has written an extended analysis of Gramsci's thoughts about education and revolutionary activity, *Antonio Gramsci: Conservative Schooling for Radical Politics* (London: Routledge & Kegan Paul, 1979), and Arshi Pipa has an insightful essay "Gramsci as a (Non)Literary Critic," *Telos*, no. 57 (Fall 1983): 83–92. Edward Greer's essay "Antonio Gramsci and 'Legal Hegemony,'" in *The Politics of Law*, ed. David Kairys (New York: Pantheon, 1982), may be of interest also, as is Joseph A. Buttigieg, "The Exemplary Worldliness of Antonio Gramsci's Literary Criticism," *Boundary* 2, 11, nos. 1/2 (1982/83): 21–39. Jerome Karabel has written one of the major critical statements on Gramsci: "Revolutionary Contradictions: Antonio Gramsci and the Problem of Intellectuals," *Politics and Society* 6 (1976): 123–72.

5. This question is one place where the work of Jean Baudrillard has useful

if also somewhat uncertain applications, since on one side it is directly engaged with theorizing the contemporary marketplace and its logics while on the other it denies the usefulness of frameworks concerned with use-value, moral force, and the questions of work and production (see n. 3 to chap. 1 above).

6. Douglas Kellner's essay "Ideology, Marxism, and Advanced Capitalism," *Socialist Review* 42, vol. 8, no. 6 (November/December 1978), pursues the topic of "ideological regions" and thereby manages to distinguish separable theoretical areas within the general mix or messiness (the contradictory coexistence of highly diverse, semiautonomous terrains) in North American social reality. Kellner also offers a brief critique of Gouldner, among others, and makes considerable sense of the potentially cryptic notion of a Utopian or emancipatory element coded (enfolded) within hegemonic cultural coherence. The Ideology-and-Utopia theme, so important to Jameson's position in *The Political Unconscious*, can be elaborated as a series of discontinuities both within and among ideological regions. By way of anticipating my reading of Jameson's strategic use of that theme—a theme that holds open room for dissent, subversion, and potentially liberating difference—let me note that my resistance in the argument that follows is directed against the insufficient attention Jameson has given to the constitution and circulation of critical knowledge (critical work), which is itself a perfect candidate for the dialectical scrutiny of the Utopia/Ideology perspective. In sum, critical activity is simultaneously a reproductive "surplus" of our dominant (high) culture and a counteracting, anti-ideological event. Each side of that entangled intellectual formation (a well-organized yet somewhat malleable institutional ensemble) requires inspection as *coincidentally transformative and stabilizing*, as does the interaction between the two.

7. Lentricchia, *Criticism and Social Change*, p. 10.

8. Fredric Jameson, *The Political Unconscious: Narrative as a Socially Symbolic Act* (Ithaca: Cornell University Press, 1981), p. 10.

9. Fredric Jameson, "Marxism and Teaching," *New Political Science*, nos. 2/3 (Fall/Winter 1979/80), pp. 31–36.

10. Jameson, *Political Unconscious*, p. 296.

11. Ibid., p. 10.

12. Jameson, "Marxism and Teaching," p. 36.

13. Ibid., p. 35.

14. Jameson, *Political Unconscious*, p. 102.

15. Ibid., p. 181.

16. Jameson, "Marxism and Teaching," p. 34.

17. Jameson, *Political Unconscious*, p. 286.

18. Ibid., p. 287.

19. Ibid., p. 291.

20. Daniel T. O'Hara, "Revisionary Madness: The Prospects of American Literary Theory af the Present Time," *Critical Inquiry* 9, no. 4 (June 1983): 733.

21. Jameson, *Political Unconscious*, p. 290.

22. Ibid.
23. Jameson, "Marxism and Teaching," pp. 32–33.
24. Ibid., p. 33.
25. Ibid.
26. Ibid., p. 35.
27. Jeffrey Mehlman poses this issue as "a confrontation between the two interpretations" of the problem involved in "teaching reading" articulated in the well-known Derrida–Foucault debate in the early 1970s, a confrontation of "the alleged mastery of 'teaching' eroded by the constitutive instability of 'reading,' or the cult of 'reading' seen as a ruse dictated by the discursive demands of the political relation called 'teaching.' " That confrontation can be traced through (and within) Jacques Rancière's analyses of Marx's *Capital*, Mehlman suggests. More to the point here, Mehlman notes that "a term like *reading* . . . has, I would suggest, all the modesty of . . . let us say, a term like *being* in Heidegger." Thus "one might well imagine a development on the subject of *teaching reading* in which that phrase would gradually be made to buckle. The specific trickiness and instability of reading would come to unsettle the putative mastery of teaching. In the sentimental mode, this might take the form of the teacher unexpectedly learning from his student. But in a stronger and uncanny mode, the learning experience itself would be caught up in and dissolved by a bracing and exhilarating sense of disorientation born of the perversity of that general medium we accede to by *reading*." This position brings us to that euphorically situated political moment, "the privilege of *teaching* decisively disrupted by the constitutive instability of *reading*"—a moment no more able to circumvent the epistemological dilemma of reading and of "understanding" (of interpreting) than to ignore the history and responsibility of its own performance. Such an awareness leaves us siding with neither Foucault nor Derrida, as victors in their dispute, but driven to go beyond the potentially sentimental pleasure of privileging any form of discourse. Mehlman's "strong" mode of reading dissolves not only the erotics of an overly personal intersubjective exchange but also any temptation to pedagogical dogma or indoctrinating zeal. In this revised, more complex version of instruction, then, a teacher may very well be thought to "learn" from students in the double sense that (1) such people manifest various forms of cognitive defense (incomprehension, evasion, resistance, idealization, etc.) that need attending to if a teacher is to work critically within a context of learning that in some sense is always ahead of teachers and students even as it evolves or changes; and (2) this general scene of instruction remobilizes collective themes, as Jameson, for example, insists—themes that are not wholly sedimented or available within the texts under examination. The text-and-context of "teaching reading," therefore, can be discovered at work in intellectual dialogue and pedagogical activity as much as in ideological and conceptual "material" to be framed, analyzed, and interpreted.

The standoff that may result from countering Jameson's emphasis on the retrospective value of critical teaching by attempting a more immediate transformation of consciousness (as I have posed it in the pages above) might be dissolved if we looked at the art of "teaching reading" as a performance that needs to disengage itself from a hierarchy of representations which sustains institutional power but does so most often and most powerfully as deferred and genuinely *collective* activity—as, for example, the institutional action that takes place in classroom discussions. Such conversations prepare potential contests and changes in the manifestation of authority that will erupt once and many times more after students leave the classroom. This model would place the scene of instruction neither wholly in the immediate moment nor wholly in a later, retrospective mode—neither on the side of plotting disciplinary terrains (pedagogical apparatus turned against the apparatus of surveillance) nor on the side of undecidable double writing (the deferral of the text's polemical self-contestation as traces or thematic energies that are to emerge only later). It would oblige the teacher of reading to inspect, as clearly and as publicly as possible, everything available to be read as a product (and in terms) of whatever ideological and political impediments constrain the uses of that knowledge. In an older terminology than the one Mehlman employs, can this pedagogy avoid being simultaneously assertive and yet humbled (unsettled) by its task, by the search for clarity and useful access to a more democratic future, and by its need to ask strong questions and to learn how to make them take hold as critical knowledge takes hold? See Jeffrey Mehlman, "Teaching Reading: The Case of Marx in France," *Diacritics* 6, no. 4 (Winter 1976): 10–18.

28. Jameson, *Political Unconscious,* p. 17. In this ambition, one could grant Jameson the tactical advantage of having helped to arouse the recently resurgent interest in Marxism; his strategic embrace of a fairly conventional academic position for Marxism might be seen, therefore, as one of the few potentially successful institutional commitments to socially democratic energies. I would be willing to grant that. My concern, however, is this: On what critical strategies can a writer call now to move past professionalizing theoretical standoffs?

29. Ibid., p. 297. Jameson has clearly been struggling to find a way within his complex perspective to deal with these issues. See "Periodizing the 60s," *Social Text* (Spring/Summer 1984): 178–209, and "Postmodernism," *New Left Review* 146 (July/August 1984): 53–92.

30. Jameson, "Marxism and Teaching," p. 31.

31. Michel Foucault, "The Political Function of the Intellectual," *Radical Philosophy* 17 (Summer 1977): 13. This statement can also be found in Foucault, *Power/Knowledge: Selected Interviews and Other Writings, 1972–1977,* ed. Colin Gordon (New York: Pantheon, 1980), pp. 126–33.

32. Michel Foucault, "The Subject and Power," in *Michel Foucault: Beyond Structuralism and Hermeneutics,* 2d ed., ed. Hubert L. Dreyfus and Paul Rabinow (Chicago: University of Chicago Press, 1983), p. 222.

33. Ibid., p. 216.

34. Jameson, "The Ideology of the Text," *Salmagundi,* nos. 31/32 (1975), p. 235.

35. Ibid., p. 205.

36. Lentricchia, *Criticism and Social Change*, p. 7.

37. Edward W. Said, "Opponents, Audiences, Constituencies, and Community," *Critical Inquiry* 9, no. 1 (September 1982): 17.

7   On the Political Use of Critical Consciousness

1. Foucault went to considerable lengths in his late essays "Why Study Power: The Question of the Subject" and "How Is Power Exercised?" to insist that the goal of his writing for twenty years was not to examine power but "to create a history of the different modes by which, in our culture, human beings are made subjects"—that is, liable to the exercise of power. He denied the existence of "something called Power, with or without a capital letter, which is assumed to exist universally in a concentrated or diffused form," since power "exists only when it is put into action" as an interrelational event, a force that acts indirectly on people. Power is thus mediated by institutional relationships. To analyze power relations, one cannot locate or expose their "internal rationality." One must look at institutional strategies that limit and define behavior, that inhibit activity or generate movement, "choice," or pleasure for productive uses. For Foucault, however, "one must analyze institutions from the standpoint of power relations, rather than vice versa," because "the fundamental point of anchorage of the relationships, even if they are embodied and crystallized in an institution, is to be found outside the institution" in the antagonism and interplay that mark strategies of domination and those of resistance and opposition.

Now all of this is a fairly forceful and straightforward way of countering the charges that his concept of power is infinitely dispersed, a plastic unity. But even in these last formulations Foucault was still committed to a "subjectless history," a history in which mechanisms of subjection supersede the willful exercise of human perversity, choice, and freedom (of human creativity) and both enable exploitation and domination and "entertain complex and circular relations with other forms" of production and behavior. In other words, Foucault remained dedicated to a structural (it may in fact be a structuralist) definition of power as something innate and, if not thoroughly "continuous," nevertheless indestructible and more or less integrated with the cultural and institutional order of a given society. Power is the constant against which human liberation, to the extent it can be acted upon (and not merely theorized), works as a strategy of evasion, subversion, or revolt.

Power, in sum, defines the possibilities of human action. And human action, from this perspective, derives its motives and options from the structure of power in place. Foucault's concluding paragraph to his late essay "How Is Power Exercised?" reveals a struggle to accommodate the idea of resistance as a counteracting force that shapes society and limits power, mostly by complicating its effect. Note that domination (both coercive and productive) is the crucial outcome of the systematic operation of technologies of subjection that

leave the human subject essentially reactive and "free" only within the latitude of reigning cultural and ethical practices:

> Domination is in fact a general structure of power whose ramifications and conse-
> quences can sometimes be found descending to the most incalcitrant fibers of
> society. But at the same time it is a strategic situation more or less taken for
> granted and consolidated by means of a long-term confrontation between adver-
> saries. It can certainly happen that the fact of domination may only be the tran-
> scription of a mechanism of power resulting from confrontation and its conse-
> quences (a political structure stemming from invasion); it may also be that a
> relationship of struggle between two adversaries is the result of power relations
> with the conflicts and cleavages which ensue. But what makes the *domination* of a
> group, a caste, or a class, together with the *resistance* and revolts which that domi-
> nation comes up against, a central phenomenon in the history of societies is that
> they *manifest in a massive and universalizing form*, at the level of the whole social
> body, *the locking together of power relations with relations of strategy* and the results
> proceeding from their interaction. [Emphasis mine.]

The "results proceeding from their interaction," a deliberately vague phrase,
most often lead, in Foucault's judgment, to ever more subtle forms of administering populations—an increase in power by the state, both violent power
and the power of surveillance and of political (and cultural) containment. We
have a view, then, in which knowledge serves the interests of power without
much room for "relations of strategy" (of subversion and revolt, of informed
political opposition) to erode domination and sustain open choice. The "liberal" objection to Foucault's view of power is that it denies the actual achievement of civil liberties and democratic freedom. Mine is that it does not promote (or for that matter find any conceptual basis for) group solidarity and
collective political action. (Foucault's essays "Why Study Power" and "How Is
Power Exercised?" are printed as an afterword to Hubert L. Dreyfus and Paul
Rabinow's *Michel Foucault: Beyond Structuralism and Hermeneutics,* 2d ed.
[Chicago: University of Chicago Press, 1983].)

2. Paul Bové, "Intellectuals at War: Michel Foucault and the Analytics of
Power," *SubStance,* nos. 37/38 (1983): 49. In Said's favor here is a point worth
remembering later in this chapter, that his position at its most politically acute
moments is taken on behalf of his fellow Palestinians, who, without a national
homeland, in effect sanction (by dint of their plight) his right to adopt a
nonspecific (non-Foucauldian) rhetoric that has historical ties to the making
of the modern nation-state. Bové's critique of Said's estimation of Foucault is
nonetheless a gentle disagreement when it is brought alongside the much
more furious attacks that any writer who enters these troubled waters is likely
to endure.

3. Edward W. Said, *The World, the Text, and the Critic* (Cambridge: Harvard
University Press, 1983), p. 220.

4. An ironic affirmation of that estimation can be found in the ruling of a
National Labor Relations Board judge, George S. McInerny, that Boston
University faculty members are not free to unionize because they act on

behalf of the university as managers and supervisors. They are, in brief, agents of the university's power and authority. Such a ruling throws the stakes involved in defining intellectual identity and the humanist's critical and political function into the brightest possible light (see Nina McCain's article on p. 1 of the *Boston Globe,* July 4, 1984).

5. Said, *World, Text, and Critic,* p. 224.

6. Michel Foucault, *Language, Counter-Memory, Practice: Selected Essays and Interviews,* ed. Donald F. Bouchard (Ithaca: Cornell University Press, 1977), p. 191. Foucault's reference to "drugs" suggests a third, nonintellectual, relation to cognition: an evasion of logic or purposiveness or both. Such a reference inevitably calls up the sort of critique to be found in Perry Anderson's charge that Foucault and his cohorts Deleuze and Guattari move in "unbridled subjectivity" that culminates in "the capsizal of psychic structures themselves into a subjectivity pulverized beyond measure or order" (*In the Tracks of Historical Materialism* [London: Verso, 1983], pp. 54–55). Foucault's rather matter-of-fact statement here seems designed less to push the psychedelic than to take stock of Deleuze's concerns, on one hand, and, on the other, to place thought in a distinctly subversive form of hyperskeptical detachment from conventional rationality.

7. Magali Sarfatti Larson, "The Production of Expertise and the Constitution of Expert Power," in *The Authority of Experts,* ed. Thomas L. Haskell (Bloomington: Indiana University Press, 1984), p. 28.

8. Said, *World, Text, and Critic,* p. 217.

9. Foucault, "How Is Power Exercised?" p. 225.

10. Michel Foucault, "Power and Sex," trans. David J. Parent, *Telos,* no. 32 (Summer 1977), p. 161.

11. Foucault, "How Is Power Exercised?" p. 220. I should note here Jonathan Arac's useful discrimination between Foucault and Habermas on "the relation of power to the 'institutionalization of discourse'" in an acute essay that draws attention to the importance of E. P. Thompson, who "is still a historical materialist, but also a humanist" long after his disavowal of political Marxism. See Jonathan Arac, "The Function of Foucault at the Present Time," *Humanities in Society* 3, no. 1 (1980): 73–86.

12. Foucault, *Discipline and Punish: The Birth of the Prison* (New York: Random House, 1979), p. 308. The overall function of the prison extends the power of surveillance which operates in factories, schools, families, and elsewhere in society. Foucault sees this as an important element in the rise of capitalism. "If the economic take-off of the West began with the techniques that made possible the accumulation of capital [in what Immanuel Wallerstein calls the "long" sixteenth century], it might perhaps be said that the methods for administering the accumulation of men made possible a political take-off in relation to the traditional, ritual, costly, violent forms of power, which soon fell into disuse and were superseded by a subtle, calculated technology of subjection. In fact, the two processes—the accumulation of men and the accumulation of capital—cannot be separated" (pp. 220–21). This position, by the way, is much closer to Peter Berger's analysis of the rise of capitalism in

England and the United States (both) than are Marxist readings that stress the imperialist appropriation of plundered capital and labor as the essential accumulative precondition for capitalist expansion. See Berger's *Pyramids of Sacrifice: Political Ethics and Social Change* (Garden City, N.Y.: Doubleday-Anchor, 1976), pp. 54–67. Berger emphasizes "private sector" autonomy as separate from political organization, precisely the definition of altogether distinct institutional regions (of a nonintegrated social pluralism) that Gramsci's analysis of capitalist cultural hegemony disputes. The greater latitude for adjustment from within that Berger's view yields opens onto the world of academic debate about "value(s)" as a separate region—or an autonomous area somehow grafted on to First World dominance. Precisely at this point, when the apparently separate realm of values and value making is asserted as distinct from the otherwise interconnected material order of commercial production and consumer culture, Jean Baudrillard's assertion of the "equivalence" of all values in our communication society complicates Berger's belief that "capitalism posits an 'agonistic' ideal of society" (p. 66). Foucault's view that surveillance and administration have replaced exploitation and brute accumulation of capital as the basis of social coherence and of interinstitutional logic separates the "technology of subjection" from two areas: from the "traditional, ritual, costly, violent forms of power" that have remained endemic to all social orders (capitalist and socialist alike) and from the ongoing stratification of class divisions that have widened and now threaten to perpetuate a permanent division of society between those who have in abundance and those many more who have very little or nothing at all. Would it be accurate to say about South Africa to this point (in its early revolutionary ferment) that its class and race divisions, maintained by various sophisticated as well as crude forms of surveillance, are essentially kept in place by such technologies of subjection that repress or quell revolutionary resistance? Or would we need to comprehend a larger history of subjection and control and to examine the coercive role of capital's traditional logic, incessantly seeking profit by any means that appear most successful? Our analysis would not end with these questions, of course, but the alternatives posed by Foucault's position demand these initial interrogations.

13. Foucault, *Discipline and Punish*, pp. 302–3.

14. Said, *World, Text, and Critic*, p. 247.

15. Foucault, *Language, Counter-Memory, Practice*, p. 207.

16. Chomsky's emphasis on the instinctive ground of personal utterance and social interaction is much like John Berger's appeal, in *Another Way of Telling*, coauthored with Jean Mohr (New York: Pantheon, 1982), to a primordial linkage in "the relation between the human capacity to perceive and the coherence of appearances" that seem for him literally to "give" themselves to sight and knowledge. This is, to say the least, a problematic position open to the charge of a romantic ideology founded on the questionable (and traditionally humanist, i.e., "bourgeois") authority of experience. This is precisely Bruce Robbins's accusation against Berger, who, he finds, "conflates 'revolution' and 'experience'" (*Boundary* 2, 11, nos. 1/2 [Fall/Winter 1982/83]: 298).

17. Foucault, "Why Study Power," p. 216.

18. Jean-François Lyotard, *The Postmodern Condition: A Report on Knowledge,* trans. Geoff Bennington and Brian Massumi (Minneapolis: University of Minnesota Press, 1984).

19. Friedrich Nietzsche, *On the Genealogy of Morals,* ed. and trans. Walter Kaufmann (New York: Random House, 1967), p. 77.

20. *Reflexive Water: The Basic Concerns of Mankind,* interviews conducted and edited by Fons Elders (London: Souvenir Press, 1974), p. 185. See Chomsky's response following Foucault's remarks, p. 186.

21. Ibid., p. 182.

22. Chomsky is certainly not alone in correlating cognitive abilities with social and communal evolution. His Rousseau-inspired understanding of the mind's innate capacity for self-direction and for a form of self-perfection (considered not as an individual's personal activity but as the development of social forms that allow the species to attain greater knowledge, diversity, and cultural expression) projects a view of human action as *independent* of the systematic domination Foucault discerns and, at the same time, *unattached* to the bourgeois liberalism that imagines a freedom dependent on market forces (a beneficent capitalist economy). Chomsky's emancipation narrative considers the individual's linguistic skill and the bonds—and also the possible improvement—of human community to be inseparable and outside the grasp of institutions, history, and incarcerating strategies. His Utopian anarchism rejects Marxism, humanism, and all forms of positivism, pragmatism, and analytic self-consciousness to argue for an attainable alliance of free people who share their labor as well as the responsibility for governing themselves and their resources in the interest of human welfare. This vision is an enormous departure from most theories of educational and scholarly aims. Whatever else it may accomplish, it permits Chomsky to imagine a future and a context for artistic skill and critical clarity—a context distinct from the institutional authority and the personal and professional competition that define human work today. "A vision of a future social order," Chomsky writes, is "based on a concept of human nature. If in fact man is an indefinitely malleable, completely plastic being, with no innate structures of mind and no intrinsic needs of a cultural or social character, then he is a fit subject for the 'shaping of behaviour' by the state authority, the corporate manager, the technocrat, or the central committee. Those with some confidence in the human species will hope this is not so and will try to determine the intrinsic human characteristics that provide the framework for intellectual development, the growth of moral consciousness, cultural achievement, and participation in a free community" ("Language and Freedom," in *For Reasons of State* [New York: Pantheon, 1973], p. 404).

23. John Schaar, "Legitimacy in the Modern State," in *Power and Community,* ed. Green Levenson (New York: Pantheon, 1970), pp. 299–300. Magali Sarfatti Larson puts this another way: "The ideological destruction of the political effected by liberal philosophy [in the British tradition stretching from Locke to the Utilitarian philosophers] provided the necessary back-

ground for an ideology of professionalism which based legitimate social power on the foundations of private monopolies of expert knowledge." This ideology is aligned with a "possessive individualism" that rests on two assumptions: "first, that freedom—conceived of as freedom from the will of others and from any relations not voluntarily assumed—is the essence of being human. Second, that 'the individual is essentially the proprietor of his own person and capacities, for which he owes nothing to society.' From this follows the reduction of human society to exchange relations and of the political order to a contrivance for the maintenance and protection of relations of exchange between free proprietors" ("Production of Expertise," pp. 32–33).

Any reference to the Bill of Rights leads one into a legal minefield. For an examination of transformations in civil rights and changes in the law regarding freedom of speech, especially in this century, see Leon Whipple, *The Story of Civil Liberty in the United States* (Westport, Conn.: Greenwood, 1927); Thomas Emerson, *The System of Freedom of Expression* (New York: Random House, 1970); and Paul Murphy, *World War I and the Origin of Civil Liberties in the United States* (New York: Norton, 1979).

24. Said, *World, Text, and Critic,* p. 239.

25. Ibid., p. 235.

26. Ibid., p. 168.

27. John Schaar, "The Question of Justice," *Raritan* 3, no. 2 (Fall 1983): 123.

28. Said, *World, Text, and Critic,* p. 28. See Said's *Orientalism* (New York: Pantheon, 1978), pp. 153–56, for a discussion of Marx's homogenizing view of Asia—in particular India and its "Asiatic" form of production.

29. Foucault, *Language, Counter-Memory, Practice,* p. 200.

30. Stanley Aronowitz, *The Crisis in Historical Materialism* (New York: Praeger, 1981), pp. 315–16.

31. Leo Bersani, noting Gilles Deleuze's observation that "the *énoncé* for Foucault hides nothing and yet is not immediately visible," somewhat forces "the compatibility of Foucault with psychoanalysis" in order to find that "Foucault offers us rigorously traced diagrams of the real historical constraints under which we live. Superficially, the extreme generality of the definition of power in *La Volonté de savior* depoliticizes the notion of power" but "invites us to reformulate our sense of violence." Since language, discourse, speech, writing, and most of all literature are confirmations of a fundamental excess both in social reality and in the desiring self, for Bersani the "sustained impersonality" of Foucault's work gives way to "the succulent orders of Foucault's prose," which as literature, as writing, carries a "joy of self-confident strength" that is itself a kind of violence. This eruption of the literary impulse (of desire, of the work of art's attempt "to master an adversary power by reducing it . . . to one's own superior version of its sense") at once *exposes the desiring,* manipulated and manipulating *subject* that Foucault is extremely evasive about and demonstrates *how discourse functions* in a conflict-ridden, power-mad social reality. For Foucault, discourse has no hidden content but, like power, is strategic: something that operates on the surface of its

tactics in the antagonism and effects it creates in others, in other strategies of power or discourse. Ironically, the submerged content (the unarticulated suggestion) in Foucault's prose which attempts to deny the possibility of buried content is its own disruptive and potentially deranged energy: the "controlled power . . . of a subversive wandering in place or lingering in even the most relentlessly programmed analytic sequences." Bersani implies (without quite saying so) that Foucault's most accurate, most alluring response to the question of discursive power is unconscious ("The Subject of Power," *Diacritics* 7, no. 3 [1977], 2–21).

32. Michel Foucault, *Power/Knowledge: Selected Interviews and Other Writings, 1972–1977,* ed. Colin Gordon (New York: Pantheon, 1980), p. 118.

33. Jean Baudrillard, "The Ecstasy of Communication," in *The Anti-aesthetic,* ed. Hal Foster (Port Townsend, Wash.: Bay Press, 1983), p. 132.

34. See chap. 15 of Martin Jay's *Marxism and Totality* (Berkeley: University of California Press, 1984), "Jürgen Habermas and the Reconstruction of Marxist Holism," esp. pp. 496–97, for Habermas's concern with speech-act theory and his ideal of an "undistorted speech" situation or community. See also chaps. 4 and 5 of Thomas McCarthy, *The Critical Theory of Jürgen Habermas* (Cambridge: M.I.T. Press, 1978). Jay later points out that in Foucault's middle period, "from *The Order of Things* in 1966 until *Discipline and Punish* in 1975, . . . discourse had nothing to do with intersubjective dialogue; it implied instead the inertial and impenetrable materiality of language which always undercut what he saw as the fiction of intended meaning" (p. 523). One might deduce that the most important result of critical work is not interpretive clarity or hermeneutic skill—the recovery of significance from statements—but a question-making power that, driven by whatever stimuli generate critical energy allows readers to assume responsibility for knowledge by seeking to create the institutional relations of a skeptical but potentially optimistic, politically grounded set of interrogations. Such a shared activity of questioning demands a high degree of commitment "to further argument about developments that presently threaten the democratic potential of our times," as John Keane advocates in *Public Life and Late Capitalism* (Cambridge: Cambridge University Press, 1984), p. 9.

35. Raymond Williams comes much closer to an accurate assessment of the force and consequences of human (as opposed to systematic discursive) action when he writes, "If ideology were merely some abstract, imposed set of notions, if our social and political and cultural ideas and assumptions and habits were merely the result of specific manipulation, of a kind of overt training which might be simply ended or withdrawn, then the society would be very much easier to move and to change than in practice it has ever been or is" ("Base and Superstructure in Marxist Cultural Theory," in *Problems in Materialism and Culture* [London: New Left, 1980], p. 37). See also n. 13 to chap. 4 above.

36. Said, *World, Text, and Critic,* p. 247.

37. Ibid., p. 242.

38. Foucault, "Political Function of the Intellectual," p. 14.

39. Said, *World, Text, and Critic*, p. 246.

40. Foucault, *Power/Knowledge*, p. 102.

41. Aronowitz finds that the four methodological principles that Foucault lays out in *The Discourse on Language* (New York: Harper & Row, 1976)—reversal, discontinuity, specificity, and exteriority—contradict his attempt to decenter metaphysics. As a historian, Foucault needs principles of some kind to explain what he finds in the record of the past, to make sense of what is "there" as a record of human practices and intentions. As a critic who means to show a certain direction of discourse and institutional activity that extends or elaborates past practices (a present institutional configuration, the "regime of truth," that needs to be undone), Foucault attempts to contest or subvert the metaphysical logos and the set of intellectual practices that shape knowledge in our era. Between the two impulses, explanation and disruption, Foucault confuses his own effort (and discoveries) by subsuming the real material facts and human actions "under the *word*"; he is thereby unable to project individual and collective choice, energy, work, and accomplishments as events distinct from the cultural systems that hold their motives, their goals or objects, and their limits.

Dreyfus and Rabinow see that Foucault "is so good at the history of *systems* of thought (practices), that he cannot deal with thoughts and practices when they are not systematically interrelated" (*Michel Foucault*, p. 206). Foucault cannot be a dominant theorist of power *and* of resistance, as Dana Polan has pointed out, as long as he opts for the rhetorical strategy of reversing (or ironizing) the momentary hope his texts sometimes hold out by showing that the horror of imprisonment is less than torture or that the contemporary compulsion to speak and write about sexuality is less repressive than Victorian strictures. The problem here is not that Foucault has an inadequate notion of *events* or of the determining role of writers and of ideologies in popular resistance, but that he ascribes to himself a curiously avant-garde position as someone who knows the obstacles to social change and the fraudulence of past intellectual leadership while mapping out the massive closures (and the small crevices) from a disengaged, somewhat sorrowful involvement with Knowledge. See Stanley Aronowitz, "History as Disruption," in *Crisis in Historical Materialism*, and Dana B. Polan, "Fables of Transgression: The Reading of Politics and the Politics of Reading in Foucauldian Discourse," *Boundary 2*, 10, no. 3 (1982): 361–81; also, for a contrast to Foucault's limited treatment of revolutionary resistance, see George Rudé, *Ideology and Popular Protest* (New York: Pantheon, 1980).

42. Foucault, *Power/Knowledge*, p. 108.

43. William E. Cain, "Authors and Authority in Interpretation," *Georgia Review* 34, no. 3 (1980): 632. I might note here, also, Cain's contribution to the reassessment of contemporary humanist purpose: *The Crisis in Criticism: Theory, Literature, and Reform in English Studies* (Baltimore: Johns Hopkins University Press, 1984). My outlook here differs considerably from Cain's, but I share his sense of an institution in upheaval and disrepair. More, I admire the breadth of his survey of current and recent disputes. Cain feels that "while it is necessary to acknowledge the 'politics of interpretation' as a

field of study, we should realize—and guard against—the dangers of under-standing literature and criticism in wholly political terms. . . . Literary pol-itics," he says quite rightly, "can all too easily become a substitute for an actual politics." From his reading of the critical establishment's present agon, it is "still devising and refining a discourse that will enable us to describe the politics of interpretation cogently—a discourse that is insightful and revelato-ry, and that remembers the differences—even as it seeks the relationships between—politics and literature" (p. 206). I think North American critics have had an example of such discourse for more than fifty years in the work of Kenneth Burke. The problem in clarifying the figures, identifications, attitudes, purposes, and rhetorics that are immediately *political* (in their intel-lectual and institutional impact) and *literary* (in their verbal and conceptual complexity) is not a lack of critical instruments. Nor is it a lack of analytic sophistication and interpretive dexterity in the North American critical com-munity. The confusion in English studies arises not because too few people are trained in reading the literary and philosophical classics, as some think, and not because too many compete for critical authority, as others think (Cain is not among them), though these factors attenuate disagreements and com-plicate any attempt to reform the main lines of professional consensus that keep criticism a conversation among a small group of theorists and well-informed onlookers.

Tzvetan Todorov, who cannot be thought of as an interpretive extremist, notes that "we possess a sufficient conceptual apparatus (even if an obviously imperfect one) to describe literature's structural properties and to analyze its historical 'inscription'; but we do not know how to speak of its other dimen-sions, and it is this deficiency which must be remedied" ("A Dialogic Crit-icism?" *Raritan* 4, no. 1 [Summer 1984]: 73). The unmarked territory Todorov has in mind is the complex process of appeal in reading, discussing, and interpreting literature whereby "literature does not reflect ideology, [since] it is one"—a hilarious if also troublesome fact that demands that critical writers not close off any dialogue that can illuminate the humanity as well as the cold conceptual promise of intellectual debates (debates that liter-ature uniquely circumscribes). Todorov's old-fashioned notion of dialogue points toward what North American criticism has lacked: professional di-alogue that seeks to know the institutional and political circumstances that ground (and motivate) interpretation. These circumstances consist largely, though not wholly, of professional conditions that have ignored—and some-times denied—the political combat and the political role of intelligent reading and teaching and writing in a society fragmented by specialized knowledge but "integrated" by commerce and cheap images of heroism. Though I be-lieve intellectuals in many areas of cultural and professional life will need courage to overcome any number of institutional as well as conceptual obsta-cles if such far-reaching forms of dialogue are to have much influence on the conduct of business and education, such courage is not an adequate basis for creating the knowledge and asking the questions that might change public discourse.

Though Cain and I disagree about what it means "to incorporate 'politics' in teaching and research" (p. xiv), we agree that something more constructive than skeptical inversions of texts and textual positions is needed. Critics in the United States now must articulate a viable, productive set of values that will no doubt initiate new debates. Toward that work, Cain's statement here makes good sense: "In teaching our classes, we might attend to one of the central 'rules' that Foucault has outlined for the intellectual philosopher. This is 'to interpolate, to intervene and ask people: What are you doing? What are you thinking? Why do you think that? Why do you behave this way?' These are questions that bear inescapably on politics, but their analytical edge is not blunted by misapplied political terms" (p. xv).

44. Foucault, *Language, Counter-Memory, Practice*, pp. 35, 188–89.

45. Said, *World, Text, and Critic*, p. 159.

46. Paul Bové, "Intellectuals at War," p. 50.

47. Ibid., p. 45.

48. Said, *World, Text, and Critic*, p. 30.

49. Foucault, "Political Function of Intellectuals," p. 12.

50. C. Wright Mills, *Power, Politics, and People* (New York: Oxford University Press, 1967), p. 612.

51. It would be a mistake to set theoretical physics up as a secular logos, a realm of potentially uninstrumental clarity and excitement for both empirical and critical activity. My point is that the theoretical scientist and the critical intellectual are now equally interested in the institutional context of the knowledge they create. Historically, the critical intellectual worked under the banner of liberation; philosophical analysis and evaluative interpretation justified themselves as emancipating labor. Science took for its aim and rationale the theoretical coherence of knowledge generally. Today the status (if not a rather mystified version of the authority) of science is complicated, in part eroded, by the same institutional and political conflicts that fracture humanist scholarship. It may become clear soon, if it has not yet for many in both realms of research, that a wholly professional and internal skirmish over narrative paradigms and the most "appropriate" procedural or theoretical grounds for intellectual legitimacy will only postpone an inevitable (and necessary) understanding of the concrete social and interinstitutional—the cultural and the political—context in which knowledge is funded, authorized, and put into the world.

52. Edward Said, "Opponents, Audiences, Constituencies, and Community," *Critical Inquiry* 9, no. 1 (September 1982): 1.

53. Said, *World, Text, and Critic*, p. 231.

54. Whatever form such efforts will take must proceed from an organization of writers and critics acting as citizens first, as intellectually trained people who strive to produce a critical "collective voice" not as an end in itself—more scholarship for the enormous holdings of our libraries—but as information and guidelines for reordering political priorities in every area of professional, institutional, governmental, and social life.

Such efforts may initially take any number of forms: perhaps an international conference of the sort that in 1985 brought together ranking scientists of the United States and the USSR to discuss the threat of "nuclear winter"; a sustained collective critical project such as the one put forward by the Society for Critical Exchange, which has organized colloquiums and reports dealing with the state of humanist education, of the humanities curriculum, of criticism, and of professional scholarship in North America at present (the Group for Research on Institutionalization and Professionalization in Literary Studies: GRIP); or some as yet unfounded organization of concerned professionals and citizens which crosses conventional disciplinary and political boundaries. The concrete results of such cooperative effort may be difficult to gauge at first, but the specifically political and social goals of that work cannot be vague.

Though goals of this sort will seem lamentable to some, if such group projects are to have much chance of succeeding they will probably need two conditions to give them strength: people of sufficient professional prestige and integrity who commit themselves (and a major portion of that prestige) to making extraordinary ambitions and affiliations viable; and changes in the outlook of sufficient numbers of people (professional and otherwise) to make the need for such affiliation apparent as a politically productive response to work relations and life relations essentially closed off and closed out of the institutional politics that determine hegemonic adjustments to just such challenges.

Any specific change that permits the coming together of intellectually trained people outside their normal areas of expertise, so that they may use their intimate knowledge of institutional management to alter the terms and forms of traditional social coherence, will have to evolve from the present-day conservatism of workers, of comfortable though sometimes disgruntled professionals, and of critical intellectuals (too, alas). It seems, therefore, that the concrete political means to build an intellectual coalition of professional and nonprofessional groups are not available. Thus the image of a collective critical and interprofessional response to our capitalist environment that (as Ronald Aronson says) "in its cultural and historical specificity, today in the United States, *means* and *includes* racism, sexual oppression, militarism, nuclearism, overdevelopment, poisonings that can induce cancer, ecocide" blurs and grows dim.

Against those facts, I think this much must be granted. First, any notion of intellectual leadership is challenged by the history of disasters, pretensions, and outright fraud and failure resulting from false leadership, from the designs of an "elitist and self-seeking" vanguard (as Gouldner saw it) that "uses its special knowledge to advance its own interests and power"—for the most part "to control its own work situation" (in the case of middle-class professionals), but in the case of many intellectuals in capitalist and socialist and mixed-government circumstances, to promote tyrannical values that cast scorn on the name of *the people* or mock the hope it carries. Second, new political energies now must come from some genuinely universally oriented group. Although cultural conditions work against it, the knowledge for such an outlook resides with critical intellectuals.

55. Said, "Opponents, Audiences," p. 24.

56. Paul Bové, "The Ineluctability of Difference: Scientific Pluralism and the Critical Intelligence," *Boundary 2*, 11, nos. 1/2 (Fall/Winter 1982/83): 159.

57. Magali Sarfatti Larson, *The Rise of Professionalism* (Berkeley: University of California Press, 1977); Thomas L. Haskell, "Professionalization as Cultural Reform," *Humanities in Society* 1, no. 2 (Spring 1978): 103–13, and "Professionalism *versus* Capitalism," in *The Authority of Experts*, ed. Haskell (Bloomington: Indiana University Press, 1984); Burton J. Bledstein, *The Culture of Professionalism* (New York: Norton, 1976).

58. Said, *World, Text, Critic*, pp. 232–33.

59. Foucault, *Language, Counter-Memory, Practice*, p. 228.

Index

Library of Congress Cataloging-in-Publication Data

Merod, Jim, 1942–
   The political responsibility of the critic.

   Includes index.
   1. Criticism—–Political aspects.   2. Criticism—–Social aspects.   I. Title.
PN98.P64M47   1987   801'.95   86–47977
ISBN 0–8014–1976–X (alk. paper)